AF871366

Building Enterprise AI Agents

Text-to-SQL and Structured Data for Answers Your Business Can Trust

Viren Shah

Copyright

Building Enterprise AI Agents

Text-to-SQL and Structured Data for Answers Your Business Can Trust

Copyright © 2026 Viren Shah. All rights reserved.

Published by Vayom AI, Edison, New Jersey.

First edition, Fall 2026.

This is the Fall 2026 edition. Product names, versions, vendor capabilities, benchmark results, and analyst positions described in this book are stated as of September 2026 and will change. Each entry in the Notes records the date its source was checked.

No part of this publication may be reproduced, distributed, or transmitted in any form or by any means, including photocopying, recording, or other electronic or mechanical methods, without the prior written permission of the publisher, except in the case of brief quotations embodied in reviews and certain other noncommercial uses permitted by copyright law.

Product and company names mentioned in this book may be trademarks or registered trademarks of their respective owners, and are used in an editorial fashion with no intention of infringement. This book is an independent publication. It is not affiliated with, authorized by, endorsed by, or sponsored by any company named in it.

The information in this book is provided as is, without warranty of any kind. The author and the publisher have taken care in its preparation but make no expressed or implied warranty, and accept no responsibility for errors or omissions, or for any loss arising from the use of the information it contains. Nothing here is legal, financial, regulatory, or other professional advice. Software products, standards, and regulations change. Verify current vendor documentation before acting on anything described in these pages.

Every web address cited in the Notes was checked on 31 August 2026.

vayomai.com

Overview

What This Book Is About

This book is part of the Enterprise AI series. It is about structured data, the data that already runs the business. That data sits in databases, in the business systems people use every day, in spreadsheets, and in the files those systems produce. What makes data structured is not where it is stored. It is structured because the shape is decided before the data arrives. A rule states what each field means, what kind of value it holds, and where that value belongs. Because the shape is set in advance, a system can read every value without guessing.[1]

Rows and columns are the form most people picture. A table holds one row for each record and one column for each field. A spreadsheet works the same way, and so does the export file a system produces at the end of a month. Rows and columns are not the only form. Time series data records the same measurement again and again, in time order. Key and value stores hold an identifier and the record that identifier points to. A graph holds nodes and the links between them, and it counts as structured when the node types and link types are defined in advance.[2]

Close to these sit formats such as JSON, XML, and YAML, which are ways of writing structured data as text a machine can read. They carry tags and a nested shape, so they are not loose text. They also allow that shape to change from one record to the next, which is why they are usually called semi-structured.[3] The line matters, because the more the shape can vary, the more work is needed before AI can rely on it. Most people meet AI and structured data through chat. You type a question in plain English, an AI writes a query, and a number comes back. It feels like the problem is solved, because the hard part looks like the query, and the AI wrote it.

That view is too small. Getting a number out is not the same as producing an answer a business can act on. A business needs to know that the question was understood, that the right tables were used, that the person asking was allowed to see the result, and that the number can be checked later by someone else.

This book moves you from asking AI for data to building AI into the data. You will see how the meaning of the business is written down so an AI can use it, how a query is checked before it runs, and how permission and cost limits are applied. You will also see how a result is tested before a person sees it, and how the decision is kept on the record. By the end you should be able to design that path, explain why each step exists, and defend it to someone who has to trust the answer.

Who This Book Is For

This book is written for three groups whose knowledge must come together for an AI project involving structured data to succeed: data professionals, business operators, and executives.

Data professionals build and maintain the systems that collect, move, organize, secure, and deliver data. You may work with ETL processes, data pipelines, databases, warehouses, data models, reports, or governance. You already know that writing a valid SQL query is only one small part of producing a trustworthy answer. The correct tables, joins, definitions, permissions, tests, and operating controls must also be in place. This book shows how those parts connect when AI becomes another user of the data.

Business operators carry out the work of the business every day. You may work in finance, sales, customer service, claims, rebates, purchasing, supply chain, or another business function. You know which information can be trusted, which exceptions matter, what must be excluded, and what business words mean in practice. Much of this knowledge may not be written in a database or procedure. This book shows how that knowledge can guide an AI system while the meaning of the business and the final judgment remain with the people responsible for the work.

Executives sponsor, approve, and fund large data and AI projects. You may receive presentations, proposals, budgets, diagrams, and technical explanations from several teams, with each one describing a different part of the project. This book uses simple language to show how those parts fit together and how AI works with structured data from the first business question to the final reviewed answer.

The purpose is not to train executives or business operators to build the technical system, or to replace the technical knowledge of data professionals. It is to give all three groups a shared understanding of what AI can do, where it needs support, and where important limits remain. This understanding can help executives set realistic expectations and fund the right foundations, help business operators explain the knowledge behind their decisions, and help data professionals build systems that use that knowledge safely.

Most material stops after AI writes SQL. The query is not the whole process. Someone must define the business meaning, connect it to the right data, check the query, control who may see the result, test the answer, approve its use, and keep a record of what happened. This book covers that complete path so data professionals, business operators, and executives can plan and evaluate the work together.

What You Will Be Able To Do

By the end of this book you will have acquired the knowledge to bring structured data into AI. You will know why AI cannot simply read your database, and what has to happen to your tables, rows, and columns before a model can work with them at all. You will know how your own knowledge of the data gets carried into the AI. Which table is the real one, which field can be trusted from when, what has to be excluded, and what your business words mean, so the agent writes SQL with what you would have used.

You will know why AI writes good SQL against a sample database and poor SQL against yours, and what it is about a real system that causes the difference. You will know what a trustworthy answer from structured data needs beyond the query itself, and how to tell one from a number that only looks right. You will know how structured data travels through an AI workflow from the question to the recorded decision, and where a person still belongs in it.

What This Book Does Not Cover

AI is a very large subject. Images, speech, code generation, forecasting, documents and the search that goes with them, and a long list of things people are building right now. Most books pick a corner of it. This book takes one corner and stays there: getting structured data to AI, and getting a trustworthy answer back. Rows, columns, and the systems that hold them. What has to be in place before a model can work with your tables, and what has to happen around its answer before anyone acts on it. A few nearby subjects are out. Documents, PDFs, and text search. Building or repairing the database itself. Anything written for one vendor's product. Where they touch this one, they are named and left there.

Table of Contents

Introduction

Researchers at Yale University introduced a benchmark called Spider in 2018. It contained 10,181 natural-language questions and 5,693 distinct complex SQL queries, across 200 databases with multiple tables. The train, development, and test splits used different databases, requiring systems to generalize to schemas they had not seen during training. Spider, together with SParC and CoSQL, formed a challenge series that attracted more than 300 submissions from research labs. On 5 February 2024 the maintainers announced that they would no longer accept submissions for Spider 1.0 evaluations or update its leaderboard.[1]

Spider 2.0 followed. It was introduced as a benchmark for real-world enterprise text-to-SQL workflows, and the published version contained 632 real-world workflow problems drawn from enterprise database use cases. Its databases often contain more than 1,000 columns. Its tasks span several SQL dialects, and solving them can require searching database metadata, consulting dialect documentation, and working through project-level codebases. The required workflows can involve multiple SQL queries and can exceed 100 lines.[2]

In the paper published at the International Conference on Learning Representations (ICLR) in 2025, the authors reported that their o1-preview-based code-agent framework solved 21.3 percent of Spider 2.0 tasks. For comparison, the paper reports execution-accuracy figures of 91.2 percent on Spider 1.0 and 73.0 percent on the BIRD benchmark; these are benchmark-specific results and are not directly interchangeable measures. The authors conclude that language models still require significant improvement for adequate real-world enterprise performance.[3] That is the published record. The live leaderboards have moved since, so the following snapshot was checked on 21 August 2026.

Spider 2.0 is currently presented in separate settings. On Spider 2.0-Snow, where database metadata and documentation are prepared and supplied, Genloop's Sentinel Agent v2 Pro leads with 96.70 percent. On Spider 2.0-DBT, which requires working through a project's own codebase, SignalPilot Agent leads with 65.60 percent.

On Spider 2.0-Lite, the listed DeepSeek-R1 entries are AutoLink + DeepSeek-R1 at 52.28 percent, LinkAlign + DeepSeek-R1 at 33.09 percent, RSL-SQL + DeepSeek-R1 at 30.53 percent, and Spider-Agent + DeepSeek-R1 at 13.71 percent. The highest of the four is 3.81 times the lowest, a spread of 38.57 percentage points. Scores are reported on the Spider 2.0 leaderboard.[4] The maintainers warn that scores can change as they continue checking the evaluation metrics. Check them yourself if a number matters to your decision.

Look again at what Spider 2.0 introduced to make its tasks resemble enterprise data work. Databases with more than a thousand columns. Several SQL dialects. Metadata that may need to be searched, documentation that may need to be read, and project code that may need to be followed. Those are benchmark facts. Here is the reading this book takes from them. The benchmark details matter because they point to the conditions that make enterprise data difficult to use well. They are not just properties of the benchmark; they are properties of an organization's own data.

Your data has its own version of that list: its own scale, dialects, structures, and history. It also has decisions, conventions, and exceptions that may never have been written down for a machine. Those details are what turn a schema into an organization's data. That is why the challenge is not only to generate SQL. An AI system must also learn which data represents the business, which definitions apply, and which unwritten rules must be made explicit before an answer can be trusted.

A model is one input. Around it sit the things that decide whether its answer can be used: what it is told before it answers, what it is allowed to look up, what is checked after it writes, and what happens to the result before a person acts on it. What follows starts there. The shapes structured data takes inside a working organization, how each one behaves when an AI system tries to use it, and what has to be done before an agent can write SQL with the knowledge a person inside that organization would have brought to the task.

Each piece is explained through the thing that goes wrong without it, because that is how you tell a step that earns its place from a step that only adds delay.

Chapter 1: What Is Structured Data?

Navigate: Contents · Next: Chapter 2

Businesses run on software, as do large organizations and governments. Much of the record of their work is created and stored digitally, even though paper records, physical documents, and other forms of non-digital evidence still remain part of many organizations. Most large organizations do not run on a single system. They have different systems for finance, sales, supply chain, human resources, and the other functions that keep the business moving. They accumulated over time, as different teams chose or built different systems to solve different problems; a large organization may be running hundreds of them at once.

Some are small and straightforward-a screen used by one person to take a payment at a counter. Others are enormous, following goods as they move across the world. They all process information and produce results, but their architectures and behavior can be radically different. A particular business operation may follow a sequence of steps, which is often called a workflow. Software, however, is not limited to a straight line: it can branch, repeat, run asynchronously, or respond to events. Consider a simplified payment at a counter. The system may ask who is paying, how much they are paying, and which method they will use before saving the record and printing a receipt.

In that example, the application may enforce the order. It can require an amount before saving the payment and prevent the user from completing the transaction out of sequence. Each question on the screen can have its own field and validation rule: the date field accepts a date, the amount field accepts a number, and the customer field accepts only a customer who already exists in the system. Those decisions are made before the first payment is entered. They determine which fields exist, what each field means, and which values the application will accept.

The person at the counter may not be allowed to add a new field. A change to the application can require a formal request, approval, development, testing, and release, a process that may take weeks or months in a large organization, depending on the process. That slowness serves a purpose. Because the fields are governed, payments saved through the application generally follow the same defined schema. When the payment is saved, it becomes a record with named fields in a defined schema: who paid, how much, when, and by what method. The next payment has those same fields unless the schema or the application changes.

The person at the counter is not usually thinking of themselves as creating data. They are serving a customer and moving on to the next one; the record is simply what the work leaves behind. The same thing happens elsewhere. Someone in finance posts an invoice, someone in sales logs a deal, and someone in supply chain receives a shipment. None of them may think of the activity as producing a data asset, but each action leaves a record. That is one important way data becomes structured: a system or format defines fields, types, and relationships in advance, or applies those rules when the data is read. Structured systems do not all reject unexpected values; some allow nulls, extra fields, or schema evolution over time.

When people speak of "our structured data," they mean the ordinary record of the organization doing its work, accumulating year after year, with each row following the current schema, a schema that may be tightly governed but may also change.

Types of Structured Data

Structured data takes many forms. The same order may appear as a live record in one system, a historical row in another, and a raw file in a third. The customer behind it may have several identities that must be brought together before anyone can see a trusted view. Each place was built for a different purpose, so the data changes shape as it moves. Five ideas will recur as we follow that data through an organization.

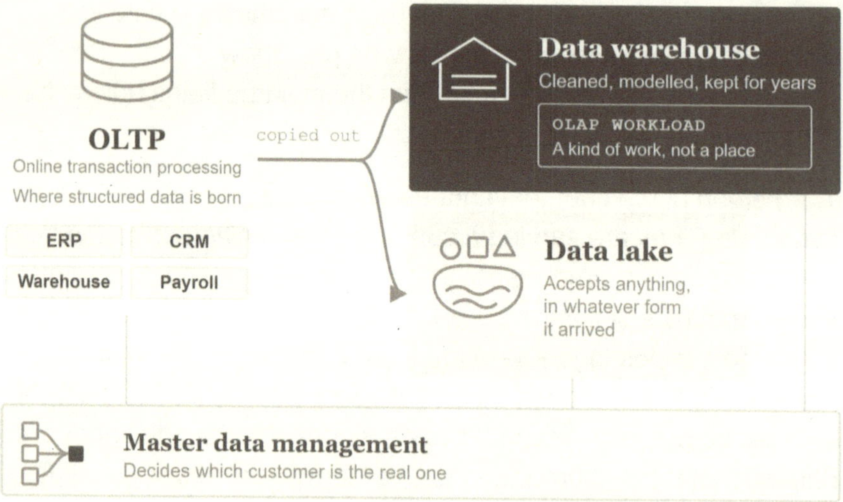

Figure 1.1 Structured data is born in OLTP systems and copied out, to a warehouse where OLAP work happens or to a lake that accepts it in whatever form it arrived. Master data management decides which customer is the real one.

OLTP. Online transaction processing is where much structured operational data is created: inside the systems people use to run the business day to day. ERP, CRM, warehouse-management, and payroll systems commonly support OLTP workloads, and many downstream datasets begin as records created there.

OLAP. Online analytical processing describes the technologies and workloads used to analyze data: reading across millions of rows, grouping them, comparing one period with another, and slicing results by region or product. Many reporting questions are OLAP questions, although not every analytical workload uses a cube or a separate OLAP system.

Data warehouse. A warehouse is one common home for OLAP work. Data may be copied from transaction systems, cleaned, reshaped into a model designed for querying, and retained for years. A well-managed warehouse can also apply shared business definitions. For example, it can define what counts as a completed order and use that definition consistently across reports.

Data lake. A data lake can hold very large amounts of data in many forms: structured tables, log files, documents, and images. Data often arrives raw, while cleaned and curated versions may be kept alongside it. That flexibility is useful, but the data may need more work before it can answer a business question.

Master data management. The same customer may appear in the CRM, ERP, and billing system under three spellings and three identifiers. Master data management helps determine which records belong to the same customer and links their source identifiers to a trusted view. Without a way to reconcile those identities, any answer that crosses systems can be wrong.

Characteristics of OLTP Data

OLTP systems are generally optimized for short, concurrent operational transactions and for keeping current-state data up to date. Think about what that looks like in practice. A customer calls to ask where an order is; someone at a counter checks an account balance; a receptionist pulls up an appointment for Thursday. These are three different systems with three different jobs, but the request has the same shape: find a record by its identifier and return it before the person finishes the sentence. In those moments, operational users usually want a small set of related records, not a total, average, or trend.

Writing follows the same pattern. The system records the payment, books the appointment, or adds a line to the order. A transaction often touches only a few rows and finishes quickly, even while many other transactions are taking place. That narrow, concurrent workload shapes the layout of the data. The resulting layout is called a normalized structure. Normalization reduces repeated facts by separating related data into tables and linking those tables with keys. A customer's name can live in the customer table rather than on every order. The order holds a customer number, and the system follows that number when it needs the customer record.

Third normal form is common in traditional relational OLTP designs. You do not need its formal rules yet; the examples that follow show its practical effect. This matters for two related reasons: consistency and the amount of work required when something changes. If the same customer name is copied into many order records, spelling differences can appear over time. Store the name once, in the customer table, and there is only one value to maintain. The same applies to a phone number. If it is repeated across many order rows, a change may require many updates; if it is stored once in the customer record, one update may be enough. For OLTP data, it helps to distinguish two kinds: master data and transaction data.

Master data usually represents the business entities that transactions refer to: customers, products, accounts, locations, and employees. It is often referenced widely and changes more slowly than transaction data, although the size and rate of change vary by domain. Transaction data records business events involving those entities: orders, payments, postings, appointments, and shipments. It is often created or changed frequently and may grow faster than master data. Many transaction rows reference master data through keys, but not every transaction table does. Here is the same basic skeleton in three unrelated systems. In each example, the key column comes first.

An order system:

```
Master
  CUSTOMER      customer_id, name, tax_id, status
```

```
  PRODUCT       product_id, description, unit_of_measure
  ADDRESS       address_id, customer_id, city, country

Transaction
  ORDER_HEADER  order_id, customer_id, order_date, currency
  ORDER_ITEM    order_id, item_no, product_id, qty, price
```

An order is split across two tables: one row in ORDER_HEADER and twelve rows in ORDER_ITEM when it has twelve line items. The customer name appears in neither table.

An Accounting System

```
Master
  PARTY         party_id, name, date_opened, status
  ACCOUNT       account_id, party_id, account_type, currency

Transaction
  POSTING       posting_id, account_id, post_date, amount

Current state
  BALANCE       account_id, as_of, ledger_bal, available_bal
```

The third group is worth pausing on. The balance could be calculated from the postings, but this example keeps a current balance instead. If the application updates the posting and the balance in one database transaction, atomicity ensures that both changes either succeed together or fail together.

An appointment system:

```
Master
  PERSON        person_id, family_name, given_name, birth_date
  PROVIDER      provider_id, provider_name, specialty_code
  LOCATION      location_id, location_name, address_id

Transaction
  APPOINTMENT   appt_id, person_id, provider_id, start_time
  APPT_NOTE     note_id, appt_id, created_at, note_text
```

Although the systems have nothing else in common, the pattern is recognizable: a small group of master tables that change slowly, a larger set of transaction tables around them, and keys linking the two so related facts can be referenced rather than copied. Step back far enough and many relational OLTP systems show some version of this pattern, although real designs vary and may include denormalized or specialized tables. Related facts are separated, so even useful questions may require joins. To show one order with the customer's name, for instance, the system must follow the customer key into another table.

To answer a question about one order, that lookup is exactly what the system is designed to do: it is narrow and touches little data. But ask which customer placed the largest order last quarter, and the character of the work changes. A design that is excellent for a small lookup becomes less comfortable when the question expands.

OLAP and the Cube

The primary job of an OLTP system is operational: record what happens, find records when somebody asks, and keep current state correct. It is generally optimized for those tasks rather than for looking across three years of records at once, although an OLTP database can support analytical queries too. Yet those are precisely the questions the business wants answered. Which product group grew last quarter? Which customers stopped ordering? How does this March compare with last March? Did the discount change anything, and in which cities? Read those questions together and a common structure emerges. Each asks for something to count or add up, a way to group the result, and a boundary that determines which records belong in the calculation.

Growth is measured by product group over the last quarter; revenue is compared by city for March and the same month last year. The quantity being added is usually called a measure, and the way the result is grouped is a dimension. Those are dimensional-modeling concepts, not requirements of every analytical question: some questions ask for detail, a single value, or a comparison without a grouping dimension. Now look at where those pieces sit in the order system. The measure is in ORDER_ITEM: quantity and price belong to the line. The dimensions are scattered elsewhere. The date is in ORDER_HEADER, the city is two tables away in ADDRESS, and the product group is in PRODUCT.

Normalization put them there deliberately, and it was a sensible choice for a system that writes one order at a time. It can be a less convenient shape for a question that reads a million orders, although indexes and query optimizers can make normalized designs perform well. Depending on the indexes, partitions, materialized views, and execution plan, a query against the live tables may scan many order lines and follow several keys to determine what was sold, who bought it, and where. It may not have to do all that; the work can be reduced by caching or pre-aggregation, but the shape of the problem remains.

Analytical designs therefore often reshape the data on purpose. They may flatten or copy data, accepting some duplication in exchange for simpler access or faster reads. Modern columnar systems can also query normalized or external tables efficiently, so this is a trade-off rather than a rule. One common reshape is the star schema: a central table holds the measures, with dimension tables arranged around it.

```
Fact
  FACT_SALES     date_key, customer_key, product_key,
                 quantity, line_amount

Dimension
  DIM_DATE       date_key, day, month, quarter, year
  DIM_CUSTOMER   customer_key, customer_name, city, country
  DIM_PRODUCT    product_key, description, product_group
```

Compare DIM_CUSTOMER with the normalized version. The customer name, city, and country now sit together in one dimension row, while the fact rows carry the customer key rather than repeating those attributes. The design accepts some duplication in the dimensions in exchange for simpler analytical access. In this simplified design, the fact table holds one row per order line, and the shown columns are keys and measures. Real fact tables can contain other attributes or can even be factless, depending on the grain and purpose of the model.

Even this simplified star schema answers the question more directly than the live tables did. There is one join per dimension rather than a chain of joins, and every grouping column is close at hand. The numbers are still added up when someone asks for them. A cube takes that optimization one step further by working out common totals in advance. With three dimensions, the name is easy to picture: time runs along one edge, product along another, and customer along the third. Each point in the resulting space represents one combination of those dimensions and stores a total the cube can return quickly. The cell for fasteners in Ohio in March gives the total line amount for those three dimensions.

Real cubes may have more than three dimensions and are still called cubes, because the geometry stops being drawable long before the concept stops being useful. Dimensions are not flat lists; they are usually organized into levels, or hierarchies.

```
Measures
  quantity, line_amount, order_count

Dimensions and levels
  Time        Year > Quarter > Month > Day
  Customer    Country > City > Customer
  Product     Product Group > Product
```

A cube can expose totals at each supported level and combination of levels: fasteners in Ohio in March, all products in Ohio for the quarter, or fasteners everywhere for the year. Whether a total is precomputed, calculated on demand, or omitted depends on the cube design and engine. Those movements have names. Drilling down moves from quarter to month; rolling up reverses that direction. Slicing fixes one dimension and looks across the others, while pivoting swaps the dimension that runs down the page with the one that runs across it. They are not queries in the usual sense, but ways of moving through a structure designed for exploration.

The payoff is that a question that would have scanned millions of order lines becomes one the cube is already shaped to answer. That convenience comes with three costs. Traditional cubes may be processed and refreshed on a schedule, so their data can be only as current as the last processing operation. Other designs support incremental processing, query-time aggregation, or near-real-time updates. The number of possible combinations grows fast. Four time levels, three customer levels, and two product levels give 24 combinations of those levels before considering additional all-members or alternate hierarchies. Add a dimension and the number multiplies again. In sparse data, many cells may be empty, and engines and cube designs handle sparsity in different ways.

Dimensions are fixed for a given cube design. A question needing an unmodeled cut cannot be answered from that cube as currently modeled. It may be answered from the underlying warehouse or after the model is extended, and the timing depends on the implementation. Cube technology is mature, but many newer analytical systems emphasize columnar warehouses, lakehouses, semantic models, and query-time aggregation, which can reduce the need for some traditional precomputed cubes.

Cube products such as Essbase and Microsoft Analysis Services are still available and remain in use, including for financial close, regulatory reporting, and spreadsheet-based reporting. In an organization with a long technology history, a cube may still sit in the reporting stack, with users who may trust its numbers more than those from newer systems. The cube may have faded from center stage, but the star schema underneath it has not. Facts in the middle, dimensions around the edge, duplication accepted in exchange for speed. That shape has outlasted much of the technology built on top of it, and it will appear again.

The Data Warehouse

A data warehouse is generally built for reading and analysis, although modern platforms also support writes. It may reshape the source data, flatten or duplicate it for performance or usability, and often uses the same star-schema form introduced in the previous section. In practice, the difference is often one of scope, although implementations vary widely. A cube is an analytical model made of measures, dimensions, and hierarchies. It may use a fixed set of dimensions chosen during its design and is often built from data that has already been modeled. That data frequently comes from a warehouse, making the cube a layer on top, but cubes can also use other sources, and a warehouse does not require a cube.

There is a classical description of that work. As is common knowledge, In 1992, Bill Inmon described a data warehouse as subject-oriented, integrated, time-variant, and nonvolatile. More than three decades later, those four terms remain widely used, even though modern implementations vary. Subject-oriented means that the warehouse is organized around the business rather than around the source software: there is a customer area and a sales area, not an ERP area and a CRM area. Integrated means that data from many source systems is reconciled into one consistent model. It is the property that matters most, and usually the one that costs the most.

Consider a customer that exists in the CRM and ERP. Each system holds the version its own job requires, so the records may carry different identifiers, spellings, and fields. Add billing and a third version may appear. None is necessarily wrong; each may be correct for the system where it lives. To answer a question about that customer across systems, the warehouse must recognize that the three records belong together and apply a consistent identity. Someone has to decide that they represent the same company, choose which name to use, and build a mapping that survives future loads. Matching the records is only the beginning.

The values can disagree as well: one system stores weight in kilograms and another in pounds; one records dates as year-month-day and another the other way around. Currencies differ, along with the exchange rate used and the date on which it was taken, while product codes may overlap between systems even when they mean different things. Then there are the definitions, which are often harder still. When, for example, does an order become an order: at quote acceptance, entry, confirmation, or dispatch? The sales and finance systems may disagree because they are asking different questions. The same problem appears in the definition of revenue, the date assigned to it, the treatment of cancelled orders, and the question of whether internal transfers count at all.

A governed warehouse usually documents or encodes these choices before publishing a trusted metric. Different definitions can still coexist in the wider data environment when they serve different purposes. A conformed dimension is one common way to preserve that consistency: define a customer dimension once and share it across the fact tables that need the same customer definition.

```
Shared dimension
  DIM_CUSTOMER   customer_key, customer_name, city, country

Fact tables using it
  FACT_SALES     date_key, customer_key, product_key, amount
  FACT_PAYMENTS  date_key, customer_key, amount_received
  FACT_SUPPORT   date_key, customer_key, case_count
```

All three fact tables point to the same customer dimension, so sales, payments, and support cases can be related to one customer definition. They can be brought into a single query when their grains and relationships are compatible and the measures are handled correctly. Without that shared definition, they remain three separate stories about three customer lists. Time-variant means that the warehouse keeps history, which is where it differs most clearly from the OLTP systems described earlier. An OLTP system is built around current state. If a customer moves from Columbus to Memphis, a simple current-state record may overwrite the old address because the operational system needs to know which address is valid now.

A warehouse has a different responsibility. It must be able to show what the orders looked like when the customer was still in Columbus and continue to show that history years later. The dimension therefore carries its own history.

```
DIM_CUSTOMER, keeping history
  customer_key, customer_id, name, city, valid_from, valid_to
```

The same customer now occupies two rows. One is valid until the move, and one is valid from the move onward. Each order can point at whichever row was current on the day it was placed. One common warehouse approach is a Type 2 slowly changing dimension, which is what this example shows. The choice between overwriting the old value and keeping both is one of the more consequential decisions anyone makes in a warehouse. In Inmon's classical description, non-volatile means that once data has landed, it is not edited in the way an OLTP row is edited. Modern analytical warehouses may still update, merge, or delete data while retaining history through snapshots, audit records, or other change history.

The reconciliation happens during loading, usually called ETL, for extract, transform, load, or ELT, for extract, load, transform, depending on whether the reshaping occurs before or after the data arrives. This is where identifiers are matched, units converted, definitions applied, and history written. A well-governed warehouse aims to give people one place to ask questions, shared customer and product definitions, a common calendar, and documented measures with history behind them. The source systems and their lineage may still matter when a result needs to be explained, and eventually an AI agent will be pointed at the warehouse too.

Every reconciliation embodies a judgment. Someone decided which name should win, which definition of revenue should apply, whether a cancelled order counts, and whether the address should be overwritten or preserved. The warehouse therefore contains the results of those decisions, which creates the problem this book takes up. The tables an analyst or an AI agent queries may show the final customer key, revenue value, or order status without revealing why the rule was chosen. That reasoning may live elsewhere, in transformation code, mapping rules, documentation, tickets, or the knowledge of the people who designed the process.

Master Data

We have already encountered master data twice in this chapter, but neither encounter showed the whole picture. In the OLTP section, master data was one of two kinds of table inside a single system: it described the business entities, while transaction data recorded the events involving them. A payment is a transaction; the customer who made it, the product it paid for, the account it landed in, and the employee who approved it are all master data. Inside one system, that definition is easy to live with. The warehouse section left one job unfinished without naming it: someone still has to decide that three records in three systems represent the same company.

That is where the term changes weight. Inside one system, master data is a kind of table; across many systems, it becomes a discipline with its own software and, in many organizations, its own team. The discipline is called master data management. The usual domains are customer, product, supplier, location, employee and asset. Some organizations add cost centre, general ledger account, or material. Master data tends to have three properties that make it difficult to manage: it is referenced widely, it may change more slowly than transaction data so that drift goes unnoticed, and it may live in many systems at once. That last property is the source of the difficulty, so it is worth being precise about why it happens.

Any system that touches a customer may maintain or reference a customer record. It may build the attributes needed for its own work, or obtain them from a shared service or master-data source.

The CRM needs a customer to sell to: the buying organization, the contacts inside it, the territory, the industry, and the history of what was pitched and when. The ERP needs a customer to bill, including a legal entity, tax number, payment terms, credit limit, bill-to address, and ledger account. Supply-chain and warehouse systems need a customer to deliver to, so they care about ship-to locations, delivery windows, unloading requirements, and the distribution centre that serves them. The billing platform needs a payer, which may not be the same legal entity as either the buyer or the receiver.

None of those four records is necessarily wrong. Each may be correct for the question its system was built to answer, even though the systems were created at different times by different teams and some customer information was entered manually in more than one place. Product presents the same problem in a different form. Engineering holds a part with a drawing number and revision; the ERP holds a material with a weight, unit of measure, and valuation class; the sales system holds a sellable item with a list price; and the warehouse holds a storage unit with a pallet configuration. It may be one physical thing, but it arrives as four records with four identifiers and four sets of attributes.

The same company can therefore arrive in the warehouse looking like this; the names below are illustrative.

```
The same customer, four systems, four identities

  CRM         ACC-40912     Meridian Freight Inc.
  ERP         0001048372    MERIDIAN FREIGHT INC
  Billing     C-88231       Meridian Freight
  Warehouse   SHIP-2201     Meridian Frght Inc, Columbus
```

Ask for total revenue by customer and the consequence becomes clear. Without something that knows those four rows represent one company, the warehouse produces four customers where there is one and splits the revenue four ways. The query can be correct while the answer is not, which is why data-warehouse work so often exposes master-data problems. What gets mastered is more than an identifier, and this is where much of the work sits.

```
Identifiers
  master ID, source system IDs, and external identifiers
  such as tax number, VAT number, DUNS, GLN, GTIN
```

```
Names
  legal name, trading name, former names, local spellings

Addresses
  registered, bill-to, ship-to, remit-to

Classification
  industry code, customer group, product hierarchy, brand

Attributes that drive behaviour
  payment terms, credit limit, tax status, delivery terms

Relationships
  parent company, subsidiaries, sold-to and ship-to links

Lifecycle
  active, blocked, obsolete, valid from and valid to
```

The identifiers matter most to the mechanics of this book, while the relationships often determine how badly an answer can go wrong. Consider the parent company. A large customer may buy through eleven subsidiaries, each with its own contracts and credit terms. Ask for the top customer by revenue and the honest answer depends on whether you mean the legal entity that placed the order or the group that owns it. Both definitions are legitimate, and they produce different lists. The relationship must be recorded somewhere authoritative and made available to the query; without it, neither a human nor an AI agent can reliably know which definition of customer the question requires.

In practice, the work usually comes down to four moves. Matching determines which records refer to the same real thing. Deterministic matching uses an exact key, such as a tax number. Probabilistic matching scores similarity across several fields, so a near-identical name at a similar address may become a likely match even when no reliable identifier matches exactly. The threshold is a business decision: set it too loose and two different companies are merged; set it too tight and duplicates survive.

Once records are matched, survivorship determines which value wins when they disagree. The rule is set per attribute, not per record: the

ERP might be trusted for the tax number and legal name, the CRM for the contact, and the warehouse for the ship-to address. The resulting master record is assembled from several sources, which is why it is often called a golden record. Cross-referencing preserves the link. A table maps each source identifier to the master identifier, allowing an ERP row and a CRM row to be traced back to the same company and forward to the same answer.

Stewardship handles what the rules cannot. Ambiguous matches go to a data steward, who decides; some platforms now propose matches for a steward to confirm rather than making the decision alone. Organizations usually implement this in one of a few common ways. A registry leaves source records alone and maintains only the cross-references. A consolidation model builds golden records for reporting without changing the sources. A coexistence model pushes agreed values back into the source systems. In a centralized model, the master-data platform becomes the place where new customers and products are created, and the sources receive them.

There is a market of products for this. As of April 2026, Gartner's Magic Quadrant for Master Data Management Solutions positioned Profisee, Reltio, Salesforce (Informatica), Semarchy, and Stibo Systems as Leaders.[1] Other established platforms include SAP Master Data Governance, IBM InfoSphere MDM, TIBCO EBX, Ataccama, and Syndigo. Product-heavy organizations often start with a product information management tool and grow into multi-domain master data from there. Many organizations manage master data without any of those products. A mapping table, a set of agreed rules, and someone who owns them can carry a smaller estate a long way. The discipline matters more than the software, and the software cannot supply the discipline.

Without that work, revenue splits across duplicate customers and nobody sees the real relationship size. Credit exposure may be assessed against one identity while the group owes money under three others. Inventory may sit under two part numbers for the same item, and screening or reporting obligations may be checked against a name that does not match the contract. Cross-system reports can be quietly wrong in a way the number itself does not reveal; this is where the issue becomes important for an AI agent.

A warehouse may contain more than one customer table: a mastered dimension, staged copies from source systems, and older tables that remain in the environment. Several may hold customer identifiers, but only one represents the identity the business has chosen for the purpose at hand. An agent that joins on the wrong identifier can produce syntactically valid SQL, run without error, and return a number calculated against the wrong customer identity. The schema alone may not tell it which table or key carries the governed definition.

By now, the pattern should be visible. The OLTP system depended on knowledge beyond the individual record; the warehouse applied decisions whose reasoning may live elsewhere; and the master-data layer decided which identities belong together. The schema alone may still not tell an agent which governed definition to use. Knowing which key is the master key is not a SQL skill; it is organizational knowledge that has to reach the agent from somewhere.

The Data Lake

The section on types named five ideas; four are now behind us, and the fifth comes last because it is the newest and is still changing. A data lake is both a storage pattern and an architecture. It often uses relatively inexpensive object storage or a distributed file system, allowing data to arrive in many forms without requiring one strict analytical schema before it lands. That last point is the heart of the idea, and it reverses the assumption this chapter has been building from the beginning. OLTP systems and many warehouse pipelines use schema on write. Someone designs the table, agrees the columns, settles the definitions, and validates the data before or during ingestion.

Many lake architectures defer some schema decisions: data can land first and receive structure when someone reads or transforms it. That is schema on read. Governed lakehouses can also enforce schemas and control schema evolution, so the boundary is not absolute. For a while, this flexibility was a poor bargain. Deferring the decision often meant that nobody made it at all. Organizations filled object storage with extracts nobody could navigate, in formats nobody had documented, without any guarantee that two files written at the same moment would agree. The word that stuck was data swamp. Several developments changed the trade-off, and they are worth separating because they arrived at different times.

Object storage is often less expensive at scale than traditional database storage, and cloud architectures can separate storage from compute. The economics vary by provider, retention policy, access pattern, and warehouse design. Keeping raw extracts for years can therefore be cheaper than it was in older architectures, but it is not free. Cloud lake architectures can also make compute elastic. Storage and compute are separated, so processing power can be directed at files for a workload and scaled back when the workload ends. This is common in cloud environments, although not every lake uses the same operating model.

The file formats matured as well. Data in a lake is often converted to a columnar format such as Parquet, which can compress well and lets a query read only the columns it needs rather than every column in the row. Other common formats include CSV, JSON, Avro, and ORC, which stands for Optimized Row Columnar. On top of the files, an open table format such as Apache Iceberg, Delta Lake, or Apache Hudi can add metadata and table-management behavior to the collection. The table-format layer is the part most people miss.

```
Query engines    Spark, Trino, warehouse engines
Table format     Iceberg, Delta Lake, Hudi
File format      Parquet
Storage          Object storage
```

An open table format can add capabilities that an unmanaged folder of files does not provide by itself, including transactions or atomic commits, schema evolution, time travel, and partition management. The exact guarantees depend on the format, engine, configuration, and retention policy. Iceberg originated at Netflix and is now an Apache project designed to work across many engines. Databricks open-sourced Delta Lake in 2019, and it has grown beyond its original ecosystem. The two formats overlap in important capabilities, including transactions, schema evolution, and time travel, while still differing in implementation and ecosystem support. With transaction and schema capabilities available, many lakehouse teams organize data into layers. A common pattern uses three layers and is usually called medallion architecture.

```
Bronze
  Often raw or minimally transformed data from source systems

Silver
  Often cleaned, typed, validated, deduplicated, or conformed data

Gold
  Often business-ready tables shaped for particular questions
```

Read that list alongside the previous two sections and the pattern should look familiar. Silver performs much of the integration work described in the warehouse section, while gold is shaped for questions rather than storage. Organizing lake data this way is one common lakehouse pattern, bringing warehouse-style management and analytics to data stored in the lake. That brings us to the lake's place alongside everything else in this chapter: it does not replace any of those systems. The OLTP systems still run the business, while a lake may be where raw extracts land first. Some pipelines preserve those extracts as received; others transform, filter, or reformat the data before it arrives. Whether the original source record survives depends on the architecture and retention policy.

Columnar files and elastic compute have reduced the need to precompute every combination in many systems. Cubes, semantic models, materialized views, and other aggregates remain useful when their performance, governance, or audit characteristics fit the workload. A warehouse may feed from the lake. In a lakehouse design, the gold layer can also perform much of the analytical work traditionally handled by warehouse tables and data marts. The star schema introduced earlier can appear here too. The lake makes one part of master-data work easier. Matching customers across four systems requires all four versions to remain available side by side in their original state, and the lake is a natural place to keep them. For this book, the most important point is what the lake preserves.

A curated warehouse may publish one agreed answer while the underlying source values and disagreements remain elsewhere. A lake often retains more of that raw and intermediate evidence. The CRM extract may still be there with the customer name spelled as the salesperson typed it; the bronze layer may preserve what arrived before anyone reconciled it; and time travel may show what a table contained before a rule changed, when the table format supports snapshots and the relevant history has been retained. The evidence behind a number is therefore more likely to survive. That is a real gain, but it should not be oversold: evidence still existing is not the same as the reasoning being recorded, and finding it usually requires knowing where to look.

For an agent, this creates a difficult trade-off. A data lake may contain many more tables than a warehouse. These tables may be spread across bronze, silver, and gold layers, along with older tables that have accumulated over time. Several tables may describe the same data at different processing stages. A query against a bronze table may run without errors but use raw, unreconciled data. That is almost never the data the user meant to ask about. The warehouse was curated. The lake gives up some curation for flexibility and lower cost, leaving you to decide which data to trust.

Chapter 2: The Shapes of Structured Data

Navigate: Contents · Previous: Chapter 1 · Next: Chapter 3

The opening was about where structured data lives. This chapter is about what shape it takes when it gets there. Those are two different questions, and people mix them up all the time. A data warehouse is a place; a time series is a shape. The same shape can exist in several places, and one place can contain several different shapes. Several shapes were mentioned in passing to show what structure means. Here they are grouped properly.

```
Tables of record
  Transactional tables
  Analytical tables

Ordered by time
  Time series
  Event and audit records

Connected shapes
  Hierarchical
  Graph

Specialized shapes
  Geospatial
```

The groups describe different ways of asking questions, not just different ways of storing data. Each shape therefore needs its own SQL approach. Tables of record are the most familiar form: rows and columns, usually with one row for each business object or event. They support most everyday business questions. Ordered data adds sequence to the meaning. In a time series or event record, reading values in the wrong order can hide trends, changes, or the relationship between an event and its correction.

Connected data makes relationships central. A product hierarchy and a company-ownership network both require you to follow links between records, but they may need different SQL techniques. Specialized data supports questions that ordinary rows and columns cannot answer well. Geospatial data represents locations and shapes, so queries usually ask about distance, containment, or intersection instead of exact-value matches. Key-value stores are another structured form. They are left aside here because application code generally accesses them through a purpose-built interface rather than SQL. The focus here is on asking questions in SQL.

The sections that follow examine these forms one at a time, beginning with tables of record. They are the form most likely to appear in a business question and the form underlying most of the examples so far.

Tables

Go back through the last chapter and count the shapes. There is only one: tables. The order system was built from them, as were the account system, the star schema, and the conformed dimension. The bronze, silver, and gold layers were organized around tables as well. These examples come from different parts of the data estate and serve different purposes, but the underlying shape is the same.

That is worth stating plainly because a warehouse or a lake can sound as though it must contain something exotic. In practice, both organize structured information into tables, although they arrange those tables for different jobs. At its simplest, a table is a grid with a rule attached. Each row follows the same schema, each column describes one aspect of the thing being recorded, and the rule is what allows a database engine to read the ten millionth row without being told anything new. What changes from one environment to another is not the basic shape, but the design decisions made within it.

An OLTP system usually spreads information across many narrow tables: customer details in one, addresses in another, order headers in a third, and order lines in a fourth. That arrangement makes short writes and targeted updates efficient, but a useful answer often requires several joins. A warehouse usually favors fewer, wider tables. Descriptive columns that were separated in the transaction system may be brought together on a dimension row, sometimes repeated for each customer. Such tables are less convenient to update, but they are often easier to read across for analytical work. A lake can preserve both kinds of organization at different layers, while also introducing a third form that is not a table in the usual database sense. We will come to that at the end of this section.

The next question is what turns a collection of tables into a model. A table on its own answers very little. `ORDER_ITEM` may know a product key and a quantity, but it does not know the product's name. That name lives in `PRODUCT`, and the model needs a way to state that the two columns refer to the same thing. This is the job of keys. A primary key is a column, or set of columns, that identifies a row uniquely. In `CUSTOMER`, for example, `customer_id` should identify one row and should not be empty. Sometimes one column is not enough. In the twelve-line order from the last chapter, `order_id` appears on every line and `item_no` repeats across different orders. Neither is unique by itself, but together they identify one line. That pair is a composite key, a common pattern in transaction tables.

A foreign key connects that row to a related table. `ORDER_ITEM.product_id`, for example, points to the corresponding product record in `PRODUCT`. In effect, it says, "this line is for that product," in a form the database can use. Relationships also have cardinality. One customer may have many addresses, one order may have many lines, and one product may appear on many order lines. Those are one-to-many relationships, a common pattern in business data. A many-to-many relationship needs an association table. A product may be bought from several suppliers, while each supplier may provide several products, so a small table in between records the pairings, one row for each combination.

The most important idea here is simple: the same business information can be arranged in different table shapes for different jobs. A sales transaction, for example, may be split across several narrow tables in an order system, combined into a fact table and several descriptive dimensions in a warehouse, or stored as a collection of event records in a data lake. The business subject is still sales, but the structure changes with the system's purpose.

In a transaction system, the tables are designed to record and update individual business events safely. An order may be in `ORDER_HEADER`, its products may be in `ORDER_ITEM`, and the product details may be in `PRODUCT`. Keys connect those tables. The important point is not whether every analytical platform enforces those relationships. The important point is that the relationships explain how the pieces fit together and which tables must be connected to answer a question.[1]

An entity relationship diagram shows this kind of design as boxes and lines. It is useful when you need to understand how a transaction system is assembled. In the order system, the diagram might include `CUSTOMER`, `ADDRESS`, `PRODUCT`, `ORDER_HEADER`, and `ORDER_ITEM`. Each box represents a table, and each line shows a relationship between tables. The line can also show whether one customer can have many orders or whether one order can contain many items. This diagram tells you how the system is connected. It does not tell you which table the business has approved for a particular report. It is a map of the roads, not a route.

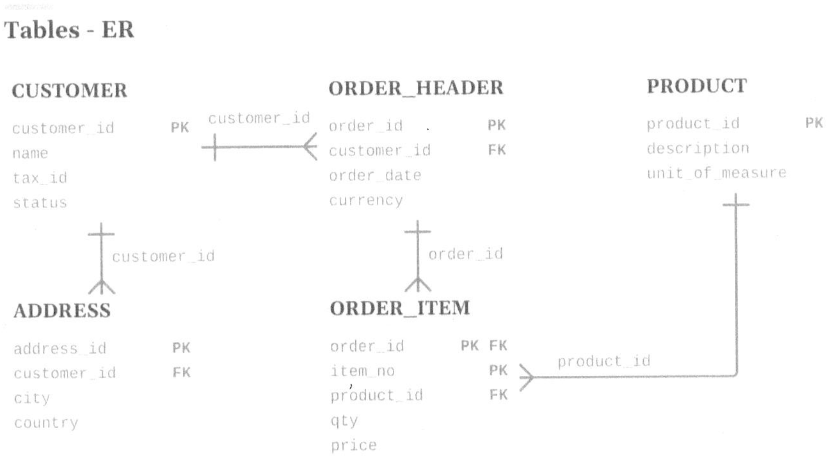

Figure 2.1 The order system drawn as an entity relationship diagram. Five tables, four one to many relationships, and the columns each join runs on.

A warehouse usually arranges the same information for analysis rather than for individual updates. A star schema places a central fact table, such as `FACT_SALES`, beside descriptive tables such as `DIM_DATE`, `DIM_CUSTOMER`, and `DIM_PRODUCT`. The fact table records measures, such as sales amount and quantity. The dimension tables explain those measures by date, customer, product, region, or other business descriptions. Most questions begin with the fact table and move outward to the dimensions.

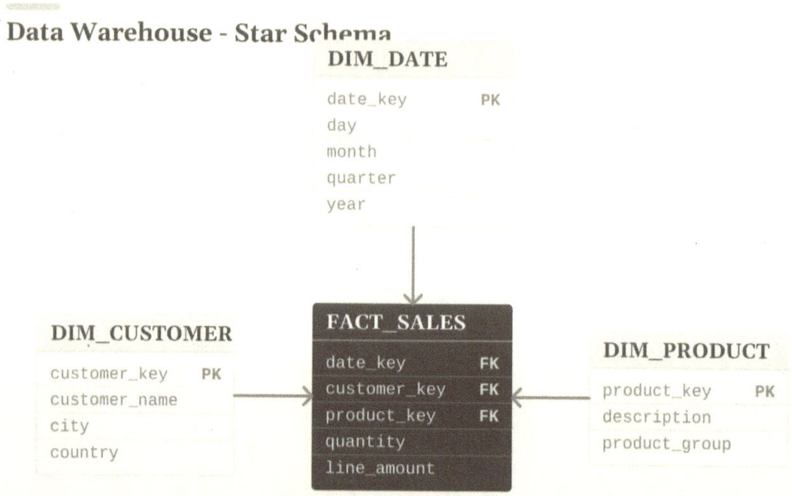

Figure 2.2 A star schema. FACT_SALES at the centre carrying the measures and the keys, with each dimension one join away.

A snowflake schema takes the same general approach but separates some descriptive information into additional tables. A customer table might point to a city table, which in turn points to a country table. This can reduce repeated information, but it also creates more steps in the path to an answer. A star schema is often easier for people to read because the route is more direct. A snowflake schema can be more normalized, but every additional join is another place where the data or the query can go wrong.

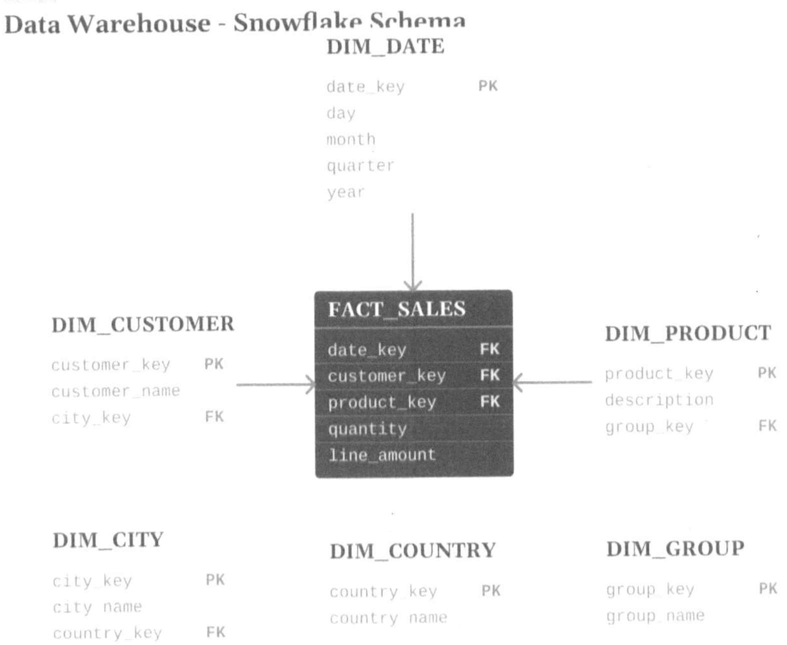

Figure 2.3 A snowflake schema. The same star with city, country and product group normalized back out, so each value is stored once and reached in more joins.

The storage technology adds another difference. In a database, the engine manages the tables and their storage. In a data lake, the same logical table may be represented by files in object storage plus metadata that explains what the files contain. A sales table in the lake might be a set of files containing raw order events. Another set of files might contain customer changes or product updates. The files can still represent familiar rows and columns, but the system has to use metadata to understand which files belong together and what version of the data they represent.

Many data lake files use Parquet. A traditional database commonly stores the values for one complete row together. Parquet stores the values for a column together instead. That difference affects how the data is read. A query that needs only dates and sales amounts can read those columns without reading every other field in the files. The result is still a table from the user's point of view, but its physical layout is different and can be better suited to large analytical reads.

A collection of Parquet files is not automatically a reliable table. The files may have schemas, but something still has to record which files belong to the current table, how the schema changed, and what the table looked like at an earlier point in time. Open table formats such as Iceberg and Delta provide that layer of metadata. They allow several engines to work with the same data while preserving a table-like view of the files.[2]

This distinction is important for an AI agent. When the agent sees the word table, it cannot assume that every table has the same shape or the same purpose. One table may contain one row per order. Another may contain one row per order item. A warehouse fact table may contain one row per sales event or one row per daily summary. A lake table may contain raw records that have not yet been reconciled. The names alone do not tell the agent which one it should use.

To read enterprise data correctly, the agent needs metadata that explains the table's grain, purpose, relationships, business definitions, and place in the data environment. It needs to know whether a table is meant for updates, reporting, historical analysis, or raw investigation. The table may be stored in a database, a warehouse, or a lake, but the real question is always the same: what does one row mean, and how should this table be used to answer the business question?

Time Series

The opening of this chapter grouped time series and event records together because both give sequence a central role. A time series adds that sequence through repeated measurements. To see the difference, go back to the account system from the last chapter. It held a balance table with one row per account, containing the current figure and updating it in the same transaction that recorded the posting. That table answered one question: what is the balance now? Now imagine keeping one row per account per day instead.

```
Current state, as it stood earlier
  BALANCE
    account_id PK, as_of, ledger_bal, available_bal

The same measure kept over time
  BALANCE_DAILY
    account_id PK, as_of_date PK, ledger_bal, available_bal
```

Two things changed, and both matter. The key gained a column. An account no longer identifies a row by itself. The account and the date do. It is the same composite-key idea from the previous section, now doing a different job. Nothing is overwritten either. Yesterday's row is still there tomorrow, so the table grows rather than replacing the past. That is the basic shape of a time series: the same measurement, for the same thing, recorded repeatedly over time.

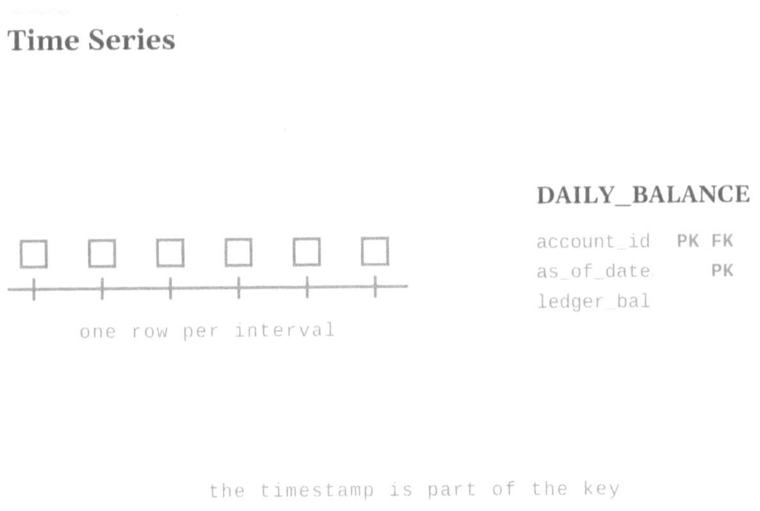

Figure 2.4 A time series. One row per interval, with the timestamp part of the key.

The rows do not have to arrive in order. You can sort them whenever you need to because the date is part of each row. What matters is that one row says very little on its own. A ledger balance of forty thousand tells you almost nothing without a comparison. Forty thousand today against thirty thousand yesterday tells you something. Forty thousand today against forty thousand every day for six weeks tells you something else. The information has moved out of the individual rows and into the distance between them.

When the interval is regular, a row may be written even when nothing happened. An account with no transactions on Tuesday can still receive a Tuesday row, and that row is not empty. It says that the balance did not move, which may be exactly the fact someone needs. That is why a missing row creates a real interpretive problem. In a time series, no row may mean that nothing was measured, or that the measurement failed to arrive. The table looks the same in both cases unless the system records the distinction somewhere else.

The questions people ask of a time series are different from the questions they ask of a single current-state table. They want to know how a value changed, what its trend looks like, when it crossed a threshold, or how this month compares with the same month last year. Each question involves several rows. Aggregation can summarize those rows, but it cannot by itself preserve every comparison between them. Window functions help because they allow each row to see related rows while remaining a row in the result. Previous values, next values, running totals, and moving averages over the last thirty days all depend on that ability to look sideways.

Then there is the question that sounds simple but is not: what was the balance on the fifteenth? If a row exists for that date, the answer is straightforward. If it does not, someone must decide how to interpret the gap. The system might carry the last known value forward because a balance persists until something changes it. It might return no value because no measurement was taken. Or it might estimate a value between the neighboring observations, which may be reasonable for a temperature but not for a balance. All three approaches can be defensible. The right choice depends on what is being measured and how the answer will be used, and the schema rarely records that decision by itself.

The same kind of decision appears in the table's grain and in the way late data is handled. The interval is chosen when the table is designed. Daily rows may be rolled into monthly figures, but monthly rows cannot be broken back into daily ones. Whoever chose the grain also chose which questions would remain answerable years later. Data can arrive late as well. A reading for Tuesday may not appear until Thursday. Should Tuesday's figure change when the reading arrives, or should Tuesday remain as it was first reported? Financial reporting may use one convention, while operational monitoring may use another. The table alone cannot tell you which rule this organization follows.

Time series appear throughout the systems described in the last chapter. Transaction systems produce them as balances, readings, and stock levels. Warehouses store them as fact rows with date keys. Lakes often partition them by date, which is one reason partition handling matters. Specialized databases are built for measurements arriving thousands of times per second and are optimized for this kind of workload.

Now put an agent in front of one of these tables. Ask for the balance on the fifteenth when the series has a gap on that date. The agent can write a query that returns nothing, and that query may be correct. It can also write a query that carries the previous value forward, and that query may be correct as well. Both are valid SQL against the same table, yet they return different answers. Nothing in the column names necessarily tells the agent which convention the organization uses. The decision may live in loading code, a reporting standard, or the memory of the person who built the system. That is the same problem the last chapter described, arriving through a different door.

There is one more shape in this group, and it takes the idea further. In a time series, rows are added according to a schedule. In the next shape, rows are added because something happened, and the records are designed not to be changed afterward.

Event and Audit Records

A time series adds a row because the clock says it is time to record another measurement. An event log adds a row because something happened. The last chapter already showed an example of the second kind: the account system held a posting table, with one row for each movement of money, next to the balance it updated.

```
From the account system
  POSTING
    posting_id PK, account_id FK, post_date, amount
```

Nothing about that table looks unusual until a posting turns out to be wrong. In most tables, the wrong value is corrected by updating the row. Here, the original remains exactly as it was. A second row is written to cancel it, and sometimes a third records what should have happened. The mistake stays on the record because preserving the history is the point. This is an append-only table: rows are added, but existing rows are not changed or removed.

That rule can sound inconvenient, yet it is what makes the record useful as evidence. If a record can be edited, there is no reliable way to distinguish the original entry from a later alteration. In an append-only record, the story can change only by adding to it, and the addition remains visible. This reverses the problem from the time-series section. A missing row in a time series may indicate a gap in measurement. In an event log, the absence of an event may itself be meaningful, provided the log is complete and the system records all relevant events.

Event and Audit Records

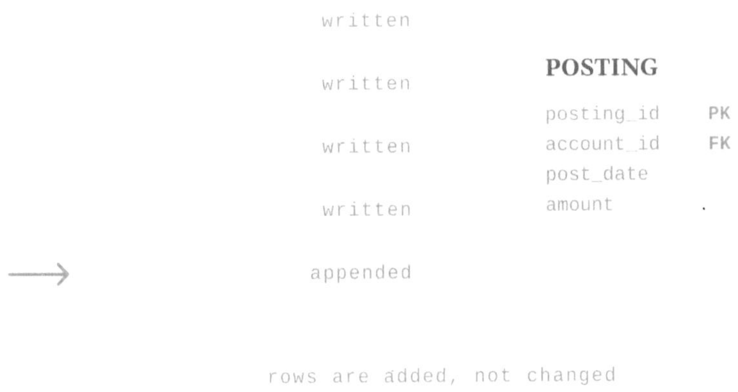

Figure 2.5 An append-only event log. Rows are added, never changed, so the record of what happened stays intact.

Events also bring another complication: time. Many events have both the time when something happened and the time when the record arrived in the system. A payment made on the twenty-eighth may not be recorded until the second day of the following month. The distinction matters because a request for last month's total can produce different answers depending on which clock is used. Financial reporting may organize the result around the date to which the event belongs, while operational monitoring may organize it around the date on which the event was seen. The column names do not always make that distinction obvious, so a query written against the wrong date can still look perfectly valid.

There is an additional consequence, which explains an issue left unresolved in the previous chapter. If every movement is recorded as an event, then the current state can be derived by replaying or aggregating those events. The balance is calculated from the postings, while a separate balance table may be maintained for fast lookups. That is why the last chapter showed both structures. Recomputing a balance from millions of rows every time someone asks for it is not what an

OLTP system does best. The same figure can therefore exist twice: once as a stored number and once as a derivation from the event history. In an event-sourced design, the events are the authority and the balance is a convenience built on top of them. The same pattern appears outside accounting wherever a system keeps both a running state and the record of changes that produced it.

Audit records use a similar structure for a different purpose. Instead of recording money moving, they record people and systems acting: who changed a credit limit, what the value was before and after, when the change occurred, and whose approval allowed it. They may record who ran a report or granted access. When designed as an append-only trail, the rows accumulate rather than being edited. This makes audit records the closest thing in the chapter to the reasoning that the earlier sections found missing. An audit table can record who made a decision, when it was made, and sometimes why.

That answer has limits. Audit tables record activity that occurs inside the systems that maintain them. They may show that a credit limit changed, but they may not show that someone on the warehouse team decided in 2019 to exclude cancelled orders from a revenue measure. Important decisions often take place in meetings, transformation code, tickets, or informal conversations, none of which may leave an audit record in the data estate.

For an agent, event and audit records offer history but demand interpretation. The agent must know which clock a question refers to. When someone asks for March, does March mean events that happened during March or records that arrived during March? It must also understand that corrections are additions. A naive sum of the amount column may count the original error, the reversal, and the corrected entry as three separate pieces of business. Every row is real, but only the correct interpretation produces the answer. The next two shapes are different because they are not about when things happened. They are about how things are connected.

Hierarchical

Everything so far has treated a row as a thing in its own right: a customer, an order, or a balance on a Tuesday. Hierarchical data is different. The rows still exist, but the important information lies in how they connect. The most common example is a tree, such as the product-group structure that appeared in the last chapter.

It might be stored like this:

```
PRODUCT_GROUP
  group_id PK, group_name, parent_group_id FK
```

The third column does something new. `parent_group_id` points back to `group_id` in the same table, so the table refers to itself. That single relationship can represent a tree of several levels. Fasteners can sit under Hardware, Hardware can sit under Industrial Supplies, and Industrial Supplies can sit at the top with no parent. Read the rows as a list and the structure is invisible. Follow the keys and the shape appears. The storage is a table, but the meaning comes from the connections between its rows.

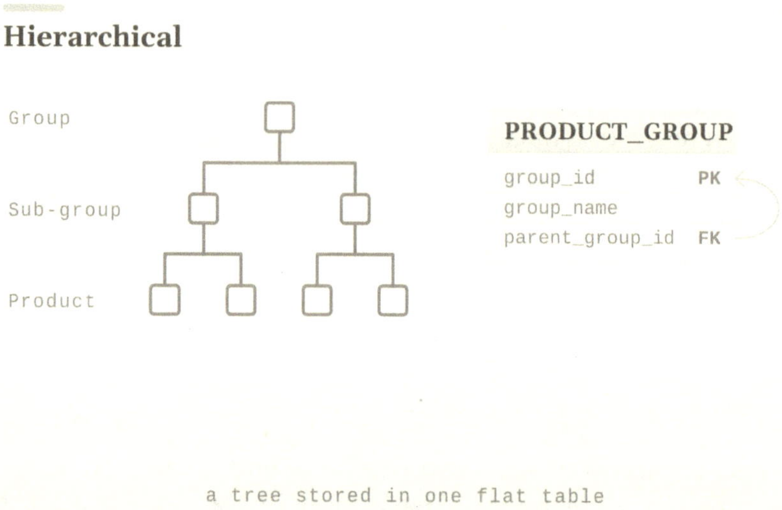

Figure 2.6 A hierarchy. A tree of product groups held in one flat table, where parent_group_id points back at group_id in the same table.

The difficulty becomes clear when someone asks a normal business question. To show all products under Industrial Supplies using ordinary joins, the query must know how deep the hierarchy is. Three levels require three joins, six levels require six, and a new level may require the query to be rewritten. Recursive SQL removes that fixed limit. A recursive query starts at one row and follows the parent relationship until there are no more levels to visit. Other designs store the full path in a column or assign each node a numbered range so that descendants can be found through a lookup. Each approach trades write cost against read cost, and all are common enough to appear in real systems.

Hierarchies also explain the ladder of totals that the cube section showed earlier. Sales can be calculated for Fasteners, then for Hardware including Fasteners, and then for Industrial Supplies including everything below it. The hierarchy supplies the levels at which those totals make sense. Real hierarchies, however, are rarely as neat as the diagram suggests. They are often ragged, with one branch four levels deep and another stopping after two. Any calculation that assumes every branch has the same depth will eventually fail.

Hierarchies change as well. Product groups are reorganized, cost centers are restructured, and territories are redrawn. When that happens, last year's numbers may have been reported under a structure that no longer exists. This is a more difficult version of the slowly changing dimension problem. A question about last year may need the hierarchy that existed at the time, so that the result reconciles with what was published, or the current hierarchy, so that old and new figures can be compared on the same basis. Both approaches are legitimate, and organizations sometimes use both.

This is why hierarchical questions need more than a table definition. An agent must know which level the business means, how the levels are named, whether branches can stop early, and which version applies to the period being asked about. Without that context, valid SQL can still produce a result that is precise, plausible, and wrong. The hierarchy's structure and history therefore need to be made explicit before an agent can use its totals with confidence.

Graph

A tree gives each node one parent, but most real relationships are not so tidy. The last chapter exposed a decision worth making explicit: when a large customer buys through eleven subsidiaries, "customer" can mean the legal entity that placed the order or the corporate group that owns it. Both definitions are legitimate, but they produce different answers. The relationship therefore needs to be recorded somewhere authoritative and made available to the query; without it, neither a human nor an AI agent can reliably know which definition the question requires. The answer to a question about the biggest customer depended on whether customer meant the entity that placed the order or the group behind it. Ownership is not always a tree. A subsidiary may have two owners, companies may hold stakes in each other, and a corporate structure can contain relationships that do not fit a single-parent model.

When nodes can connect to one another in different directions and through different relationship types, the shape is a graph. One business-oriented way to represent this is to keep one list of the things the business tracks and another list showing how those things are connected:

```
NODE
  node_id PK, node_type, node_name

EDGE
  from_node_id PK FK, to_node_id PK FK, edge_type
```

Graph data describes things and the connections between them. A thing might be a company, a person, an account, a product, or a location. A connection explains how two things are related. One company may own another, supply it, share a director with it, or sell to it. These relationships are part of the meaning of the data, not just a path to another piece of information.

Graph

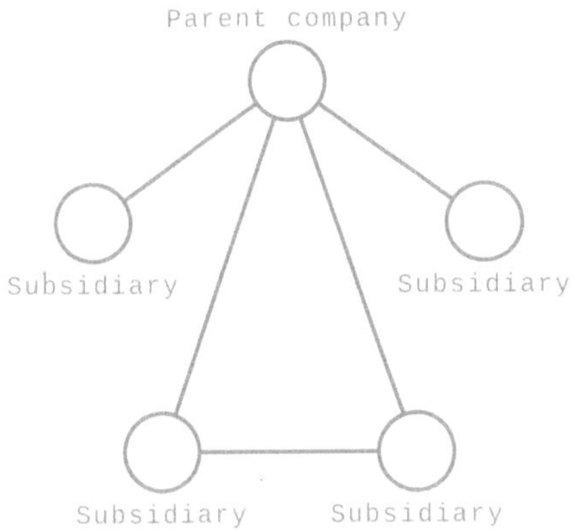

NODE

node_id	PK
node_type	
node_name	

EDGE

from_node_id	PK FK
to_node_id	PK FK
edge_type	

many to many, and no single root

Figure 2.7 A graph. Things and the connections between them, held in two tables, with no single root.

Consider three companies: Acme owns Beta, Beta buys materials from Gamma, and Gamma supplies a product to Acme. Each connection has a different meaning and may have its own details, such as an ownership percentage, a contract date, or a product category. The same two companies can have several connections at once. A system that stores only one relationship between them would lose important business information.

Graph data is useful when the question requires following connections through several steps. Which companies are ultimately controlled by Acme, even if the ownership chain has several levels? Which suppliers do our two largest customers have in common? Is there a connection between two bank accounts, and how many steps does that connection contain? Which products were handled by the same supplier as a product that was recalled? In each case, the path matters as much as the individual companies, accounts, or products.

Following those paths can become difficult as the network grows. A simple hierarchy has one direction, such as an employee reporting to a manager or a subsidiary belonging to a parent company. A business network can branch in many directions. A company can have several suppliers, those suppliers can serve several customers, and the connections can eventually lead back to a company already visited. A search must keep track of where it has been so that it does not follow the same loop forever. The answer may be technically correct, but the logic can still be difficult to read and easy to get subtly wrong.

Some systems are designed specifically to search these connections. They treat the relationships as important information rather than reconstructing every path from separate pieces of data. This can be useful for corporate ownership, supply-chain analysis, fraud detection, recommendations, and identity resolution. A bank, for example, might follow connections among accounts, devices, addresses, and transactions to identify a pattern that would be difficult to see by looking at one account at a time. The performance depends on the system, the design, and the question being asked. It also brings another system with its own data loads, controls, and governance. SQL:2023 added property graph queries in Part 16 of the standard, so some graph questions can now be expressed in SQL.[3] Support varies across products, but graph analysis does not always require a separate graph system.

Return to the question of the largest customer. If customer means the organization that placed the order, the answer is a normal total. If customer means the entire corporate group, the answer requires following ownership connections through as many levels as needed and adding revenue to the correct parent. The business question sounds the same, but the word customer changes the calculation. An agent may have access to the ownership information, but it still needs to know whether ownership should be followed, how far the search should go, and which relationships count as ownership. Without that business knowledge, it can produce an answer that is technically valid but wrong for the business.

The connected shapes are now complete.

Geospatial

Most of the examples so far have compared values by matching them or testing their size. Is this customer key equal to that one? Is this date inside that range? Is this amount greater than the threshold? Geospatial data opens a different kind of business question: where is something, and what is near it? An address written as a city and country can tell us how many customers are in Ohio or which orders shipped to Memphis. To ask which customers are within eighty kilometres of a depot, the data also needs to describe each location as a position.

A location record can include the address details people use, together with a geometry value that represents its position or shape. Three basic shapes cover many business examples. A point represents one position, such as a depot, customer address, utility meter, or vehicle at a particular moment. A line is an ordered set of points, such as a delivery route, pipeline, river, or road. A polygon is a closed boundary around an area, such as a sales territory, delivery zone, warehouse catchment, or country boundary.

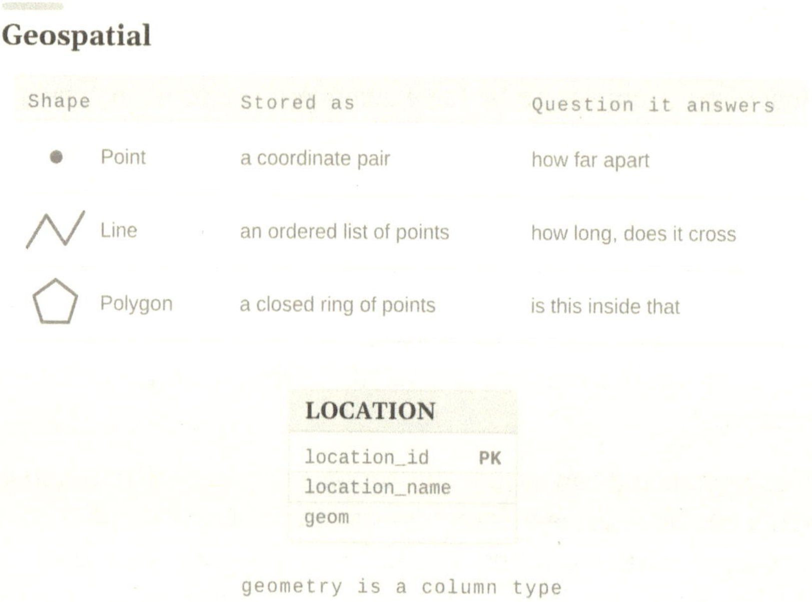

Figure 2.8 Geospatial data. Point, line and polygon, what each is stored as, and the question each one answers.

The questions asked of these shapes are spatial rather than arithmetic. A business can calculate the distance between a depot and a customer, find the customers inside a delivery zone, determine whether a road crosses a sales territory, or identify which service locations are near a pipeline. These operations extend the kinds of questions an AI agent can answer. Spatial indexes can help the system first focus on a likely region before it performs the detailed calculation.

Every position also uses a coordinate reference system, which gives the numbers their meaning. A coordinate is not simply a pair of numbers. It describes a location relative to a model of the earth. Many systems are in use, and databases often identify them with an integer code. WGS 84, the World Geodetic System of 1984, is a common geographic system that expresses latitude and longitude in degrees. Web Mercator is a projected system that uses a flat map and linear units, and it is widely used in web mapping. These are common examples, not universal choices.

The coordinate system and the units are part of the business meaning of a geospatial question. A request for everything within eighty is incomplete until the query establishes whether eighty means degrees, metres, kilometres, or another unit. Distance on a curved earth also differs from distance on a flat projection. A projection that works well for a local delivery radius may not be the best choice for a continental calculation. The geographic area and the purpose of the question help determine the appropriate approach.

Geospatial data gives an agent a richer way to understand the enterprise. A customer is no longer only a name and an account number. The customer can also be located in relation to a depot, route, territory, service region, or other business asset. To use that context well, the agent needs to inspect the geometry type, coordinate reference system, units, and intended business use. When that information is available, the agent can turn location data into practical answers about coverage, logistics, service, territory planning, and operations.

What the Shapes Have in Common

Enterprise data can describe the same business in different ways. An order system records transactions as they happen. An analytical system arranges those transactions so people can study sales, customers, products, and performance. Other forms of data show timing, sequence, ownership, reporting relationships, connections between organizations, or the location of a customer or asset. The structure changes because the business question changes.

That structure also affects the meaning of the information. Customer may mean the organization that placed an order or the corporate group that owns it. A date may describe when an event occurred or when the system received it. Product group may refer to a particular level or version of a product structure. A period with no records may describe a quiet period or data that has not arrived yet. A location becomes useful for distance and territory questions only when its measurement system and units are understood.

These details are business definitions expressed through data. They may be described in metadata, policies, mappings, process documentation, or the knowledge of experienced people. The names of fields and systems provide useful clues, but the full meaning comes from the organization that created and uses the data.

That meaning is what an AI agent needs to work with enterprise information. A model can write SQL and recognize common data patterns, but it needs the organization's definitions to select the right source, combine information correctly, and explain the result in business terms. The rest of this book shows how to make that knowledge available so that AI can move from finding data to answering trusted questions and carrying out useful work.

Chapter 3: Metadata

Every business object has its own form, behavior, and distinguishing characteristics. A customer, order, account, or product is shaped differently and follows different rules. The information that describes those forms, rules, relationships, and characteristics is called metadata. It helps people and systems understand not only what data exists, but what it means and how it should be used. Metadata is what gives structured data its business context.

The standard definition of metadata is data about data. That is true, but almost useless on its own. A more workable definition is this: metadata is everything a system knows about a column except the values stored in it. By that definition, you have been reading about metadata from the beginning without calling it by name. A column called `order_date`, a type that says the column holds a date, and a declaration that `customer_id` is a key are all metadata. None of them is business data. They are the database describing itself.

Metadata comes in three kinds, and telling them apart is the point. Technical metadata is what the engine records because it needs it to operate: table and column names, data types, whether a column can be empty, which columns are keys, how a table is partitioned, and roughly how many rows it contains. Every database keeps some version of this information and usually exposes it through a catalog that can be queried like any other table. It is generally available without anyone writing separate documentation, but it says very little about meaning.

Business metadata is the meaning. It explains what a column represents, what its values stand for, who owns it, what counts as included or excluded, and which of several similar tables the business has agreed to use. The database does not produce this information.

Someone writes it down, or nobody does. Operational metadata records what has happened to the data: where it came from, what transformed it, when it was last loaded, whether the load completed, and whether the data passed its checks. Some systems record this automatically, many record only part of it, and most record less than people assume.

Technical metadata describes how data is stored: table and column names, data types, keys, and other details the database needs to operate. Business metadata explains what the data means and how business users should use it. This book also calls it the business meaning, which is the same idea in plainer words. For example, it can identify the approved customer table, explain what an empty day in a time series means, specify which date column to use, define the level meant by a hierarchy term, or describe how a financial measure is calculated. A coordinate reference system is a technical detail because it describes how a geographic value is stored; the other issues are about business meaning. The database knows the structure of the data, but not what that data means to the business.

Metadata should stay where an agent can easily access it. That may be inside the source system, but it may also be in a separate catalog, semantic layer, or other system outside the source. The right location is the one that keeps the definitions, relationships, ownership, and usage rules available when the agent is deciding how to answer a question.

A source system has its own overheads and constraints. It may be designed for transactions, operational stability, security, or vendor compatibility, and the AI models and agents we use may not be able to access all of it directly. Keeping metadata in the source system is therefore not always practical or necessary. Metadata can live elsewhere, provided it remains connected to the data and is easy for the agent to retrieve.

This architecture must be designed jointly by business and technology. Technology determines how the metadata is stored, connected, secured, maintained, and made available to agents. The business must define the meaning of the data, because business users decide what the values in a dataset represent, which definitions are approved, which tables should be used, and how measures should be interpreted. Neither side can make this decision alone.

The rest of the discussion takes each shape in turn and asks three questions. What does the database already record? What does it leave out? What would the missing information look like if someone documented it properly? The third question matters most. Saying that documentation is missing achieves very little. Showing the specific fields that would have prevented a particular wrong answer gives someone a task they can actually complete.

Tables

Start with tables, because they carry the most information and because the database already knows more about them than most people realize. Ask any database what it holds and it can provide a precise technical description without anyone having written a word of business documentation. In most database engines, built-in catalog views expose table and column names, data types, lengths, keys, and relationships. SQL-standard `information_schema` views cover many of these fields, while approximate row counts and storage size often require vendor-specific catalog views. Exact fields and names vary by database.[1] That may be a complete technical description of `DIM_CUSTOMER`, but it is still almost no help to an analyst or an agent.

The catalog will not say that `DIM_CUSTOMER` is the mastered dimension while `STG_CUSTOMER` is a staging copy that nobody should query. It will not say that `status` contains three codes or explain what those codes mean. It will not say that one of them has been excluded from revenue reporting since a decision made several years ago. The earlier chapters spent a great deal of time on exactly this problem. Knowing which key is the master key is not a SQL skill.

The values below show a generic current-state snapshot from a database catalog. They are concrete example values for the book, not placeholders and not a claim about a particular customer database.

What the database can show about the object

The database can describe the object itself. It can identify where the object lives, what kind of object it is, how much data it contains, how it is organized, and when it was last refreshed.

T3.1 Database object inventory and refresh metadata.

Object name	Object type	Database	Schema	Status
DIM_CUSTOMER	Table	Customer Analytics	ANALYTICS	Active
FACT_SALES	Table	Customer Analytics	ANALYTICS	Active
DIM_PRODUCT	Table	Customer Analytics	ANALYTICS	Active

Object name	Approximate row count	Organization
DIM_CUSTOMER	1,250,000	Partitioned by month on EFFECTIVE_FROM
FACT_SALES	48,600,000	Partitioned by month on SALE_DATE
DIM_PRODUCT	82,400	Not partitioned

Object name	Last refresh
DIM_CUSTOMER	2026-08-23 02:15 UTC
FACT_SALES	2026-08-24 01:55 UTC
DIM_PRODUCT	2026-08-23 02:05 UTC

That is the database's description of the object. It tells us that DIM_CUSTOMER is a table in the ANALYTICS schema, that it contains about 1.25 million rows, and that its data is organized by the month in which each customer record became effective.

What the database can show about the columns

The database can also describe the individual columns and the rules declared for them.

T3.2 Column definitions and relationship metadata for a selected table.

Column name	Data type	Nullable	Primary key
CUSTOMER_KEY	INTEGER	No	Yes
SOURCE_CUSTOMER_ID	VARCHAR(40)	No	No
CUSTOMER_NAME	VARCHAR(200)	Yes	No
STATUS_CODE	VARCHAR(10)	No	No
EFFECTIVE_FROM	DATE	No	No
EFFECTIVE_TO	DATE	Yes	No
REGION_KEY	INTEGER	Yes	No

Column name	Foreign key
CUSTOMER_KEY	No
SOURCE_CUSTOMER_ID	No
CUSTOMER_NAME	No
STATUS_CODE	No
EFFECTIVE_FROM	No
EFFECTIVE_TO	No
REGION_KEY	Yes

Now the technical picture is visible. The database tells us the name and type of each column, whether it can be empty, whether it identifies a record, and whether it connects to another object.

It still does not tell us whether `DIM_CUSTOMER` is the approved customer source, whether `SOURCE_CUSTOMER_ID` is trusted across systems, what the status codes mean to the business, or whether a customer record represents a legal entity, a household, or an account. Those definitions are the business metadata that must be added next.

Some of this information can be collected automatically. For example, you can check a table's grain by counting its rows and unique key combinations. If the numbers match, the grain is probably correct. This check can run every night and send an alert if the grain changes.

You can also find the possible values in a column by scanning it and listing its distinct values. However, this only tells you the codes, not what they mean. Someone still needs to document that. Loading tools usually record when data was refreshed, but that information often stays inside the loading system instead of being stored where a query or an AI agent can access it.

Business metadata is expensive because it requires expert knowledge. Writing it down makes that knowledge reusable. Analytical tables need two extra details: the fact table's grain and how its measures can be added. One row per order line is different from one row per order, even if the tables look similar. Revenue can usually be summed across dimensions, but balances cannot be summed across dates, and averages cannot be averaged. Measures are therefore classified as fully additive, semi-additive, or non-additive. Without this guidance, an agent may sum a semi-additive measure simply because it is numeric, producing a mathematically correct but financially meaningless result.

Time Series

A time series records observations in relation to time. A row may represent an account balance on a particular date, a product's inventory at the end of an hour, or a sensor reading at a specific moment. The important feature is not only the values in the rows, but also the order in which those rows occur.

In a database catalog, a time series may look like an ordinary data object with a date or timestamp column. The catalog shows the columns, their data types, whether they can be empty, and the keys declared for them. It provides the technical structure of the data, but it does not necessarily identify the object as a time series or explain how the organization uses it.

System-provided structure for `BALANCE_DAILY`

The database can describe the individual columns and the rules declared for them.

T3.3 BALANCE_DAILY column definitions and key relationships.

Column name	Data type	Nullable	Primary key
ACCOUNT_KEY	INTEGER	No	Yes
AS_OF_DATE	DATE	No	Yes
BALANCE_AMOUNT	DECIMAL(18,2)	No	No
CURRENCY_CODE	CHAR(3)	No	No
ACCOUNT_TIMEZONE	VARCHAR(64)	No	No
BALANCE_CLASS	CHAR(1)	No	Yes
RECORDED_AT	TIMESTAMP	No	No
SOURCE_SYSTEM_CODE	VARCHAR(30)	No	No
LOAD_BATCH_ID	BIGINT	No	No

Column name	Foreign key
ACCOUNT_KEY	Yes
AS_OF_DATE	No
BALANCE_AMOUNT	No
CURRENCY_CODE	No
ACCOUNT_TIMEZONE	No
BALANCE_CLASS	No
RECORDED_AT	No
SOURCE_SYSTEM_CODE	No
LOAD_BATCH_ID	No

The declared keys show that ACCOUNT_KEY, AS_OF_DATE, and BALANCE_CLASS together identify a row. That structure allows one account to have more than one balance category for the same date. BALANCE_AMOUNT stores the measured value, while CURRENCY_CODE identifies the unit associated with that value. ACCOUNT_TIMEZONE records the timezone associated with the account. RECORDED_AT, SOURCE_SYSTEM_CODE, and LOAD_BATCH_ID show when the record was recorded, where it came from, and which load supplied it.

BALANCE_CLASS contains a short code rather than a business description. The codes may be defined in business metadata as P - Payables, L - Loans, R - Receivables, and I - Interest. A single time-series table can therefore hold balances for several business areas while keeping the stored value compact and consistent.

This gives us the technical information that the database exposes: the column names, data types, nullable settings, keys, timezone field, balance classification, source details, and load details. It still does not tell us what kind of accounts are included, what each balance represents, which account population should be used, or how the codes map to the organization's business terms.

That distinction matters when an AI model writes a query. A question about Receivables may require the model to filter for R, while a question about Loans may require L. A question about Interest may require I, while a question about Payables may require P. The model needs written metadata that connects those codes to Payables, Loans, Receivables, Interest, and other business terms. It also needs the account definitions, date rules, and reporting requirements. The database supplies the structure. Business metadata supplies the meaning needed to select the correct information and write a useful query.

Event and Audit Records

Event and audit records are usually functional-area agnostic. They are not designed for one business process such as lending, sales, or customer service. A common log can record activity from many modules and systems. The rows look like ordinary relational data, but their meaning comes from what the system was doing, what object it touched, whether the action succeeded, and what time each timestamp represents.

System-provided structure for SYSTEM_AUDIT_LOG

The database can describe the generic columns and rules declared for the log.

T3.4 SYSTEM_AUDIT_LOG column definitions and key relationships.

Column name	Data type	Nullable	Primary key
AUDIT_EVENT_KEY	BIGINT	No	Yes
EVENT_TIME	TIMESTAMP	No	No
RECORDED_AT	TIMESTAMP	No	No
MODULE_NAME	VARCHAR(100)	No	No
TABLE_NAME	VARCHAR(128)	Yes	No
COLUMN_NAME	VARCHAR(128)	Yes	No
ACTION_CODE	VARCHAR(20)	No	No
SYSTEM_ACTION	VARCHAR(100)	No	No
STATUS_CODE	VARCHAR(20)	No	No
ERROR_CODE	VARCHAR(50)	Yes	No
ERROR_MESSAGE	VARCHAR(2000)	Yes	No
CORRELATION_ID	VARCHAR(100)	Yes	No
ACTOR_ID	VARCHAR(100)	Yes	No

Column name	Foreign key
AUDIT_EVENT_KEY	No
EVENT_TIME	No
RECORDED_AT	No
MODULE_NAME	No
TABLE_NAME	No
COLUMN_NAME	No
ACTION_CODE	No
SYSTEM_ACTION	No
STATUS_CODE	No
ERROR_CODE	No
ERROR_MESSAGE	No
CORRELATION_ID	No
ACTOR_ID	No

The catalog tells us that the log can identify the module involved, the table and column affected, the action performed, and the resulting status. SYSTEM_ACTION can record the system activity in a more direct form, such as starting a load, updating a column, validating a record, or sending a notification. It also shows that the log can keep an error code and error message when an operation does not succeed. EVENT_TIME and RECORDED_AT provide two separate clocks. One may describe when the activity occurred, while the other describes when the log entry was written.

The technical structure does not tell us what each action or status code means. A status such as SUCCESS may mean that a file was received, a row was updated, or a complete module finished processing. An ERROR status may identify a rejected row, a failed load, or a system failure. The column list alone cannot distinguish those cases. It also does not tell us which events must be retained, which messages are safe to show to a business user, or whether the log is complete for every module.

The same generic structure can therefore support many uses. One report may count errors by module. Another may find which column was updated. A third may trace a single operation across systems by using CORRELATION_ID. An AI model needs written metadata that defines the action codes, status codes, timestamps, retention rules, and completeness expectations before it can choose the right filters and write a useful query. The records look relational, but their meaning comes from system activity and operational context.

Hierarchical

Hierarchical data can look like an ordinary relational object. It has rows, columns, identifiers, names, and dates. The difference is that one identifier points to another identifier, creating a parent-child path. The object is stored in a relational system, but it is not just a flat list of records. Its meaning depends on how the records connect and on what each entity represents.

System-provided structure for ENTITY_RELATIONSHIP

T3.5 ENTITY_RELATIONSHIP column definitions and key relationships.

Column name	Data type	Nullable	Primary key
CHILD_ID	BIGINT	No	Yes
PARENT_ID	BIGINT	Yes	No
ENTITY_TYPE	VARCHAR(50)	No	No
ENTITY_NAME	VARCHAR(200)	No	No
LEVEL_NUMBER	SMALLINT	No	No
EFFECTIVE_FROM	DATE	No	No
EFFECTIVE_TO	DATE	Yes	No
VERSION_CODE	VARCHAR(20)	No	No
STATUS_CODE	CHAR(1)	No	No

Column name	Foreign key
CHILD_ID	No
PARENT_ID	Yes
ENTITY_TYPE	No
ENTITY_NAME	No
LEVEL_NUMBER	No
EFFECTIVE_FROM	No
EFFECTIVE_TO	No
VERSION_CODE	No
STATUS_CODE	No

The catalog tells us that PARENT_ID points to another entity and that CHILD_ID identifies the entity below it. ENTITY_TYPE can identify what kind of entity is being connected, such as a Sales Rep, Product, Department, or Category. LEVEL_NUMBER stores a numeric depth, while the effective dates and version identify when the relationship applies.

The column names and keys do not tell us what the parent-child relationship means. A Sales Rep may report to a Manager. A Product may belong to a Category. A Department may belong to a Division. The same relational pattern can represent all three, but the rules for moving through the relationship are different. Business metadata must identify the permitted entity types, the names of the levels, the root, and whether each child can have one parent or several.

Business metadata must also explain whether level 1 means division, level 2 means category, and level 3 means product group. It must state which level a report should use, which hierarchy version applies to a historical period, and whether history is restated under the current structure or preserved as it was originally published.

For an AI model, these details determine how the parent-child path should be followed and where the result should be grouped. A question about sales by category is different from a question about sales by product group, even though both may use the same object and the same measure. The data appears as a relational object, but the query must treat it as a hierarchical structure and use the business level that the question requires.

Graph

Graph data can also be stored as ordinary relational objects. One object stores nodes, and another stores connections between nodes. It may even resemble a hierarchy because one record points from one entity to another. It is not a hierarchy, however. A hierarchy normally follows a parent-child structure with defined levels, while a graph can contain several relationship types, several paths between the same entities, multiple connections in both directions, and cycles. The rows may look familiar, but the meaning is carried by the connections, their direction, and the type of relationship.

System-provided structure for node records

T3.6 Graph node record columns and relationship metadata.

Column name	Data type	Nullable	Primary key
NODE_KEY	BIGINT	No	Yes
NODE_TYPE_CODE	CHAR(1)	No	No
NODE_NAME	VARCHAR(200)	No	No
SOURCE_SYSTEM_CODE	VARCHAR(30)	No	No
EFFECTIVE_FROM	DATE	No	No
EFFECTIVE_TO	DATE	Yes	No

Column name	Foreign key
NODE_KEY	No
NODE_TYPE_CODE	No
NODE_NAME	No
SOURCE_SYSTEM_CODE	No
EFFECTIVE_FROM	No
EFFECTIVE_TO	No

System-provided structure for connection records

T3.7 Graph connection record columns and relationship metadata.

Column name	Data type	Nullable	Primary key
EDGE_KEY	BIGINT	No	Yes
FROM_NODE_KEY	BIGINT	No	No
TO_NODE_KEY	BIGINT	No	No
RELATIONSHIP_CODE	CHAR(1)	No	No
OWNERSHIP_PERCENT	DECIMAL(5,2)	Yes	No
EFFECTIVE_FROM	DATE	No	No
EFFECTIVE_TO	DATE	Yes	No

Column name	Foreign key
EDGE_KEY	No
FROM_NODE_KEY	Yes
TO_NODE_KEY	Yes
RELATIONSHIP_CODE	No
OWNERSHIP_PERCENT	No
EFFECTIVE_FROM	No
EFFECTIVE_TO	No

The catalog tells us that a connection has a starting node and an ending node. It shows that the connection can have a type, an ownership percentage, and effective dates. It does not tell us which direction the relationship follows or what the short code means. In business metadata, O might mean Ownership, S might mean Supplies, and D might mean Shared Director. Those relationships may connect the same two entities without making the data a hierarchy.

That distinction is essential. Two companies may be connected by ownership, by a supply agreement, and by a shared director. These are three different business relationships, even if they use the same pair of node identifiers. A query about ultimate ownership should follow only the relationship defined as Ownership. It should not follow every connection in the graph.

The AI model also needs to know whether a percentage threshold applies, how deep a traversal may go, how to guard against cycles, and whether a result should roll up to the ultimate parent or remain with the entity that placed the order. The records look like ordinary rows and can resemble a hierarchy, but the question is answered by walking through typed connections and applying graph rules.

Geospatial

Geospatial data may look most like a conventional relational object. It has identifiers, names, codes, dates, and a column that appears beside the others. The important difference is that the geometry column does not hold a simple number or ordinary text. It holds a location shape that can be compared by distance, containment, and intersection.

System-provided structure for DELIVERY_ZONE

T3.8 DELIVERY_ZONE column definitions and key relationships.

Column name	Data type	Nullable	Primary key
ZONE_KEY	INTEGER	No	Yes
ZONE_NAME	VARCHAR(100)	No	No
ZONE_SHAPE	GEOMETRY(POLYGON, 4326)	No	No
ZONE_CLASS	CHAR(1)	No	No
VALID_FROM	DATE	No	No
VALID_TO	DATE	Yes	No
SOURCE_SYSTEM_CODE	VARCHAR(30)	No	No

Column name	Foreign key
ZONE_KEY	No
ZONE_NAME	No
ZONE_SHAPE	No
ZONE_CLASS	No
VALID_FROM	No
VALID_TO	No
SOURCE_SYSTEM_CODE	No

This looks like a familiar relational structure. The database still provides a key, a name, data types, nullable settings, and declared relationships. The difference is the data type of ZONE_SHAPE. GEOMETRY(POLYGON, 4326) identifies a polygon shape and the coordinate reference system used to describe it. The value represents a closed boundary made from ordered points, such as the outline of a delivery zone.

The catalog can provide the geometry type and coordinate reference identifier. It does not necessarily tell us whether the zone represents a delivery area, a sales territory, a warehouse service area, or a legal boundary. It also does not tell us whether the boundary is current, how complete the geocoding is, or which distance unit a report should use.

The AI model needs this information before it can choose the right operation. A question about customers inside a delivery zone requires a containment relationship. A question about two overlapping territories requires an intersection relationship. A question about customers within a given distance of a depot requires a distance calculation and an appropriate unit. These are not ordinary equality or numeric comparisons.

The same principle applies to points and lines. A point may represent a customer or depot, while a line may represent a road, pipeline, or delivery route. The database can describe the shape type. Business metadata explains what the shape represents, which version is current, and how the organization expects it to be used.

Across these four sections, the catalog presents familiar technical objects. The difference is in the shape of the data and the operation required to answer a question. Event records depend on time and correction links. Hierarchies depend on parent-child paths and levels. Graphs depend on typed connections and traversal. Geospatial data depends on geometry and spatial relationships. An AI model needs business metadata that tells it which interpretation and operation apply before it writes the query.

Metadata Is Data Too

Metadata is part of the information an AI model needs to produce a reliable response. The data provides the values, but metadata explains what those values represent, how they relate to one another, which definitions the business has approved, and how the information should be used. Without that context, a model may select the wrong table, interpret a code incorrectly, join records at the wrong grain, or calculate a plausible number that does not answer the intended question.

Technical metadata gives the model the structure: table and column names, data types, keys, relationships, partitions, and refresh details. That structure is necessary, but it does not explain whether a table is authoritative, what one row means, which date applies to a business measure, whether a balance can be summed, or how a term such as "customer," "revenue," or "current" is defined. Business metadata supplies those meanings and connects the technical objects to the language used in the question.

Some of this context can be verified automatically. Grain can be tested by counting rows and key combinations. Codes can be profiled. Hierarchy depth can be checked by traversing parent-child relationships. Coverage, freshness, and completeness can be measured. These checks cannot create business meaning, but they can reveal when documented assumptions no longer match the data.

Metadata also needs the same care as any other operational asset. Definitions become outdated, ownership changes, tables are replaced, and business rules evolve. A description that was accurate when it was written can become actively misleading when nobody maintains it. Facts that are measured automatically should be monitored, and facts that require judgment should have clear owners responsible for keeping them current.

When definitions, relationships, ownership, validation rules, and usage guidance are available, they can be stored in a catalog, semantic layer, source system, transformation code, or a combination of these. The important requirement is that the information remains connected to the data and can be retrieved when the model is deciding what the question means, which sources to use, and how to combine them.

Reliable AI responses therefore depend on both data and metadata. Data tells the model what values are present. Metadata tells it what those values mean and how they should be interpreted. Without the first, there is nothing to query; without the second, there is no dependable way to know whether the query answers the question.

Chapter 4: How an AI Model Reads Structured Data

Navigate: Contents · Previous: Chapter 3 · Next: Chapter 5

Here is a question, written the way somebody actually asks one. Who were our ten biggest customers last quarter, and how does that compare with the same quarter last year? Nobody would call that difficult. A person who works in the business could answer it, and would know within a second or two roughly where to look and what to be careful about. Give it to a model with access to a database and something has to happen in between. The remainder of this section explains the underlying process. It focuses on how an AI system interprets structured data and translates business questions into reliable queries, not on the mechanics of language models themselves. You do not need to understand transformer architecture, and the principles remain relevant even as model architectures evolve.

It is about a narrower thing. A model never reads your data. It reads text about your data, assembled by something else, and then produces text that happens to be SQL. Everything explored so far has to survive that translation, or it may as well not exist.

What the Question Does Not Say

"Who were our ten biggest customers last quarter, and how does that compare with the same quarter last year?"

Read the question again and take an inventory of what is technically present in it. There is no table name. No column name. No key. No join. No filter expression. No aggregate function. No dialect. Nothing that appears in a schema appears in that sentence. That is not a flaw in how the question was asked. It is what a business question is. If it contained table names it would be a query, and the person asking would not have needed to ask. Now take a second inventory, of what is present but undefined. The word `biggest` has no meaning until somebody says biggest by what. Revenue, order count, margin, units shipped, contribution: all defensible, all producing different lists.

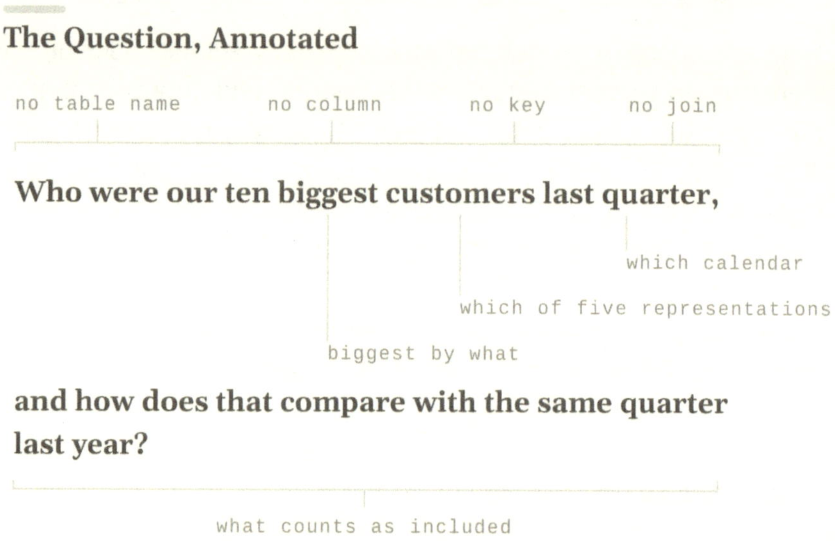

Figure 4.1 The question as asked. What it does not contain is marked above, what it leaves undefined below.

The word `customer` has already been the subject of two sections. The first established that the same company can exist in four systems, with four identifiers. The second established that the largest customer is a different company depending on whether you mean the entity that ordered or the group above it. The words `last quarter` assume a calendar, but calendar quarters and financial quarters are frequently not the same. An organization with a financial year starting in April will produce a different answer from one with a year starting in January. And the whole question assumes a definition of what counts: cancelled orders, internal transfers, credit notes. The warehouse section listed exactly these and pointed out that somebody settles them before a single number leaves the building.

So the question contains no technical content, and its business content is ambiguous in at least four places. A person handles that without effort, because they are not working from the sentence. They are working from everything they know about the organization, and the sentence is only the part they had to say out loud. A model has the sentence, and nothing else. Unless that organizational knowledge is supplied separately, the model must fill in the gaps itself, turning each unstated assumption into a guess. That is why a question can be perfectly clear to a person and still be underspecified for a model.

Entities and Edges

Before a model can find a table, it needs to know what things exist and how they relate. Not tables, but things. This is knowledge of a different order from anything in the last three chapters, and separating it cleanly matters. A schema describes storage. What is needed here describes the business, and it would still be true if every system in the organization were replaced tomorrow. Build it from what this book has already used.

T4.1 Business entities and their plain-language definitions.

Entity	Description
Customer	An organization or individual that purchases products or services
Address	A physical or mailing location associated with a customer
Product	An item offered or sold by the business
Supplier	An organization that provides products
Order	A purchase request placed by a customer
Order Line	A specific product and quantity included in an order
Account	A financial or business account held by a customer
Posting	A financial transaction recorded against an account
Legal Entity	A legally recognized organization

T4.2 Business relationships connecting the entities in the knowledge graph.

Source Entity	Relationship	Target Entity
Customer	places	Order
Order	contains	Order Line
Order Line	is for	Product
Customer	ships to	Address
Supplier	supplies	Product
Customer	holds	Account
Account	records	Posting
Legal Entity	owns	Legal Entity
Customer	is a	Legal Entity

Nine things and nine connections. Every one of them appeared somewhere in the first three chapters, and none of them is a table. That distinction is the first thing to notice. A table is a way of storing records. An entity is a thing the business recognizes, whether that thing is stored in one table, several tables, a warehouse dimension, or a collection of files. A relationship describes how two entities are connected, even when the systems storing them use different keys or different names.

For example, the business may store customers in `CUSTOMER`, `DIM_CUSTOMER`, and `MDM_PARTY`. Those are three physical representations, but they can all describe the same business entity: `Customer`. Likewise, an order may appear in `ORDER_HEADER` in one system and in a fact table in another. The knowledge graph describes the business objects and their connections without choosing a storage location.

This is a knowledge graph: a map of the business concepts an organization cares about and the relationships between them.

It is not a map of tables and columns.

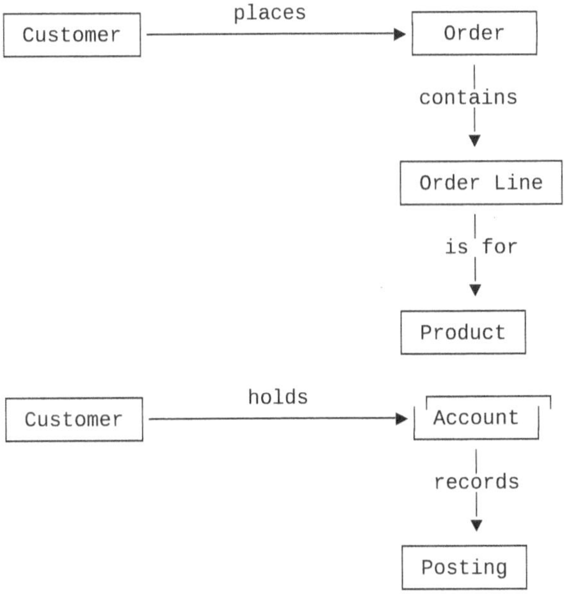

The graph describes business relationships such as:

- A `Customer` places an `Order`.
- An `Order` contains an `Order Line`.
- An `Order Line` is for a `Product`.

- A `Customer` holds an `Account`.

These relationships remain true even if the underlying systems, tables, keys, or joins change. That is why a table is not itself the knowledge graph:

```
┌──────────────────────────────────────┐
│ Physical data layer                  │
│                                      │
│ ORDER_HEADER                         │
│ ORDER_ITEM                           │
│ DIM_CUSTOMER                         │
│ DIM_PRODUCT                          │
└──────────────────────────────────────┘
                  │ mappings
                  ▼
┌──────────────────────────────────────┐
│ Business meaning layer               │
│                                      │
│ Customer places Order                │
│ Order contains Order Line            │
│ Order Line is for Product            │
└──────────────────────────────────────┘
```

A database catalog defines the technical path:

```
ORDER_HEADER.customer_key
          └──── joins to ──── DIM_CUSTOMER.customer_key
```

The knowledge graph expresses the business meaning:

```
Customer
   └──── places ───▶ Order
```

The first describes how the data is connected technically. The second describes what the connection means to the business.

The two layers are connected through mappings:

```
**T4.3** Business entities mapped to their physical table
representations.

| Business entity | Physical representation |
|---|---|
| Customer | `DIM_CUSTOMER.customer_key` |
| Order | `ORDER_HEADER.order_id` |
| Order Line | `ORDER_ITEM.order_id`
`ORDER_ITEM.item_no` |
```

The relationship can be visualized like this:

```
┌──────────┐
│ Customer │
└──────────┘
     │ represented by
     ▼
DIM_CUSTOMER.customer_key


┌────────┐
│ Order  │
└────────┘
     │ represented by
     ▼
ORDER_HEADER.order_id


┌────────────┐
│ Order Line │
└────────────┘
     │ represented by
     ▼
ORDER_ITEM.order_id + ORDER_ITEM.item_no
```

The knowledge graph establishes what the business means. The physical mapping explains where that meaning is stored in a particular data environment.

This separation allows an AI agent to work in two stages:

```
1. Understand the business question
                    │
                    ▼
2. Follow the correct business relationship
                    │
                    ▼
3. Identify the physical tables and columns
                    │
                    ▼
4. Generate the query
```

In other words:

```
Business meaning first
        +
Physical mapping second
        =
A query grounded in the correct business path
```

Look at what the question needs from it. Suppose someone asks:

```
Which customers bought products last quarter?
```

`Customer` and `Order` are both entities, and `places` is the relationship that connects them. That single edge tells the model that the question is answerable at all. It says that orders belong to customers in a business sense, even before the model knows which columns implement the connection. Without it, customers and orders are two unrelated lists. The model might see a column called `customer_id` in one table and a similar column in another, but a matching name is only a clue. The relationship confirms that the two objects belong on the same path.

The edge also helps the model interpret direction. `Customer places Order` means the customer is the party that makes the purchase request. That is different from `Order is placed by Customer`, although both describe the same connection from opposite directions. If the question instead asks which salesperson handled the order, the model needs a different entity and a different edge. A customer may be assigned to a salesperson, while an order is placed by a customer. Those relationships should not be confused simply because both can eventually lead to a person.

`` `Order `` contains `Order Line`, and `Order Line` is for `Product`. These edges extend the knowledge graph from the customer who placed an order to the product that was actually sold. Consider this question:

```
Which products did our ten largest customers buy?
```

The business path is:

```
Customer
  places Order
    contains Order Line
      is for Product
```

The knowledge graph identifies the business meaning first. The physical table mappings then show how to implement that meaning:

```
Customer
  represented by DIM_CUSTOMER.customer_key

Order
  represented by ORDER_HEADER.order_id

Order Line
```

```
  represented by ORDER_ITEM.order_id and ORDER_ITEM.item_no

Product
  represented by DIM_PRODUCT.product_key
```

The model should therefore translate the path into table logic:

```
DIM_CUSTOMER
  joins to ORDER_HEADER through customer_key
ORDER_HEADER
  joins to ORDER_ITEM through order_id
ORDER_ITEM
  joins to DIM_PRODUCT through product_id or product_key
```

A possible relational path is: **S4.1 (SQL fragment)** Shows the joins that connect customers, orders, order lines, and products for a product-level question in sequence.

```
FROM DIM_CUSTOMER c
JOIN ORDER_HEADER o
    ON o.customer_key = c.customer_key
JOIN ORDER_ITEM l
    ON l.order_id = o.order_id
JOIN DIM_PRODUCT p
    ON p.product_key = l.product_key
```

The order header alone may identify the customer and contain a total, but it does not usually identify every product and quantity sold. Those details belong to the order lines. To answer a product-level question, the model must follow the graph from `Order` to `Order Line`, and then from `Order Line` to `Product`. Without those edges and mappings, it might stop at the order total or invent a direct relationship between an order and a product table.

In these examples, colon-prefixed names such as `:period_start` and `:current_seq` are bind placeholders supplied by the calling application. They must be adapted to the parameter syntax of the approved execution tool.

The graph also explains the grain of the table logic. One `Order` can contain many `Order Line` records, and one `Product` can appear on many order lines. After joining a customer to order lines, the result is normally at the grain of one row per order line:

```
Customer 1 —— many Order
Order    1 —— many Order Line
Product  1 —— many Order Line
```

That means the model must decide what to aggregate at each stage. To find the ten largest customers by gross order-line value, it may first aggregate that value by the stable customer identity:

S4.2 Calculates gross order-line value by customer for a period, excludes cancelled orders, ranks customers, and returns the ten highest totals.

```
WITH customer_totals AS (
    SELECT
        c.customer_id,
        MIN(c.customer_name) AS customer_name,
        SUM(l.quantity * l.unit_price) AS
gross_line_value
    FROM DIM_CUSTOMER c
    JOIN ORDER_HEADER o
        ON o.customer_key = c.customer_key
    JOIN ORDER_ITEM l
        ON l.order_id = o.order_id
    WHERE o.order_date >= :period_start
      AND o.order_date < :period_end
      AND o.order_status <> 'CANCELLED'
    GROUP BY
        c.customer_id
)
SELECT
    customer_id,
    customer_name,
    gross_line_value
FROM customer_totals
ORDER BY
    gross_line_value DESC
FETCH FIRST 10 ROWS ONLY;
```

It can then use those ten stable customer identifiers to find the products bought through every applicable customer-dimension version:

S4.3 Finds products purchased by the ten customers with the highest gross order-line value and ranks products by that same value.

```
WITH top_customers AS (
    SELECT
```

```
        c.customer_id
    FROM DIM_CUSTOMER c
    JOIN ORDER_HEADER o
        ON o.customer_key = c.customer_key
    JOIN ORDER_ITEM l
        ON l.order_id = o.order_id
    WHERE o.order_date >= :period_start
      AND o.order_date < :period_end
      AND o.order_status <> 'CANCELLED'
    GROUP BY
        c.customer_id
    ORDER BY
        SUM(l.quantity * l.unit_price) DESC
    FETCH FIRST 10 ROWS ONLY
)
SELECT
    p.product_key,
    MIN(p.product_name) AS product_name,
    SUM(l.quantity) AS units_bought,
    SUM(l.quantity * l.unit_price) AS gross_line_value
FROM top_customers tc
JOIN DIM_CUSTOMER c
    ON c.customer_id = tc.customer_id
JOIN ORDER_HEADER o
    ON o.customer_key = c.customer_key
JOIN ORDER_ITEM l
    ON l.order_id = o.order_id
JOIN DIM_PRODUCT p
    ON p.product_key = l.product_key
WHERE o.order_date >= :period_start
  AND o.order_date < :period_end
  AND o.order_status <> 'CANCELLED'
GROUP BY
    p.product_key
ORDER BY
    gross_line_value DESC;
```

The exact SQL depends on the organization's approved measure and table mappings. In this example, `quantity * unit_price` is deliberately labelled gross order-line value, not governed revenue. The graph supplies the customer-to-order-to-line path, and the physical mappings and grain metadata turn that path into table logic. It also warns that joining a header total to line-level rows can duplicate the header amount once for every line.

The remaining connections provide similar guidance:

```
Customer    ships to    Address
Supplier    supplies    Product
Customer    holds       Account
Account     records     Posting
```

For example, the question "Which customers are within eighty kilometres of our depot?" needs the `Customer ships to Address` relationship before it can use location data. The customer may be the business entity, while the address is the physical location. Joining a customer directly to a depot without passing through an address would be a different question and could produce the wrong result.

The question "Which products are supplied by companies in Ohio?" follows another path:

Supplier supplies Product Product is sold through Order Line Order Line belongs to Order Order is placed by Customer That path connects suppliers to the products they provide and then to the customers who bought those products. It is not enough for the database to contain a `supplier_id` and a `product_id`. The model needs to know that `supplies` is a business relationship, rather than assuming that two similarly named columns should be joined.

`Customer` and `Account` are also different entities. A customer may hold several accounts, such as a checking account, a loan account, or a receivables account. The relationship `Customer holds Account` tells the model that one customer can be connected to many accounts. Then `Account records Posting` tells it where the financial movements are recorded. A question about a customer's current balance may use the account's current-state value. A question about how that balance changed may need to follow the posting history instead. The graph identifies the business path; the metadata for each object explains which representation answers the particular question.

And the last edge in the list is the one that has been causing trouble since the master data section. A `Legal Entity` can own another `Le-`

gal Entity, and a Customer is a Legal Entity. Those two lines together are the entire ownership problem, written in five words.

Suppose Meridian Freight Inc. places orders, but its parent company is Meridian Holdings Inc. The question "Who is our largest customer?" could mean the legal entity that placed the orders or the entire corporate group. The graph makes the possible path visible:

Customer is a Legal Entity Legal Entity owns Legal Entity The model can therefore recognize that revenue may need to be rolled up through an ownership chain. If Meridian Freight owns a subsidiary and that subsidiary also places orders, the model may need to follow several owns edges before calculating the group total. If the business instead defines customer as the ordering entity, it should stop at the first Customer node. The graph does not decide which interpretation the organization approves, but it prevents the model from overlooking the distinction.

Notice something about that graph. It says nothing about where any of it is stored. There is no mention of a table, a warehouse, a key, or a join. It would read the same in an organization running one system or forty.

That is deliberate. The graph might later be mapped to physical structures like these:

Customer represented by DIM_CUSTOMER.customer_key

Order represented by ORDER_HEADER.order_id

Order Line represented by ORDER_ITEM.order_id and item_no

Product represented by DIM_PRODUCT.product_key Those mappings are useful, but they are a separate layer. The knowledge graph first establishes what the business means. A physical mapping then explains where that meaning can be found in a particular data environment. If the organization replaces its order system, the Customer places Order relationship should remain true even though the table names, keys, and joins change.

That separation is what allows the graph to connect the question to the right data without confusing business concepts with storage details. It tells the model which things exist, how they relate, which paths are possible, and where a question may require a choice. The tables and columns are still necessary, but they are the implementation of the knowledge, not the knowledge itself.

Now let us see this at work. Start with the question.

Who were our ten biggest customers last quarter? Nothing about that sentence is unusual. It is the kind of thing somebody types on a Monday morning without pausing to consider it. Alongside it, the model receives a description of what is available.

You have access to the following tables.

CUSTOMER	customer_id, name, tax_id, status
STG_CUSTOMER	customer_id, name, load_date
CRM_CUSTOMER_RAW	account_id, account_name, owner
DIM_CUSTOMER	customer_key, customer_id, customer_name, city, country
ORDER_HEADER	order_id, customer_id, customer_key, order_date, order_status, currency, total_amount
ORDER_ITEM	order_id, item_no, product_id, quantity, unit_price

S4.4 Produces a plausible but incorrect customer ranking by joining operational customer records to order header totals.

```
SELECT
    c.name,
    SUM(o.total_amount) AS total
FROM CUSTOMER c
JOIN ORDER_HEADER o
    ON o.customer_id = c.customer_id
WHERE o.order_date >= '2026-01-01'
  AND o.order_date < '2026-04-01'
GROUP BY
    c.name
ORDER BY
    total DESC
LIMIT 10;
```

Look at that query on its own terms. The syntax is clean. The join has a condition. The dates are bounded correctly. It groups, sorts and cuts at ten. Anybody reviewing it as SQL would pass it. It runs. It returns ten rows with names and numbers. Nothing errors, nothing warns, and the figures are the right order of magnitude. It is also wrong in four separate ways. `CUSTOMER` is the operational table, not the governed one. A company that exists under four identifiers appears as four different customers, and its revenue is divided between them. The one that belongs at the top of the list may not appear on it at all.

`total_amount` is a header total. Nobody told the model what it contains, and header totals commonly include tax and freight, and commonly still include lines that were later cancelled. The number is a number. It is not revenue. The quarter is a calendar quarter. If the organization's financial year begins in April, the whole period is wrong. And the grouping is by name rather than by key, so two customers sharing a registered name merge into one row. Now the part that matters. Not one of those four is visible in the output. The result is ten rows of plausible names against plausible figures, and the person receiving it has no way to tell it apart from a correct answer.

How the model evaluates it with a graph

Same question, same tables, and this added behind them.

```
Entities

  Customer
    an organization that buys from us
    also called     account, client, buyer, sold-to party
    identified by   the governed customer_id
    join through    customer_key
    use             DIM_CUSTOMER for questions spanning time
                    CUSTOMER for current operational detail
    never use       STG_CUSTOMER, CRM_CUSTOMER_RAW

  Order
    a purchase placed by a customer
    also called     sales order, deal
    use             ORDER_HEADER
```

```
  Order Line
    one product on one order, with a quantity and a price
    also called    line item, order item
    use            ORDER_ITEM

Relationships

  Customer  places    Order
    join    DIM_CUSTOMER.customer_key
            to ORDER_HEADER.customer_key

  Order     contains  Order Line
    join    ORDER_HEADER.order_id
            to ORDER_ITEM.order_id

Calendar and period

  Calendar
    system date     2026-08-24
    quarter type    Gregorian calendar quarter
    current quarter Q3 2026
    last quarter    Q2 2026
    period start    2026-04-01
    period end      2026-07-01, exclusive

Measure and exclusions

  ranking value    gross order-line value
                   quantity times unit_price
  status rule      exclude CANCELLED orders
  identity rule    join by customer_key
                   group companies by customer_id
```

The graph included a calendar definition in addition to the business relationships. For this example, the system date was 2026-08-24, which falls in the third quarter of 2026. The model therefore interpreted “last quarter” as the second quarter, chose 2026-04-01 as the start date, and used 2026-07-01 as the exclusive end date. That means the query covers April 1 through June 30.

S4.5 Uses governed customer identity and order lines to rank customers by the documented gross order-line value.

```
SELECT
    d.customer_id,
    MIN(d.customer_name) AS customer_name,
    SUM(l.quantity * l.unit_price) AS gross_line_value
FROM DIM_CUSTOMER d
JOIN ORDER_HEADER h
    ON h.customer_key = d.customer_key
JOIN ORDER_ITEM l
    ON l.order_id = h.order_id
WHERE h.order_date >= '2026-04-01'
  AND h.order_date < '2026-07-01'
  AND h.order_status <> 'CANCELLED'
GROUP BY
    d.customer_id
ORDER BY
    gross_line_value DESC
LIMIT 10;
```

The model chose this query by following the graph from Customer to Order and then from Order to Order Line. The graph identified `DIM_CUSTOMER` as the governed source, `customer_key` as the join key, and `customer_id` as the stable company identity. It defined the ranking value as gross order-line value, not revenue, and required cancelled orders to be excluded. The calendar definition supplied the period boundaries, so the model selected 2026-04-01 as the start of the previous quarter and 2026-07-01 as the exclusive end date.

The two evaluations side by side

	Without graph	With graph
Customer table	CUSTOMER	DIM_CUSTOMER
chosen because	name matched	the entity named it
decoys ruled out	none of three	all three
The measure	total_amount	gross line value
chosen because	name looked right	the graph defined it
Cancelled orders	included	excluded
Tables joined	two	three
Grouped by	name	customer_id
The calendar	assumed	documented
Unsupported choices	hidden	none

The first evaluation resolved important choices by guessing and had no way to tell a guess from a fact. The second used a written source, identity, measure, exclusion rule, and calendar. That is the difference between an answer that can be checked and an answer that can only be believed.

And notice what the graph never did. It did not make the model better at SQL. Both queries are competent SQL. What it supplied was the ability to tell the difference between a documented measure and a column with a promising name. That is exactly why the graph is useful, and why it must contain the business rules the query claims to follow.

One Entity, Five Places

Take one entity from that graph and follow it through the places described earlier.

```
The same customer, five places

  OLTP         CUSTOMER, one narrow row, current state only
  Warehouse    DIM_CUSTOMER, wide, one row per validity period
  Cube         a member of the customer dimension
  Lake         bronze extract, silver conformed, gold dimension
  Master data  a golden record plus links to every source id
```

One entity. Five representations. All of them correct, all of them current, none of them redundant. They also disagree in ways that matter. The OLTP row holds today's address and nothing else. The warehouse row holds two rows for a customer who moved, one valid until the move and one after it. Ask what the customer's city was when an order was placed and only one of those can answer. The lake holds three versions at once. The data lake section made the point that a query against a bronze table runs perfectly and answers a question about unreconciled data.

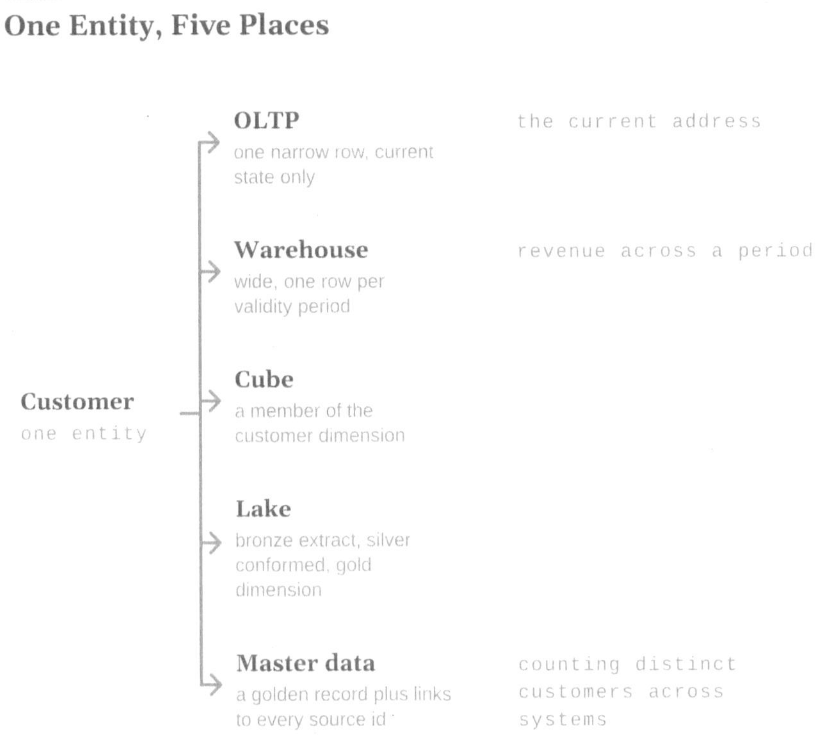

Figure 4.2 One customer in five places. Each was built for a different job, and they disagree in ways that matter.

The master data record holds the identity the business agreed on, along with the mapping back to four different source identifiers. That section closed on the line that knowing which key is the master key is not a SQL skill. So the knowledge graph says `Customer` exists. It does not say which of these five to use, and the answer is not a general one. It depends on what is being asked. For last quarter's revenue, the warehouse dimension is probably right, because the question spans time and the warehouse is the layer that keeps history. For a customer's current address, the OLTP row is right, because it is the only one guaranteed to be current.

For counting distinct customers across systems, the master data record is the only correct answer, because it is the only one that knows four identifiers are one company. That mapping, from entity to the right physical representation for a given kind of question, is a second body of knowledge sitting on top of the first. It is specific to the organization, it changes when systems change, and nothing in the knowledge graph contains it. Now do the same for `Product`. The master data section described engineering holding a part, the ERP holding a material, sales holding a sellable item and the warehouse holding a storage unit. Four records for one physical thing, and a fifth if the analytical dimension is counted.

Every entity in that nine-item graph fans out this way. The graph has nine nodes. The estate behind it has hundreds of tables.

Where It Is Least Effective

Those five places are not equally good targets. Two of them are close to hopeless, and the reasons are worth understanding before anybody points an agent at a database. Start with the one people reach for first.

Raw operational tables

An OLTP system is the obvious place to start. It holds the real data, it is current, and it is where the business actually happens. It is also the hardest surface in the estate for a model to work against, for three reasons that compound. The first is the normalization described earlier. Everything that made writes fast made reading expensive. A single meaningful record, one order with its customer, its addresses, its products, its currency and its status, is assembled from six or seven tables. A model has to reconstruct that path every time, and it has to get every hop right.

The second is volume, and it is worse than it sounds. A large operational system does not hold hundreds of business tables. It holds thousands of tables, and most of them are not business tables at all.

Configuration. Control records. Number ranges. Logging. Buffers. Intermediate structures the application uses and nobody queries. The twenty tables that answer business questions are sitting inside a few thousand that do not, and nothing in the catalog marks the difference. The third is naming. Operational table and column names are written for the application that reads them, not for a person. A model looking for customers in a system where the customer table is called something unpronounceable has nothing to match against.

Put those together and the scaffolding required becomes enormous. Not model training, which is not what this book is about. Scaffolding: an knowledge graph, a mapping, and a set of exclusions large enough to hide several thousand tables, all of it maintained against a system that changes when the vendor ships an update. It can be done. It is rarely the best use of the effort.

A reporting layer already built over operational tables

This is the subtler case and the more common mistake. Many organizations already have a reporting layer sitting over their operational systems. Somebody built views, or a reporting database, or a set of standard reports, and those reports are used and trusted. Point an agent at that and ask it to answer a question the report already answers, and consider what is actually being added. The hard work was done once, by a person who knew the data. Which tables to use. Which records to exclude. What the columns mean. How the joins go. That work is already embedded in the report, and it is correct, because it has been checked by everybody who has used the report for the last three years.

An agent regenerating that same answer has to make every one of those decisions again, from scratch, with less information than the person had. It will be slower. It will occasionally get one of them wrong. And when it gets them all right, it has produced a number that was already available. That is the honest position. Where a trusted report already answers the question, generating SQL to answer it again adds latency and a failure mode, and adds no capability.

What the two have in common

```
Raw operational tables
  thousands of tables, most of them not business tables
  a single record assembled from six or seven joins
  names written for the application, not for a reader

A reporting layer that already answers the question
  the decisions were settled once, by a person
  regenerating them adds latency and a failure mode
  the answer was already available
```

They look like opposite problems and they are the same one seen from two sides. In the first, nobody has settled what the data means, so the agent has to settle it, and it is not equipped to. In the second, somebody has already settled it and gone further, settling the question too, so there is nothing left for the agent to contribute. An agent is least valuable where the meaning has not been settled, or where the question has already been answered. Which leaves a gap between those two, and that gap is where the whole case for this technology sits.

The Data Warehouse

The data warehouse deserves separate treatment, because on paper it looks like the ideal target and the reasons it is not are less obvious than the previous two. Start by giving it its due. An earlier chapter described what a warehouse is for. Data from many source systems, reconciled into one consistent model, kept over time, organised around the business rather than around the software. Everything an agent needs and struggles to find elsewhere is present. Few tables instead of thousands. Wide tables, so a question travels one join rather than six. Table names that say what the table holds. Definitions already settled, because settling them is most of what building a warehouse consists of.

It is also a considerable advance on the cube. A cube fixes its dimensions when it is designed and answers only what was anticipated. A warehouse holds the detail underneath and can be queried in ways nobody planned for. So the warehouse is genuinely better, and for the purposes of this argument it sits in the same position as the cube. Both are a curated layer where somebody decided in advance what the numbers mean, and where reports and dashboards were then built on top of those decisions. That position brings three problems with it, and they are worth taking one at a time.

The names are not the words

Warehouse tables are wide and their columns are named by the people who built them, working to conventions that made sense inside a modelling project. They are not named for a person asking a question. Here is a fact table of the kind that actually exists.

```
FACT_SALES
  date_key, customer_key, product_key, org_key,
  qty_bu, net_amt_lc, net_amt_gc, gross_amt_gc,
  disc_amt_gc, tax_amt_gc, cogs_gc, rebate_accr_gc
```

Somebody asks for revenue by customer. Which column is revenue.

```
qty_bu          quantity in base units
net_amt_lc      net amount, local currency
net_amt_gc      net amount, group currency
gross_amt_gc    gross amount, before discount
disc_amt_gc     discount given
tax_amt_gc      tax
cogs_gc         cost of goods sold
rebate_accr_gc  rebate accrued but not yet paid
```

Seven of those eight are amounts, and all seven are legitimate answers to somebody's question about money. Gross or net decides whether discounts are deducted. Local or group currency decides whether the figures across regions can be added together at all. And the last one is the sharpest, because a rebate accrued and not yet paid is money the organization expects to give back, and whether it comes off revenue is an accounting decision rather than a data decision.

The convention in this warehouse is that revenue means net amount in group currency, less accrued rebate. That is one line of information. It is not in the column names, it is not in the data types, and it is not derivable by inspection. Somebody in finance decided it, and the whole estate has quietly agreed ever since. An agent without that line has seven plausible columns and no way to choose. An agent with a wrong version of it produces a number that is out by exactly the accrual, every time, consistently, which is worse than being obviously wrong.

The names change

Warehouses are maintained. Columns are added when a new requirement lands. Dimensions are restructured when the business reorganises. A source system upgrade brings new fields, and the loading process is extended to carry them. Every one of those changes can invalidate the context an agent depends on. Suppose the rebate treatment changes, and a new column appears carrying the post-rebate figure directly. The old column stays, because reports depend on it. Now there are two right answers and one of them is right for last year.

Nothing announces this. The scaffolding this book goes on to describe, the knowledge graph and the definitions and the verified examples, was written against the old shape and continues to run. The queries still execute. The numbers are still returned. This is not model training going stale, because no model was trained. It is the written-down knowledge going stale, which is the rot the metadata chapter named and this book returns to later. The maintenance burden is real and it is continuous, and it belongs to somebody who has to notice a warehouse change and update a definition that lives somewhere else.

Meanwhile the dashboard sitting on the same warehouse was updated by the team that made the change, in the same release, because they own both.

The questions already have answers

Which brings us to the third problem, and it is the same one the reporting layer had. A warehouse is not built and then left alone. Reports get built on it. Dashboards get built on it. Somebody has already asked for revenue by customer, and somebody has already built the view that answers it, and the definition of revenue was settled inside that view years ago. Point an agent at the warehouse and ask for the top ten customers by revenue, and the honest question is what has been added. The dashboard shows it. It shows it with the agreed definition, the agreed currency and the agreed rebate treatment, all of which the agent has to be told separately and may get wrong.

The agent is slower, it carries a failure mode the dashboard does not have, and the number it produces was already on a screen somewhere in the building.

Where that leaves the warehouse

It is not a bad target. It is a good target that has usually already been harvested. Everything that makes a warehouse pleasant to query is a consequence of somebody having done the work. And having done the work, that somebody generally went on to build the report, because building the report was the reason the work was funded. So the value an agent can add against a warehouse is not in the questions the warehouse was built to answer. Those have answers. It is in whatever is left over, which is a smaller and more specific thing than it first appears.

Master Data

Master data management is the one people are most surprised by. It sounds like it should be central. An earlier section explained why it matters that four records in four systems are recognised as one company. If that is where identity is decided, surely that is where an agent should be pointed. It is not, and the reason begins with what a master data system actually is underneath.

It is an OLTP system

Look at the shape of one.

```
Master
  MDM_PARTY             party_id, legal_name, tax_id, status
  MDM_ADDRESS           address_id, party_id, addr_type,
                        city, country, valid_from, valid_to
  MDM_ADDR_TYPE         addr_type, type_group, description
  MDM_CLASSIFICATION    party_id, scheme, code

Cross reference
  MDM_XREF              party_id, source_system, source_id,
                        confidence, last_matched

Relationship
  MDM_RELATION          parent_party_id, child_party_id,
                        relation_type, share_pct,
                        valid_from, valid_to

Stewardship
  MDM_TASK              task_id, party_id, task_type, status,
                        assigned_to, decided_at
```

Read that against the earlier description of an operational system and every characteristic is present. It is normalized. The name is in one table, the address in another, the address type in a code table, the classification in a fourth, and everything is joined by key. It is accessed one record at a time. A steward opens a match and looks at two parties. An interface asks for the master identifier behind one source record. Nobody scans it. It is built around current state, with validity dates where history is needed. It is written transactionally. A steward approves a match, and several tables change together or none of them do.

And it holds master tables alongside tables recording things that happened to them. Those were called transaction tables earlier, and `MDM_TASK` is exactly one, recording who decided what and when. So a master data hub is an operational system that happens to be about data rather than about orders. Everything this chapter said earlier about pointing an agent at operational tables applies here without amendment. Which sounds abstract until you ask it something simple.

One question, asked twice

Here is a question with no ambiguity in it at all. No measure, no calendar, no definition to settle.

```
Show me all warehouse locations of customer A
```

S4.6 Recursively walks current ownership relationships in both directions to find every group member connected to a specified customer.

```
WITH RECURSIVE group_members (party_id) AS (
    SELECT
        party_id
    FROM MDM_PARTY
    WHERE party_id = :customer_a

    UNION

    SELECT
        CASE
            WHEN r.parent_party_id = g.party_id
                THEN r.child_party_id
            ELSE r.parent_party_id
        END
    FROM group_members g
    JOIN MDM_RELATION r
        ON r.parent_party_id = g.party_id
        OR r.child_party_id = g.party_id
    WHERE r.relation_type = 'OWNS'
      AND r.valid_to IS NULL
```

```
)
SELECT DISTINCT
    p.legal_name,
    a.city,
    a.country
FROM group_members g
JOIN MDM_PARTY p
    ON p.party_id = g.party_id
JOIN MDM_ADDRESS a
    ON a.party_id = g.party_id
JOIN MDM_ADDR_TYPE t
    ON t.addr_type = a.addr_type
WHERE t.type_group = 'WAREHOUSE'
  AND a.valid_to IS NULL;
```

The recursive UNION removes repeated party identifiers, so a cycle does not keep producing the same members. Following both ends of each current OWNS relationship allows a search that starts at a subsidiary to reach its parent and siblings as well as any descendants.

S4.7 Retrieves warehouse locations for a customer from a denormalized dimension using resolved parent and location attributes.

```
SELECT
    location_name,
    city,
    country
FROM DIM_CUSTOMER_LOCATION
WHERE ultimate_parent_name = 'Customer A'
  AND location_type = 'Warehouse'
  AND is_current = 'Y';
```

One table. No joins. No recursion. No code lookup. The difference is not that the warehouse is cleverer. It is that the work was already done. Somebody walked the ownership tree during the nightly load and wrote the result into a column called `ultimate_parent_name`. Somebody resolved the address type code into the word Warehouse. Somebody applied the validity dates and set a flag. That was described earlier as denormalization, and the trade explained: storage in exchange for time. This is what the trade actually buys. The work did not disappear. It moved upstream and happens once a night instead of once a question.

For an agent, that difference is everything. The warehouse version needs one table name. The master data version needs an understanding of recursive traversal, relationship types, two separate validity conventions and a code table, all of which have to reach the model before it writes a line.

And there is nothing to add up

There is a second limit, quieter than the first. A master data hub holds no revenue, no quantities, no orders, no shipments and no payments. It holds who things are, not what they did. The only two numbers anywhere in that schema are a percentage holding and a match confidence. The first says how much of one company another owns. The second says how sure the system is that two records are the same. Neither is a business measure, and no amount of aggregation turns them into one. So even the questions that survive the join problem run into a wall. There is nothing in there to trend, compare or total.

What it can answer

There is a real set of questions master data answers well, and they are all about the data rather than about the business.

```
How many customers do we have after deduplication
How many source records map to more than one master
What proportion of parties carry a tax identifier
How many parties are blocked, and since when
How many matches are waiting for a steward
```

Those matter. They are how an organization knows whether its master data is working, and somebody should be asking them. They are not what the business means when it asks about customers.

What it is actually for

Which brings the real role of master data into view, and it is not the role of a query target. Look again at the warehouse query. It worked because `ultimate_parent_name` was already sitting on the row. That column exists because something walked the ownership tree beforehand, and the ownership tree came from `MDM_RELATION`. The same is true of the customer key on every fact row in the building. It is a master key because master data decided it was, and that decision was applied during a load rather than at query time. Master data is not where the answer comes from. It is what makes the answer groupable, and what makes an eight-word question resolvable in one table somewhere else.

The master data section said that identifying the governed key requires organizational knowledge, not SQL skills. Master data is where that key is chosen. This decision happens before anyone asks a question, but it affects every answer that follows. An agent has little to reason about when it queries master data directly. However, the decisions from master data guide everything else and help determine whether the answers are correct.

The Data Lake

Everything before this in the chapter is rigid. The structure is fixed. Somebody decided the columns before any data arrived. They named them to suit the system rather than a reader. And what those names actually mean is held somewhere the query cannot see. Rigid is not an insult. A transaction system has to be rigid or it cannot promise anything. A warehouse has to be rigid or its numbers stop agreeing with each other. That is what those systems are for, and they are good at it. It does have one consequence. A fixed shape answers the questions somebody anticipated when they fixed it, and nothing else.

The opposite is no better. Data with no structure at all gives a model nothing to hold on to. No columns, no types, no relationships. Nothing to reason about. What a model needs is both at once. Enough structure to have something to work with, and enough fluidity that the shape is not locked to a set of questions somebody guessed at years ago. A data lake is the only place in the estate that offers both. That is what this section is about.

Data lands first

In every other layer in this chapter, the shape comes before the data. A person works out the columns, settles what each one means, builds the table, and only then is anything allowed in. A lake reverses that. Data lands first, in whatever form it arrived, and the shape is applied afterwards. Those two arrangements were named earlier as schema on write and schema on read. The consequence is more interesting than the names. Because the shape is applied afterwards, it is applied by somebody who already knows what the data is going to be used for. That single difference is why lake tables tend to read differently.

An operational table's names came from the vendor who built the application. They follow an abbreviation scheme designed for a system rather than a reader, they were set years before anybody in the organization saw them, and they cannot be changed. A warehouse's column names came from a modelling project. They follow a convention that made sense inside that project, and once reports depend on them they are effectively frozen. This chapter has already shown what that produces.

A lake's consumable layer is built later, by or for the people who are going to read it, for a purpose that is already known. Nobody inherited an application schema. Nobody is bound to a convention set a decade ago. So the names tend to be the words the business actually uses.

`One number, three names`

`In the operational table: `NETWR``

A legacy abbreviation inherited from the source system. It represents the net value of the transaction.

`In the warehouse: `net_amt_gc``

A technical warehouse name that makes the measure and currency explicit: net amount in group currency.

```
In the lake's gold layer: `revenue`
```

A business-facing name chosen for the curated layer, where the column has already been defined and prepared for reporting as revenue, with amounts in multiple currencies converted to the reporting currency.

The names changed because each layer serves a different purpose. The operational system preserves the source application's naming, the warehouse adds technical precision for integration and analysis, and the gold layer uses the business term that people actually ask for. The names are not automatically interchangeable: `NETWR` may have source-system rules, `net_amt_gc` identifies a particular currency and calculation stage, and `revenue` should be used only when the gold-layer definition confirms what is included, such as discounts, tax, rebates, returns, and currency conversion.

The gold layer was described earlier as business-ready tables shaped for particular questions. That is what business-ready means in practice. Not just clean data, but a table somebody can read the name of and know what it holds. This is a tendency rather than a guarantee. A lake that nobody governs will accumulate names as bad as anywhere else, which is the data swamp warned about earlier. But when it is done properly, this is the combination named at the top of the section. Structure, because those gold tables are described, typed and joinable like any others. Fluidity, because the shape and the names were chosen after somebody knew what the data was for, rather than years before.

It is files, and that matters more than it sounds

In a database, the engine owns the file. You cannot read a table by opening it, because the storage format is the database's private business and the database is the only thing that understands it. Everything you want to do with that data has to be phrased as a request to the engine, in the language the engine accepts, which is SQL. In a lake, the file is a file. A Parquet file in object storage can be read by a query engine, a notebook, a script, a statistical library or a model, and none of them has to ask a database for permission.

This is easy to overstate, so it is worth saying exactly what has changed. Parquet is not less structured than a database table. It was established earlier that the file carries its own column definitions and types. Both are structured. The difference is who owns the shape and what is allowed to read it. A database says: I hold this, and you may query it. A lake says: this is here, and anything that can read a file may use it. That is the freedom. Not freedom from structure. Freedom from a single gatekeeper that only speaks one language.

What a lake holds that nothing else does

Here is the property that changes what an agent can do. A lake holds structured tables and everything else, in the same place, on the same storage. The order lines are there as Parquet. So are the scanned delivery notes, the supplier contracts, the free-text notes a service agent typed, the machine logs, the photographs from an inspection, the emails attached to a dispute. Nowhere else in the estate is that true. A warehouse holds tables. An operational system holds tables. A master data hub holds tables. Only the lake holds the numbers and the words next to each other.

That matters because a great many real questions have a number on one side and a document on the other. Why did this shipment miss its date. What does the contract say about this rebate. Which complaints mention the same fault. Each of those is unanswerable with SQL alone and unanswerable with documents alone. It is sometimes said that models read files better than they read databases. That is not quite it. A model handles a schema description perfectly well. The truer statement is narrower and more useful: the lake is the only layer where the material a model can read and the material SQL can read are sitting side by side.

It kept the grain

There is a second property, and it comes from earlier in this book. A warehouse aggregates. Somebody chose a grain when it was designed, and everything finer than that grain was summed away during the load. It was established earlier that grain travels one way only. Fine detail rolls up into coarse totals, and coarse totals never break back down. A lake keeps the raw event. One row per transaction, per reading, per click, per movement, with its original timestamp and its original values.

That distinction decides which questions are even possible. Anything that depends on sequence, on timing between events, on rare occurrences, or on what happened at a level of detail nobody thought to preserve, needs the raw grain. The warehouse threw it away for good reasons. The lake still has it. There is a third property, noted earlier. Where a warehouse settles a disagreement and keeps only the settlement, a lake tends to hold on to both sides, and it can usually show a table as it stood before somebody changed a rule.

So what can an agent actually do here

EEverywhere else in our exploration so far, the only move available to an agent was to write SQL. In a lake it has more than one move, and that is the real difference. - **Forecasting and projection.** Forecasting often requires the original record of each event, including exactly when it happened. For example, a model may need to examine individual orders, shipments, payments, or machine readings over time. The warehouse may have combined these events into weekly or monthly totals, which removes important patterns. The lake keeps the detailed event records, so an agent can identify trends, seasonality, delays, and changes in behavior before making a projection.

- **Anomaly and exception detection.** An agent can examine raw data before it has been cleaned, corrected, or reconciled. This makes it possible to find unusual records that the normal loading process might hide. For example, it could detect duplicate transactions, unexpected values, missing fields, incorrect dates, or a mismatch between two source systems. The warehouse may already have corrected or removed these problems, while the lake preserves the original evidence.

- **Joining a number to a document.** Many useful questions require both structured data and documents. An agent might connect an invoice amount to the specific clause in a contract that explains the charge. It could also connect a delayed shipment record to the delivery note that describes the problem. The number comes from a table, while the explanation comes from a document. Keeping both in the lake allows the agent to examine them together.

- **Reading free text alongside structured data.** Important business information is often written in service notes, delivery exception comments, inspection reports, emails, or case descriptions. An agent can read these comments and identify recurring issues, such as damaged packaging, late deliveries, or equipment failures. It can then combine those observations with structured data, such as order counts, costs, locations, and dates, to show how often a problem occurs and which customers or products are affected.

- **Sequence and cohort analysis.** Some questions depend on the order in which events happened and the time between them. For example, an agent may need to determine whether a support call happened before a customer cancelled an order, or how long new customers usually take to place their second order. This type of analysis requires the original event timestamps. Once events have been combined into monthly or quarterly totals, the sequence and the time between events are lost.

- **Resolving identity from raw source extracts.** Raw extracts preserve the original identifiers and names used by each source system. One company may appear with different spellings or identifiers in the ERP, CRM, billing system, and other applications. An agent can compare these records, identify likely matches, and provide evidence for master-data teams to review. In this way, the lake helps create or improve the master record rather than simply querying a master-data table that has already been created.

- **Reconstructing history.** The lake can preserve earlier versions of records, definitions, and calculations. This allows an agent to determine what a figure meant before a business rule changed. For example, it could show how revenue was calculated under the old rebate policy and compare it with the current calculation. The warehouse may have replaced the old definition with the new one, while the lake keeps both versions and the history of the change.

- **Building the context this book asks for.** An agent can examine what the data actually contains instead of relying only on documentation. It can profile columns, identify common values, find missing or unexpected data, detect possible duplicates, and examine how tables relate to one another. These findings can help people write clearer definitions, confirm the true grain of a table, identify trusted sources, and document rules that the business has been using informally. In other words, the lake can help create the metadata and business context that an AI agent needs to give reliable answers.

Look at that list and notice how few of the items are text-to-SQL. Most of them are things an agent can do because the raw material survived and because a file can be read by anything. Here is the difference that matters most, and it has nothing to do with names or files. Every system before the lake made one decision at the start. Somebody designed a structure, and that structure decided what could ever be captured.

Think about what that means. A schema is not just a place to put data. It is a list of the questions that will be answerable. Anything the designers did not think of has no column. Anything with no column was never stored. Not stored badly. Never stored at all. A lake does not make that decision. It takes what arrives, in whatever shape it arrives, and keeps it. Tables, documents, notes, logs, images, emails. The decision about what matters is postponed until somebody has a reason to care. Most of the time that difference is invisible. The predictable questions get asked, and the systems built to answer them do their job. Then something happens that nobody planned for.

A question nobody built a table for

Suppose two of your competitors announce a merger. The first questions are easy, and your dashboards answer them. How much do we sell in the markets where those two overlap. What is our share. What did revenue do last year. Then somebody in the room asks the real question.

Which of our customers will be worse off now that those two are one company, and what does that mean for us?

Stop and work out what it would actually take to answer that. You need to know which of your customers also buy from those two competitors. That is not a field in your order table. It sits in the notes a salesperson typed after losing a deal, in win and loss records, and in tender documents. You need to know where the merged company will now have scale you cannot match. That is their combined footprint set against your cost to serve each customer, which is partly cost data and partly delivery records. You need to know which of your contracts come up for renewal in the window where this will bite. That is in the contracts, which are documents.

You need to know which customers are price sensitive. That is in discount history, and in how often a quote turned into an order. You need to know where your products overlap with theirs. That is in specification sheets and catalogues. Now count the sources. Order data. Cost data. Delivery records. Sales notes. Win and loss records. Contracts. Product specifications. Two of those live in the warehouse. The rest are documents and free text that no schema was ever built for, because nobody knew this merger was coming.

The work is reading, not thinking

A person could answer this question. That is worth saying plainly, because the point is not that a machine is cleverer than the people in the room. The reasoning is not the hard part. Find the overlapping customers. Check the renewals. Work out where the price pressure lands. Any experienced person in the business could tell you how to do it, and would probably sketch it on a whiteboard in ten minutes. What they cannot do is read every contract, and every sales note from the last three years, and cross-reference all of it against the order data, before the decision has to be made.

So the question gets answered from a sample, or from memory, or it does not get answered at all. That is the normal outcome, and everybody in the room knows it. Now put an agent against a lake. It can read the win and loss notes and find the customers mentioned alongside those two competitors. It can pull renewal dates out of the contracts. It can set both against the order and cost data in one answer, because in a lake the contracts and the order data are in the same place.

It does not replace the judgment. Somebody still has to look at the customers it comes back with and decide what to do. What it removes is the reason the question was never answered properly, and that reason was never the thinking. It was the reading.

Where the value actually sits

This is worth being exact about, because it is easy to describe badly. The value is not faster dashboards. Dashboards are already fast. It is not automated reports. Reports already run, and this chapter has already said that regenerating one adds a failure mode and nothing else. The value is in the question nobody built a table for. The question that arrived because something changed, that no schema anticipated, and that until now was too expensive to answer properly. Those are the questions that matter most. They turn up exactly when something has shifted, and something shifting is when a decision is worth the most.

A model is at its strongest finding patterns across more material than a person can hold, in a body of information too large to search by hand. That is not a small capability. It hands a person back a question they had written off. The other layers in this chapter were built to answer known questions well, and they do. A lake is the only one holding the material for a question nobody saw coming. Structure enough to reason over, fluidity enough that nothing was thrown away for not fitting. An agent is what makes reading all of it affordable.

The cost, stated plainly

None of this comes free, and the price was already named earlier. A lake puts far more tables in front of an agent than a warehouse does. Bronze, silver and gold, alongside whatever has collected over the years, and more than one of them will hold the same thing at a different stage of processing. A query aimed at the wrong layer runs without complaint and answers a question about data nobody has reconciled yet. So the lake is simultaneously the best surface for an agent and the easiest one to be confidently wrong on. The freedom that makes it powerful is the same freedom that removes the curation a warehouse provides.

Which means everything about metadata and supplied context matters more here, not less. A lake without a catalog, without definitions, without stated grain and without somebody saying which layer answers which kind of question is a very large collection of files that an agent can read fluently and interpret wrongly. That is the trade. More capability, less protection, and the protection has to be supplied deliberately.

Two Things Called by One Name

So a lake is where an agent earns its place, and four other systems are not. Anybody who has followed this far should be asking an obvious question by now. Does that mean AI cannot be used on the other four at all? It can. The reason the question feels confusing is that two different things are being called by the same name.

Two different things

There is using English instead of a technical query. Somebody wants a number. The number is already sitting in the data. In the old arrangement they would write SQL, or ask somebody who could. Now they type the question in English and the query gets written for them. Nothing new was produced. The answer was always in there. What changed is who could reach it. Then there is using English to get a task done.

Somebody wants to know which customers will be worse off after a competitor merger. That answer is not sitting anywhere. Nothing in the estate contains it. It has to be assembled out of contracts, sales notes and order history by something that reads all of them and works out what they mean together. Something new was produced. It did not exist until somebody asked. People call the first one natural language query, or text-to-SQL, or chatting with your data. Plenty of people call it NLP. People call the second one AI. And the industry sells both of them as AI, which is why this conversation is so hard to have in a meeting.

A test that does not need the labels

Ask one question about any answer you are shown. Did this answer already exist? If somebody could have written a query in advance and got the same result, it is translation. The answer was in there and the work was reaching it. If no query would have produced it, because the answer had to be made out of several things nobody had put together, it is reasoning. The answer was not in there and the work was making it.

Real questions sit along a line between those two rather than at one end. Plenty of them need a little assembly and a lot of retrieval. But the two ends are clear enough to be useful, and most of what an organization buys sits close to one of them.

Translation works on all four, and sometimes it is the best thing available

Now the useful question. Can translation be used on the other four systems? Yes. On some of them it is the most valuable thing you can do. On operational tables, somebody in customer service asks where an order is and why it has not shipped, dozens of times a day. That question has one right query and somebody has almost certainly written it before. Today the person either learns the system or asks a colleague who has. Translation is a better front door to a query that already exists, and there is nothing wrong with a better front door.

On a reporting layer, the report already holds the answer. Translation lets somebody reach it by asking rather than by hunting through a menu of two hundred reports, most of which they have never opened. That is an improvement to the interface and it is honest about being one.

On a warehouse, translation is worth more than anywhere else. The tables are business shaped, the definitions are settled, and the joins are shallow. That is exactly the ground translation needs. And the long tail from earlier in this chapter is real. Somebody wants last quarter, but only for one region, only for customers acquired this year, with returns excluded. No report exists for that and none ever will. Translation answers it in seconds and the alternative was not answering it.

On master data, translation is the fix for the problem that section described. An eight word question about warehouse locations needed four tables and a recursive walk. The steward who wants that answer probably cannot write a recursive query and should not have to. They ask in English and the walk gets written for them. Four systems, four genuine uses. None of them is nothing.

Reasoning on those four is a different matter

Can reasoning be used on the same four? It can, and this chapter has already explained why it does not buy much. Reasoning needs several kinds of material to work across. Those four hold tables. A warehouse holds tables that have been cleaned, settled and aggregated, which is the same material with the disagreements removed and the detail summed away. So reasoning against them is possible, and the additional value is limited. Not because the technology falls over. Because there is little in there to reason over that the tables do not already state directly.

That is the whole distinction, and it explains every judgment in this chapter. Those four systems are good places to translate and poor places to reason. A lake is the only one where both are worth doing.

Why the confusion survives

One reason this gets confusing is that translation is easy to demonstrate. Someone asks a question, SQL appears, and a chart is ready in a few seconds. People are impressed.

Reasoning is harder to show. It may take longer, involve documents no one else can see, and produce paragraphs instead of a chart. So companies often buy translation because it looks better in a demo. It is usually deployed on the warehouse, where the data is already clean and the queries are straightforward.

That means they often buy the cheaper half and use it where it adds the least value.

That explains something many organizations have lived through without being able to name it. They bought a natural language layer, pointed it at the warehouse, launched it, and very little changed. Nothing failed. It worked. It answered the questions people asked, correctly, in English. It simply turned out that writing the query had never been the difficulty.

Why this matters before the next part

This distinction has to be settled here, because it decides whether everything that follows looks necessary or looks like ceremony. If an agent is a thing that turns English into SQL against a clean warehouse, then checking the query, checking permissions, testing the result and keeping a record all look like overhead. The report already does the same job and nobody validates the report every morning. If an agent is a thing that assembles an answer nobody had before, out of material nobody had joined before, then every one of those steps is the difference between something a person can act on and a paragraph nobody can check. The rest of this book is about the second one.

Querying Is Becoming Standard

Something is happening across enterprise software that changes the question. Asking in plain language and getting an answer back is becoming a standard feature. Not a product bought separately. Not a project to scope. A feature, arriving in the systems you already run and in every system you are likely to evaluate next. That matters before anybody decides to build anything, because it changes what is scarce. The capability is no longer scarce. What it needs to work still is. What follows is dated deliberately. Product names in this area move faster than the capabilities do, and everything here is as it stood in the middle of 2026. Treat the pattern as durable and the names as illustration.

It arrives with the application platforms

SAP ships Joule, an assistant embedded across its cloud portfolio. By the first quarter of 2026 SAP reported it live across thirty-five solutions. Natural-language querying of business data in S/4HANA Cloud Public Edition and Ariba was in early adopter release, with general availability planned for the third quarter of 2026, and SAP describes the answers as grounded in the underlying data models and business context rather than in general knowledge. Joule reached general availability inside SAP Datasphere, the data platform, in the first quarter of the same year.[1]

One detail in SAP's description is worth pausing on. The business context comes partly from SAP Knowledge Graph, which holds the relationships, processes and business logic that let the assistant work out what a question is asking about. That is the knowledge graph from earlier in this chapter, built by the vendor and shipped with the product.

Salesforce ships Agentforce, sitting on Data Cloud, which the company renamed Data 360 on 14 October 2025. Data Cloud is the grounding layer, and its job is the one this book gave to master data: pulling records from many systems into one resolved customer profile. It handles structured records and unstructured material together, with vector search over the unstructured side, and it can query external warehouses in place rather than copying the data in. Requests pass through the Einstein Trust Layer, which masks private data and logs what happened.[2]

ServiceNow ships Otto, which replaced Now Assist and Moveworks across its products, with an AI Agent Studio for building agents and an

AI Control Tower for governing them. The most telling detail is commercial rather than technical. In April 2026 ServiceNow stopped selling its AI capability as an add-on and bundled it into every product tier. That is a vendor saying the capability is now part of the price of the software. It is the clearest signal in this section of where the market has landed.[3]

It arrives with the data platforms

Snowflake ships Cortex Analyst, which answers natural language questions against structured data and is now generally available. Snowflake Intelligence and Cortex Agents reached general availability in November 2025.

Databricks ships Genie Agent, formerly called Genie Spaces, which does natural language to SQL and inherits the governance already defined in Unity Catalog. A Genie Agent can include up to 30 tables.[4]

Palantir ships Foundry with an Ontology that represents business objects, properties, actions, and relationships above the underlying data. Its AIP, the company's AI Platform, brings large language models and agents into that governed context. AIP Logic, AIP Assist, and the Ontology let users ask questions, retrieve information, and take controlled actions across operational and analytical workflows.

ThoughtSpot ThoughtSpot Spotter does search over an agentic semantic layer.

Notice what all of those have in common. None of them is a model. Every one of them is a place to put definitions.

They all needed the same thing

This is the part that carries the whole section, and it is not a product feature. Every one of these vendors discovered they could not do this with a schema alone. Snowflake's own documentation for Cortex Analyst says so directly. It notes that generic approaches struggle when given only a database schema, because schemas lack critical knowledge like business process definitions and metrics handling. Its answer is a semantic model, held alongside the database, describing logical tables, logical columns split into dimensions, time dimensions and measures, and the relationships that permit joins.[5] Read that description against the last four chapters.

Logical columns are the business concepts behind a question, such as categories to group by or numbers to calculate. Relationships show which business entities can be connected. Business process and metric definitions provide the context needed to understand terms like revenue, including their meaning and ownership. Cortex Analyst also supports verified queries: saved questions with approved SQL that run consistently every time. This book later calls these saved questions verified examples. In Cortex Analyst, this is a built-in product feature.

SAP arrived at the same place from a different direction and called it a knowledge graph. Salesforce arrived at it and called it Data Cloud. ServiceNow arrived at it and called it a context engine. Four vendors, four names, one conclusion. The model was never the hard part. The hard part was writing down what the business means, and none of them could avoid it.

Where the opportunity actually is

So the translation layer arrives on its own. Building a private version of it duplicates something already paid for, and duplication is the least interesting thing anybody could do with the material in this book. Three things are more interesting. The first is that all of it ships empty. The semantic model is a file with no meaning in it. The knowledge graph is a structure with your business absent from it. The verified examples are a facility with no examples in it. Every one of these products supplies a place to put definitions, and none supplies the definitions, because definitions are true only inside one organization.

That is not a gap in the products. It is the division of labour. They built the machinery. The meaning is yours, and it decides whether any of it returns a correct number. A practitioner review of one of these platforms in 2026 put the position more bluntly than the vendors do: the capability amplifies whatever is already there, and where the foundations are weak it produces mistakes faster than before. The second is that the same definitions feed all of it. You will not end up with one of these. You will have an assistant inside the application platform, another over the warehouse, and a third in whatever gets bought next. Each of them will ask you for the same definition of revenue.

Written into one, that definition improves one tool. Held once, somewhere several tools can read, it improves all of them, and it keeps improving as more of them arrive. That is the argument for treating definitions as an asset with an owner rather than as configuration inside a product, and it is why the semantic layer products that sit above any single warehouse exist at all. The third is the one worth the most. Every capability described in this section works inside its own boundary. Joule knows SAP. Agentforce knows Salesforce. Cortex Analyst knows Snowflake. Each of them knows its own data extremely well and almost nothing about the others.

Now recall the question from the last section. Which of our customers will be worse off after a competitor merger. Order data in one system, contracts in another, sales notes in a third, cost data in a fourth. No vendor assistant answers that, because no vendor owns all of it. That is the work nobody is doing for you, and it is worth more than the translation layer ever was. So the position is straightforward. Take the capability that arrives with the platform, because it is arriving anyway. Feed it the definitions only you can write, once, somewhere everything can reach. And spend what you save on the questions that cross every boundary the platforms cannot see past.

The machinery is becoming free. The meaning is yours to supply. And the value compounds, because every tool that reads it gets better without anybody building anything twice.

One Customer, Everywhere

Everything so far has been about categories. This section is about one customer. Take a company called Meridian Freight Inc., based in Columbus, Ohio. The systems below are generic, and the names and numbers are made up. The shapes are not. This is what one customer looks like across an ordinary set of systems, and everything after this is built on top of it.

In the ERP

One customer is not one record. The customer file is split across several tables. General details sit in one. Anything to do with money sits in another. Anything to do with selling sits in a third. So a company that trades with two of your legal entities already has three records here, before it goes anywhere else. The general one looks like this.

```
CUSTMAST
  CUSTNO     0001048372
  CNAM01     MERIDIAN FREIGHT INC
  CADR01     2400 RICKENBACKER PKWY
  CCITY      COLUMBUS
  CRGN       OH
  CPSTC      43217
  CCTRY      US
  CGRP       01
```

Most of that can be worked out with effort. CUSTNO is the customer number. CCITY is the city. CRGN is the region, which here means the state. CPSTC is the postal code. CCTRY is the country. CGRP is a group code that decides what kind of customer this is and which fields are allowed to be filled in. Two of them tell you something extra. CNAM01 has a number on the end, which means there is a CNAM02. The field holds a fixed number of characters, and a longer name spills into the next one. The address works the same way.

Nobody chose these names for a reader. They were chosen by whoever built the system, decades ago, under limits that no longer exist. Short field names, fixed lengths, uppercase, and abbreviations that made sense to the team at the time. They also cannot be changed now. Thousands of programs look for these exact fields, and every one of them would break. Most ERP vendors know this is a problem, and newer versions ship a readable layer over the raw tables. It is a set of views with business names in place of the abbreviations, so a program or a person can ask for the customer name rather than for CNAM01. That is the vendor doing the work this book keeps saying somebody has to do.

So why does anybody still see CNAM01? Because the readable layer covers what the vendor modelled. Fields your own people added, tables your own people built, and older installations that never got the layer are not in it. And a great many extracts into warehouses and lakes were set up years ago, reading straight off the raw tables. The abbreviations travel downstream with them and turn up in places the vendor never touched. There is one more detail about that customer number, and it causes real trouble. It is stored as text rather than as a number, and it is padded with zeros to fill the whole field.

So the database holds `0001048372`. The screen shows `1048372`. Same customer, two versions of the number, and most people only ever see the second one. Pull that field into a warehouse or a spreadsheet and you have whichever version you happened to capture. Try to match it back against the other one later and nothing matches. No error. Just missing rows. And remember the split. Payment terms are not on this record. They sit with the financial data, against the customer and the set of books together. Ask what payment terms Meridian is on and the honest answer is a question back. With which of our companies?

In the CRM

The same company, in the sales system, is a different thing entirely.

```
ACCOUNT
  AccountNumber    ACC-40912
  AccountName      Meridian Freight Inc.
  BillingStreet    2400 Rickenbacker Parkway
```

```
BillingCity       Columbus
BillingState      OH
BillingCountry    United States
AccountType       Customer
ParentAccount     points at Meridian Holdings Inc.
AccountOwner      points at the salesperson responsible
AnnualRevenue     48,000,000
```

Two things are different. The names are readable, with no separate layer needed to make them so. BillingCity is BillingCity. Anybody can look at that record and understand it. This is a newer system, built for a different kind of user, and it shows. And the contents are different. The parent account points at another record, which is how this system knows about the group. The owner points at a person, so it knows which salesperson is responsible. AnnualRevenue is an estimate somebody typed rather than anything the business measured. The ERP record has none of those. This one has no tax number and no payment terms. Neither is missing anything. Each carries what its own job asks for.

Put the two records side by side and nothing connects them. `0001048372` and `ACC-40912` have no link that either system knows about. One name is in capitals and one is not. A person can see at a glance that these are the same company. Neither system can.

In the cube

In a cube the customer is not a record at all. It is a position.

```
Customer
  United States
    Ohio
      Meridian Freight Inc.
```

That is all of it. A place in a list, three levels deep, so that numbers can be split by it. Ask the cube for the tax number and there is nothing there. Ask who owns the account and there is nothing there. A cube keeps only enough to add things up.

In the warehouse

The warehouse has a row. Often more than one.

```
DIM_CUSTOMER
  customer_key       48211
  customer_id        MDM-7741
  customer_name      Meridian Freight Inc.
  city               Columbus
  state              OH
  ultimate_parent    Meridian Holdings Inc.
  valid_from         2019-03-12
  valid_to           2024-06-30

  customer_key       52909
  customer_id        MDM-7741
  customer_name      Meridian Freight Inc.
  city               Memphis
  state              TN
  ultimate_parent    Meridian Holdings Inc.
  valid_from         2024-07-01
  valid_to
```

Two rows, one company. They moved their head office in the middle of 2024. Both versions are kept, so an order placed in 2022 still shows against Columbus. The city and state sit on the same row as the name. The parent company has already been worked out and written down as text, so nobody has to follow a chain of records to find it. And there is a customer number here that matches neither of the systems above. That last one came from somewhere else.

In master data

```
MDM_PARTY
  party_id      MDM-7741
  legal_name    Meridian Freight Inc.
  tax_id        34-2891746

MDM_XREF
  MDM-7741   ERP        0001048372   confidence 1.00
  MDM-7741   CRM        ACC-40912    confidence 0.94
  MDM-7741   BILLING    C-88231      confidence 0.87
```

Three lines in that second table, and they are the only place in the whole estate where the ERP number and the CRM number are known to be the same company. Nobody found that with a query. Something matched them, and where the match was uncertain a person agreed it. The confidence figures say how sure the system was, and the two below one are the ones somebody looked at. Everything downstream rests on those three lines. The warehouse row says `MDM-7741` because this table said so, during a load, long before anybody asked a question.

In the lake

The lake holds all of it, side by side.

```
bronze/erp_customer/      the ERP extract, exactly as it arrived
bronze/crm_account/       the CRM extract, exactly as it arrived
bronze/billing_customer/  the third one
silver/customer/          all three, cleaned and matched
gold/dim_customer/        the modelled version
docs/contracts/           the signed agreement, as a PDF
docs/notes/               sales notes mentioning Meridian
```

Two things here exist nowhere else. The raw extracts still carry the original spellings, the original numbers and the leading zeros. If anybody ever questions how these records were matched, the evidence is here. And the documents sit next to the tables. The contract is a PDF. The sales notes are free text somebody typed after a call. Neither is a row. Both are about this customer. This is the only place a question can reach the number and the sentence at the same time.

What is actually the same

Put it all on one page.

	Number	Name as stored
ERP	0001048372	MERIDIAN FREIGHT INC
CRM	ACC-40912	Meridian Freight Inc.
Billing	C-88231	Meridian Freight
Cube	a position in a list	

Warehouse	48211 and 52909	Meridian Freight Inc.
Master data	MDM-7741	Meridian Freight Inc.
Lake	all of the above	

One company. Six different numbers, and the first of those has a second version without the zeros that most people think is the real one. Three different spellings. Two rows in the warehouse for the same company at different times. And inside the ERP alone, several more records, one for each set of books and each sales team. None of that is a mistake. Every one of those is right for the job it was built to do. That is the situation any question about this customer lands in.

Ask how much Meridian bought last year, and the answer depends on which version was used, whether the parent company was included, and which of the two warehouse rows the orders attached to. Ask what payment terms they are on, and the answer depends on which set of books. Ask where their warehouses are, and the sales system has never heard of them. Ask what the contract says, and only the lake can help. Everything from here works against this picture. Not a schema and not a diagram. One company, in seven places, with three spellings, all of it correct, in a completely ordinary organization.

Chapter 5: How a Model Reads Words

Navigate: Contents · Previous: Chapter 4 · Next: Chapter 6

Language models are another kind of software. Like all software, they have a kind of syntax: a set of patterns and rules that shape how they work. The difference is that their syntax is much simpler and more familiar than the syntax of regular programs. Almost anyone can type a few words into a language model and start using it.

When you ask a language model a question, it does not retrieve an answer in quite the same way a database does. It reads the text in front of it and predicts what text is most likely to come next. That may sound like a small technical detail, but it explains much of what these systems can do and why they sometimes make mistakes.

If the instructions or information given to the model are unclear, incomplete, or wrong, the software may choose the wrong meaning, use the wrong data, or calculate the wrong result. It can still produce an answer that sounds confident and looks reasonable, even when the answer is inaccurate. We refer to these mistakes as "hallucinations." In simple terms, a hallucination is when the software gives an answer that is not supported by the available information.

Clear instructions and accurate context reduce these mistakes. They help the model understand what the user means, which data to use, and how to calculate the answer.

Let us try it ourselves, Can you finish this sentence:

```
"The shipment arrived"
```

You can't know yet, because too many possibilities remain open. The shipment could have arrived on time, arrived damaged, arrived on Tuesday, or arrived in Memphis. Each possibility would complete the sentence differently and lead you toward a different meaning. You need more context before you can finish it reliably.

"We promised Tuesday, and it left the depot on Friday. The shipment arrived"

Still unclear. Which Tuesday, and which Friday? The shipment should have arrived four days earlier than it did, but the sentence never tells us which dates those words refer to. Without the actual dates, we cannot know whether the Tuesday was the one before that Friday or a different Tuesday altogether, so we cannot work out exactly how late it was or why.

`"The driver made up two hours overnight. The shipment arrived"`

On time. Possibly early. The same four words appear all three times, yet the endings differ. Nothing was looked up, and nothing was fetched from anywhere. The only thing that changed was the text in front of those four words.

This is the point of the example: the model does not begin with a fixed answer and then retrieve the one that fits. It reads the preceding text and predicts what is likely to come next. When the context is too short, several continuations are plausible. After "The shipment arrived," the model can reasonably continue with "on time," "damaged," "on Tuesday," or "in Memphis." Each continuation creates a different meaning.

As more context is added, some possibilities become more likely and others become less likely. "We promised Tuesday, and it left the depot on Friday" suggests a delay, but still leaves the exact dates unclear. "The driver made up two hours overnight, so the shipment may have arrived early, or may simply have been two hours less late." That third version suggests the shipment may have arrived on time, or early. A human reader can understand these implications because people use situational and contextual awareness, along with experience and common sense, to fill in what has not been stated. AI models do not have that human awareness. They read the available context, identify learned patterns, and predict what words are most likely to come next. The model does not understand the situation in that human sense. It has learned patterns from large amounts of text and predicts which words usually follow similar wording and context.

The model then repeats this process one piece at a time. On the second pass, the text in front of it includes the piece it has just produced. Each new piece is therefore predicted from the original question or instruction, the earlier context, and the model's own previous words. A response is not assembled in advance. It grows sequentially, with each prediction narrowing or redirecting the possibilities that remain.

So where does the apparent understanding come from? It comes from the model having learned enough patterns to produce language that often resembles the way a knowledgeable person would respond. When the context is clear, those patterns can lead to a coherent and useful answer. When the context is incomplete or ambiguous, the model may choose one plausible interpretation without knowing that it has guessed. That is why a human must be able to understand the context supplied to the model: if the meaning is unclear to a person, the model has no reliable basis for predicting the intended answer either.

It comes from the enormous quantity of written text the model was shown and from the patterns it learned about what tends to follow what. The model did not keep those texts as a library. It retained patterns abstracted from them. That is why it cannot reliably tell you where a particular sentence came from. It no longer has the pages themselves, only patterns learned from many pages. Three consequences matter later in the book. First, the result can read as if somebody planned it. No one did. There was no outline and no first draft. Yet when each word is chosen with all the preceding words in view, the result can hold together well enough to make most readers assume that a plan existed.

Second, the beginning steers the end. Once the first sentence sets an answer in a particular direction, every sentence that follows is chosen in light of that direction. A response that starts down the wrong road rarely turns around halfway through; it tends to commit to the path it has begun. Third, the model does not always select the single most likely next piece. If it did, the same question would produce the same answer every time, word for word. Instead, it chooses among several likely possibilities. Most of the time, that variation does not change anything important. Sometimes it does.

You do not need to learn how AI works internally. You only need to learn how to make it do what you want, and to see how that can be done in practice. The story here is not about the machinery underneath, or about mathematics, diagrams, terminology, or technical components. It is about exploring what happens when a model is given words and asked to continue them. Everything else it appears to do grows out of that same operation.

It Only Reads Words

A model continues text, so anything it uses must become text first. It learns patterns, not pages. For example, customer, client, account, and buyer often appear in similar sentences. Over time, the model learns that they can have similar meanings.

The model looks at the text already written and predicts what comes next. That is all it does. A database is not text. Its structure is stored for the database engine, and its rows are arranged for fast retrieval, not reading. You do not read a database directly. You ask it a question, and it returns rows.

This creates a problem. A model receives text and produces text. Database rows are neither until something converts them. So someone must describe the database in the message sent to the model. That description may include table names, column names, and notes about what the columns contain. The model reads all of this as text.

The model does not see a table. It sees words.

```
CNAM01
```

Six characters that resemble very little of what the model has ever read, and which therefore carry almost nothing. The model can read `CNAM01` as text, and somewhere inside the software that text is represented in binary, as every piece of computer information eventually is. But that conversion does not give the name any meaning. It is like writing an unfamiliar label in another alphabet: the characters are stored correctly, yet the model still does not know whether `CNAM01` is a customer name, an address, a status, or something else. The binary form preserves the characters. It does not explain the table.

```
customer_name
```

A human immediately understands the difference because of contextual and situational intelligence. To an AI model, however, `customer_name` is no more meaningful than `CNAM01`: both are simply text represented internally as binary. The model can read the characters, but the binary representation does not tell it what they mean. That meaning comes only from the context supplied around them.

Now consider a common enterprise setup. A company uses an Enterprise Resource Planning (ERP) system to run its daily business and a separate data warehouse to support reporting. Both systems contain customer information, but they store it differently and serve different purposes.

In the ERP, customer records are stored in a table called `CUSTMAST`. The column `CNAM01` contains the full customer name as stored in the ERP. During the warehouse load, that information is prepared for reporting and stored in `DIM_CUSTOMER.customer_name`.

Column-level information

ERP system

T5.1 ERP customer column descriptions supplied as model metadata.

Environment	Table name	Column name	Description supplied to the AI model	Example value
ERP system	CUSTMAST	CNAM01	Contains the full customer name stored in the ERP. Use this column as the primary source whenever a query retrieves the customer name from ERP data. Unless this field is blank, do not refer to another column for the customer name.	MERIDIAN FREIGHT INC

Data warehouse

T5.2 Data warehouse customer column descriptions supplied as model metadata.

Environment	Table name	Column name	Description supplied to the AI model	Example value
Data warehouse	DIM_CUSTOMER	customer_name	Contains the full customer name approved for reporting in the data warehouse. Use this column whenever a reporting query needs the governed customer name. Unless this field is blank, do not refer to another customer name column.	Meridian Freight Inc.

Table-level information

T5.3 Table-level descriptions supplied as model metadata.

Environment	Table name	Description supplied to the AI model
ERP system	`CUSTMAST`	Customer master table used by the ERP to maintain customer records for daily business operations. It includes the full customer name maintained in the source system and follows the naming and maintenance rules of the ERP.
Data warehouse	`DIM_CUSTOMER`	Customer dimension table used for reporting and analysis. It stores customer identity and descriptive information prepared for warehouse reporting and provides the governed customer name used in reports and analytical queries.

A model that sees only the column names cannot know this relationship. It may recognize that both columns appear to contain names, but it does not know which system each column belongs to, how one maps to the other, or which column the organization has approved for a particular purpose.

These descriptions give the model that missing context. They identify the environment, name the table and column, explain what the column contains, describe the purpose of the table, and provide a rule for selecting the correct field. If a fallback is allowed when the value is blank, that fallback should also be supplied as a separate business rule. The model should not invent one.

The model already brings a general ability to write SQL. It does not need another lesson on how to use `SELECT`, `JOIN`, or `WHERE`. What it needs from the organization is the meaning behind those operations and the mapping between business terms and actual data.

Once the model receives the table definitions, the column descriptions, the relationships shown in the entity relationship diagram, and the approved business mappings, it can choose the correct field. For a reporting question about the full name of a customer, it can use `DIM_CUSTOMER.customer_name` instead of guessing between `CUSTMAST.CNAM01`, `AccountName`, or another similarly named field.

The SQL is then generated from the supplied business and technical context. The model provides the general SQL skill, while the organization provides the knowledge that makes the query relevant to its own systems.

ERP customer table

T5.4 ERP customer table columns, examples, meanings, and model descriptions.

Table	Column	Data type	Example value
CUSTMAST	CUSTNO	Text, 10 characters	0001048372
CUSTMAST	CNAM01	Text, fixed length	MERIDIAN FREIGHT INC
CUSTMAST	CNAM02	Text, fixed length	Empty
CUSTMAST	CADR01	Text, fixed length	2400 RICKENBACKER PKWY
CUSTMAST	CCITY	Text	COLUMBUS
CUSTMAST	CRGN	Text, 2 characters	OH
CUSTMAST	CPSTC	Text	43217
CUSTMAST	CCTRY	Text, 2 characters	US
CUSTMAST	CGRP	Text, 2 characters	01

Table	Business meaning	AI Description
CUSTMAST	ERP customer number	Use this as the customer identifier only within ERP data. The value is stored as text and padded with leading zeros, so do not convert it to a number or remove the zeros when joining to ERP tables. This identifier is not the same as the CRM account number, billing customer number, or warehouse customer key unless an explicit cross-reference is supplied.
CUSTMAST	First part of the customer name	Contains the first portion of the customer name as maintained by the ERP. Because the ERP uses fixed-length fields, a long name may continue in CNAM02. Do not assume that CNAM01 alone always contains the complete name. Use the ERP name fields together when the complete source-system name is required.
CUSTMAST	Continuation of the customer name	Contains the continuation of a customer name when the name exceeds the length available in CNAM01. Concatenate this field only when a complete ERP customer name is required, and preserve the original ERP spelling and capitalization. Do not treat an empty value as a missing customer record.

Table	Business meaning	AI Description
CUSTMAST	First part of the customer address	Contains the first line of the address stored in the ERP. The address may use abbreviated street names and may have additional address content in continuation fields. Use this field for source-system address reporting, not as proof that the address is the current legal or registered address.
CUSTMAST	Customer city	Contains the city recorded by the ERP for this customer record. It reflects the operational source-system value and may differ in spelling, formatting, or currency from the governed warehouse value. Do not use it to determine historical or current customer location without applying the ERP's validity or company-code rules.
CUSTMAST	Customer region or state	Contains the ERP region code, which represents the state for the United States example. Interpret this field according to the ERP country and region-code rules; do not assume that every country uses a two-character state code.
CUSTMAST	Customer postal code	Contains the postal code stored in the ERP. Treat it as text because postal codes may contain leading zeros, letters, spaces, or hyphens. Do not perform arithmetic on this field or use it as a numeric geographic measure.

Table	Business meaning	AI Description
CUSTMAST	Customer country code	Contains the ERP country code. Use the ERP country-code reference when displaying a country name or filtering by country. Do not assume that the code is interchangeable with a warehouse country name such as `United States`.
CUSTMAST	Customer group code	Identifies the ERP customer group and may control which fields are permitted or how the customer is treated in ERP processes. Do not interpret the code as a business segment, parent company, or customer type unless the ERP code definition explicitly states that meaning.

Data warehouse customer dimension

T5.5 Data warehouse customer dimension columns, examples, meanings, and model descriptions.

Table	Column	Data type
DIM_CUSTOMER	customer_key	Integer
DIM_CUSTOMER	customer_id	Text
DIM_CUSTOMER	customer_name	Text, up to 120 characters
DIM_CUSTOMER	city	Text
DIM_CUSTOMER	state	Text, 2 characters
DIM_CUSTOMER	ultimate_parent	Text, nullable
DIM_CUSTOMER	valid_from	Date
DIM_CUSTOMER	valid_to	Date, nullable
DIM_CUSTOMER	is_current	Character flag
DIM_CUSTOMER	source_system	Text

Table	Example value	Business meaning
DIM_CUSTOMER	48211	Warehouse surrogate key
DIM_CUSTOMER	MDM-7741	Governed master-data identifier
DIM_CUSTOMER	Meridian Freight Inc.	Governed customer name
DIM_CUSTOMER	Columbus	Registered customer city for this version
DIM_CUSTOMER	OH	Registered customer state
DIM_CUSTOMER	Meridian Holdings Inc.	Top-level ownership entity
DIM_CUSTOMER	2019-03-12	Start of row validity
DIM_CUSTOMER	2024-06-30	End of row validity
DIM_CUSTOMER	Y	Current-row indicator
DIM_CUSTOMER	MDM	Origin of governed customer identity

Table	AI Description
DIM_CUSTOMER	Use this key to join DIM_CUSTOMER to fact tables such as FACT_SALES. It identifies a version of a customer record, not necessarily the company itself. The key can change when customer details change, so never use it to count distinct companies or to group results across time unless the question specifically asks for customer-record versions.
DIM_CUSTOMER	Use this identifier when grouping, counting, or filtering companies across warehouse history. It represents the governed customer identity established by master data management and may appear on multiple dimension rows when a customer has more than one validity period. Count distinct `customer_id`, not distinct `customer_key`, when the question refers to companies or customers as business entities.
DIM_CUSTOMER	Contains the registered legal name approved for warehouse reporting, normally based on the signed contract or governed master record. Use it for reporting and display when an exact legal customer name is required. It may differ from ERP capitalization, CRM naming, trading names, or informal names used in sales notes. If grouping by `customer_id`, do not also group by `customer_name`; select one governed name, such as `MIN(customer_name)`, unless the question asks for name history.
DIM_CUSTOMER	Contains the city associated with the customer's registered address during the row's validity period. A customer may have multiple rows with different cities over time. Use the row whose validity period covers the requested business date; do not assume the current city applies to historical transactions.

Table	AI Description
DIM_CUSTOMER	Contains the standardized two-letter United States state code for the customer's registered address during the applicable validity period. Use the governed code format for grouping and filtering. Do not join it to ERP region values without confirming that both systems use the same code set.
DIM_CUSTOMER	Contains the ultimate parent determined during the master-data and warehouse loading process. Use it when the question asks for reporting by corporate group or ultimate parent. An empty value means that no parent was identified, not that the customer should be excluded. Do not independently traverse ownership relationships when this governed value is appropriate.
DIM_CUSTOMER	Indicates the first date on which this version of the customer dimension row applies. For historical analysis, keep rows where `valid_from` is on or before the requested date. This column describes customer-attribute history and is not automatically the date when a transaction occurred.
DIM_CUSTOMER	Indicates the last date on which this version of the row applied. An empty value means the row is currently in force, not that the end date is unknown. For current-state questions, filter to `valid_to IS NULL`. For a historical date, use `valid_from <= requested_date` and `valid_to >= requested_date`, while handling the empty current-row value explicitly.
DIM_CUSTOMER	Indicates whether the row is the current warehouse version of the customer record. Use `is_current = 'Y'` for present-state questions when the warehouse standard identifies this flag as authoritative. Do not use it for historical reporting, because historical rows are expected to have `is_current = 'N'` even though they are valid for past dates.

Table	AI Description
DIM_CUSTOMER	Identifies the system or process that supplied or governed the dimension record. Use this field for lineage, reconciliation, and source analysis. Do not use it as a substitute for `customer_id`, and do not assume that a value such as `MDM` identifies the original ERP or CRM record. Source-specific identifiers must be resolved through the master-data cross-reference.

The ERP table preserves the source application's customer information for operational processing. The warehouse dimension provides governed customer information for reporting and historical analysis. These tables must not be joined by name. An approved master-data mapping connects the records from the two systems. For reporting, use the warehouse table and its governed customer information. ### One customer, two SQL dialects

The same customer lookup can require different SQL because the two tables live in different database systems. The ERP customer table runs in Oracle. The governed customer dimension runs in Amazon Redshift.

ERP Customer Lookup: Oracle

S5.1 Looks up one ERP customer in Oracle, combines name fields, trims text, and returns standardized address and grouping values.

```
SELECT
    CUSTNO AS customer_number,
    TRIM(CNAM01)
        || NVL2(
              TRIM(CNAM02),
              ' ' || TRIM(CNAM02),
              ''
          ) AS customer_name,
    TRIM(CADR01) AS address_line_1,
    TRIM(CCITY)  AS city,
    TRIM(CRGN)   AS state,
    TRIM(CPSTC)  AS postal_code,
    TRIM(CCTRY)  AS country_code,
    TRIM(CGRP)   AS customer_group
FROM CUSTMAST
WHERE CUSTNO = '0001048372';
```

This query uses Oracle SQL. It preserves the ERP customer number as text and combines `CNAM01` and `CNAM02` when necessary with Oracle's `NVL2` function.[1] The metadata for this example declares `CUSTNO` unique. If the lookup returns more than one row, the execution process reports a data-quality problem instead of silently choosing one.

Customer Information Lookup: Amazon Redshift

S5.2 Looks up the current governed customer record in Amazon Redshift after the legal name has been resolved to one customer identifier.

```
SELECT
    customer_id,
    customer_name,
    city,
    state,
    ultimate_parent,
    valid_from,
    valid_to,
    source_system
FROM DIM_CUSTOMER
WHERE customer_id = :customer_id
  AND valid_to IS NULL;
```

Before this query runs, the application resolves the requested legal name to one governed `customer_id`. If the name maps to no entity or more than one entity, it stops and asks for clarification. In this table, `valid_to IS NULL` identifies the current record. More than one current row for the resolved identifier is a data-quality problem, so the query does not hide it with `LIMIT 1`.[2]

What the model already knew

There is no ambiguity about what "training" means here. It means the pretraining performed by the model developer before the model was deployed and used in this conversation. That pretraining gave the model a general ability to recognize SQL grammar and common

Oracle and Redshift patterns. The exact training data and process depend on the model provider and are not specified by this example.

We did not need to give the model an additional lesson in SQL grammar or dialect syntax. We supplied two environment facts: the ERP backend is Oracle, and the data warehouse backend is Amazon Redshift. Those facts allowed the model to select the appropriate common dialect patterns automatically.

The model still needed organization-specific metadata. That metadata identified the tables, columns, field meanings, customer information, and rule that an empty `valid_to` value identifies the current warehouse record.

The pretraining supplied general SQL grammar and common dialect patterns. The metadata supplied the meaning of this organization's data. Pretraining did not reveal the organization's private table names, column definitions, historical rules, or business definitions. Without that metadata, the model could produce valid Oracle or Redshift SQL against the wrong table, column, or business definition. The generated queries should therefore still be reviewed and tested against the target database.

Where the Grammar Came From

The grammar had to come from somewhere. It came from reading queries, not a few thousand carefully chosen ones but an enormous quantity of SQL written by an enormous number of people over several decades. Tutorials and documentation, code sitting in open repositories, forum answers, bug reports, migration scripts, and the working guts of systems whose source anybody can look at. Read enough of that and certain things become impossible to miss.

SELECT is followed by columns and never by nothing. A query that selects always carries a FROM, because there is nowhere else for rows to come from. A JOIN is not one thing but several, and writing

JOIN on its own quietly means INNER, which returns a different answer from LEFT without saying so. An ON belongs with the JOIN and the thing will not run without it. WHERE filters rows and HAVING filters groups, and putting the wrong one in the wrong place is a mistake common enough that the model has watched it being corrected thousands of times.

Then the flavours, because it read Oracle queries and Redshift queries and MySQL queries and SQL Server queries, and picked up not only the rules they share but the places where each one goes its own way. None of that required understanding anything. It required exposure at a scale no person could match. A good analyst might write a hundred thousand queries across a whole career, and the model had read orders of magnitude more than that before anybody asked it a single question. So the grammar arrives free, and it arrives good.

What none of that reading contained was your data. None of those queries mentioned your tables because your tables were named by people inside your organization for reasons that made sense at the time. Nobody outside the company had written about them. That is the part someone has to provide, and it already has a name: metadata. Metadata is data about data. It may sound administrative, but it is not. It contains the facts that determine whether a query answers the question correctly. Take "revenue by customer." What would the model need to know?

The model needs more than a table name and a column name. It needs the decisions that determine which data represents the business question. For "revenue by customer," the required context is as follows.

Revenue definition

T5.6 Revenue definition metadata identifying the engine, sources, joins, stable identity, measure, period, and exclusions.

Metadata item	Definition
Query engine	Amazon Redshift
Customer table	`DIM_CUSTOMER`
Sales fact	`FACT_SALES`, at one row per order line
Customer relationship	Join `FACT_SALES.customer_key` to `DIM_CUSTOMER.customer_key`.
Customer identity	Use `customer_key` only for the join. Group, count, and filter companies by stable `customer_id`.
Measure	Calculate revenue as `SUM(FACT_SALES.net_amount - FACT_SALES.rebate_accrual)`.
Business meaning	Net invoiced value after discount and before tax, less accrued rebate.
Date relationship	Join `FACT_SALES.date_key` to `DIM_DATE.date_key`.
Reporting period	Use `DIM_DATE.fin_quarter_seq`; the previous complete financial quarter is `:current_seq - 1`.
Exclusions	Exclude cancelled orders. Required NULL values must pass validation before calculation.
Tables in scope	`FACT_SALES`, `DIM_CUSTOMER`, and `DIM_DATE`.

Table descriptions

T5.7 Approved table descriptions for revenue reporting, stable customer identity, and financial-quarter filtering.

Table name	Description
FACT_SALES	Order-line fact table containing the approved sales amounts, rebate accrual, order status, customer join key, and date join key. Use it as the primary source for revenue calculations.
DIM_CUSTOMER	Governed customer dimension. Join through `customer_key`, but group, count, and filter companies by stable `customer_id`.
DIM_DATE	Governed date dimension. Join through `date_key` and use `fin_quarter_seq` for complete relative financial quarters.

Measure description

T5.8 Approved revenue measure definition and calculation rules.

Measure name	Definition
revenue	Sum FACT_SALES`.net_amount - ` FACT_SALES`.rebate_accrual` after the required inputs pass NULL validation. Exclude cancelled orders. Do not add tax, use `net_amount` by itself, or subtract the rebate more than once.

The relationships and approved sources are shown in the following excerpt from the entity relationship diagram.

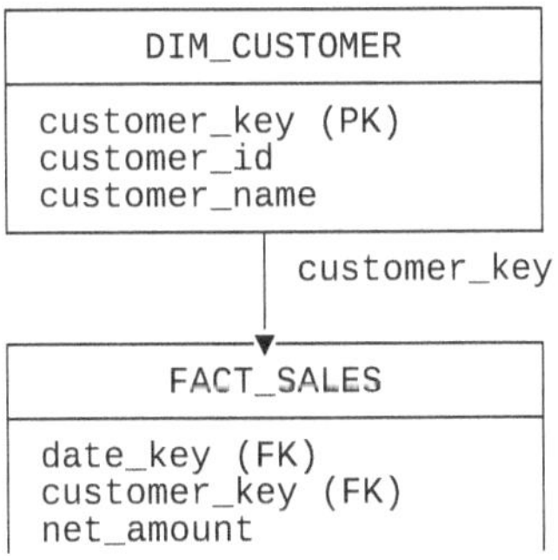

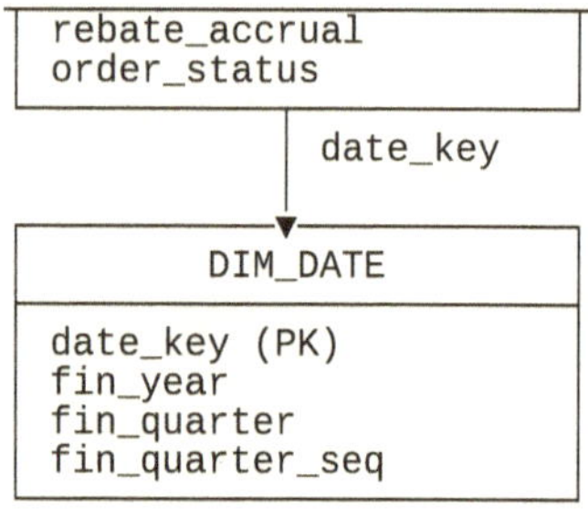

The diagram makes the approved path explicit. Revenue comes from `FACT_SALES.net_amount - FACT_SALES.rebate_accrual`. Sales rows join to the governed customer dimension through `customer_key`, while company-level results use stable `customer_id`. The reporting period comes from the financial-quarter sequence in `DIM_DATE`.

The tables, column definitions, and entity relationship (ER) diagram are all here. Each contains information your organization already knows but that could not have been inferred from the model's training. Now bring these three pieces together and watch the model answer a question.

S5.3 Calculates revenue by customer for the previous financial quarter from documented joins, exclusions, and the approved rebate rule.

```
SELECT
    c.customer_id,
    MIN(c.customer_name) AS customer_name,
    SUM(f.net_amount - f.rebate_accrual) AS revenue
FROM FACT_SALES AS f
JOIN DIM_CUSTOMER AS c
    ON c.customer_key = f.customer_key
JOIN DIM_DATE AS d
    ON d.date_key = f.date_key
WHERE f.order_status <> 'CANCELLED'
  AND d.fin_quarter_seq = :current_seq - 1
GROUP BY
    c.customer_id
ORDER BY
    revenue DESC;
```

The question asked for revenue by customer for the previous financial quarter. The metadata explained what that meant in this business:

use `FACT_SALES` for order lines, `DIM_CUSTOMER` for governed customer information, and `DIM_DATE` for financial-quarter details. It also supplied the joins, the rule to group by stable `customer_id` rather than version-specific `customer_key`, and the revenue definition: `SUM(net_amount - rebate_accrual)`, excluding cancelled orders. The model's training supplied the general SQL ability, while the engine metadata supplied the Redshift dialect and syntax.

The model did not discover the revenue formula from the column names or determine the SQL dialect from the data. It matched the question to the supplied definitions. "Revenue" selected the finance-approved calculation. "By customer" selected the stable master identifier and `MIN(customer_name)` for display. "Last quarter" selected the previous complete financial quarter using the financial calendar and quarter sequence, rather than a calendar quarter or an arbitrary 90-day period. The model also used the supplied rule to filter cancelled orders by adding `WHERE f.order_status <> 'CANCELLED'`, excluding any rows whose order status was `CANCELLED` from the revenue calculation. The model assembled these decisions into SQL, but the decisions came from the question and metadata.

In short, the question provided the requested result, the metadata explained what those words meant and where to find the data, and the training provided the ability to express the result in SQL. The model already knew how to write SQL. It could not know which amount this business calls revenue, which quarter the business means, which customer identifier to use, or which tables are trusted. People solved the technical language problem during the model's training. The organization's business meaning still had to be documented.

Validate required values before calculating

The execution process runs the following validation over the same financial-quarter window as the calculation. The application supplies the window boundaries. If `rows_requiring_review` is not zero, it stops and reports the affected rows. It does not replace missing values with zero.

Validation query Counts missing revenue inputs or order statuses in the calculation window before any aggregation is allowed to run.

```
SELECT
    COUNT(*) AS rows_requiring_review
FROM FACT_SALES f
JOIN DIM_DATE d
    ON d.date_key = f.date_key
WHERE d.fin_quarter_seq BETWEEN :window_start_seq
                            AND :window_end_seq
  AND (
      f.net_amount IS NULL
      OR f.rebate_accrual IS NULL
      OR f.order_status IS NULL
  );
```

The revenue query runs only after this count is zero. S5.3 uses the previous-quarter window, and S5.5 uses the preceding twelve complete quarters.

Table Metadata and Column Metadata

In the examples we provided earlier, the column descriptions and table descriptions were metadata. Metadata means data about data. It tells the model what a table is for, what one row represents, what a column contains, which values are allowed, how tables connect, and which rules apply when a value is empty. The model already knows how to write `SELECT`, `JOIN`, and `WHERE`. What we supplied was the information needed to use those instructions against our data correctly.

Table metadata answers the questions somebody would ask before using a table at all. Is this the right table. What does one row represent. How current is it, who owns it, and which similar tables should be avoided.

Column metadata answers the questions that arise once you are inside. What does this column mean. What kind of value does it hold. Can it be added, compared, or used in a join. What does an empty value mean. Written out for the customer dimension, this metadata looks like this.

Metadata is simply information that explains other information. A table contains data about customers, orders, or products. Metadata explains what that data means and how it should be used. For example, a column may contain a date, but its metadata can explain whether that date means when an order was placed, shipped, or paid.

Good metadata helps people and software avoid guessing. It can explain that a customer table keeps earlier details so historical reports remain accurate. It can also explain that an empty end date means the current customer details. These details may seem small, but they can change the result of a query.

Table: `DIM_CUSTOMER`

Description:
The `DIM_CUSTOMER` table stores governed customer information for reporting. It keeps older customer details so historical reports can use the information that was valid at the time.

- **Grain:** One row per customer for each period of validity.
- **Historical data:** Older customer details remain available when information changes.
- **Governed:** Yes. Use this table for customer reporting across time.
- **Use instead of:** `STG_CUSTOMER`, `CRM_CUSTOMER_RAW`, or `CUSTOMER`.
- **Refresh schedule:** Nightly at 02:00 from the master data hub.
- **Approximate row count:** 340,000.

- **Owner:** Master data team.

Column: `DIM_CUSTOMER.customer_name`

Description:
The customer's registered legal name as recorded on the signed contract. Use this column for governed reporting and legal-name display.

- **Type:** Text, up to 120 characters.
- **Meaning:** The registered legal name for the customer.
- **Important note:** This is not the customer's trading name, which is not stored in this table.

Column: `DIM_CUSTOMER.city`

Description:
The city associated with the customer's registered address during the period represented by the row.

- **Type:** Text.
- **Meaning:** The city of the registered address for the applicable validity period.
- **Usage note:** Because the value may change over time, use the row whose validity period covers the date being analyzed.

Column: `DIM_CUSTOMER.state`

Description:
The standardized state or region associated with the customer's registered address.

- **Type:** Text, exactly 2 characters.
- **Allowed values:** Standard two-letter state codes.

Column: `DIM_CUSTOMER.ultimate_parent`

Description:
The company at the top of the customer's ownership chain, as determined during the nightly data load.

- **Type:** Text; may be empty.
- **Meaning:** The customer's ultimate parent company.
- **Important note:** An empty value means that no parent company was identified.

Column: `DIM_CUSTOMER.valid_from`

Description:
The date on which these customer details became effective.

- **Type:** Date; never empty.
- **Meaning:** The first day on which these customer details applied.

Column: `DIM_CUSTOMER.valid_to`

Description:
The final date on which these customer details were effective.

- **Type:** Date; empty for the current customer details.
- **Meaning:** The last day on which these customer details applied.
- **Important note:** An empty value means that these are the customer details currently in force.

Nothing in there is clever, and none of it took specialist knowledge to write. Somebody on the master data team could produce the whole thing in twenty minutes, because every line is something they already know. What matters is what happens when a model reads it. Those descriptions are sentences, and sentences are the one thing a model is unquestionably good with. Registered legal name pulls in everything it has ever read about names, companies, registration and contracts. The company at the top of the ownership chain pulls in parents, groups, holdings and subsidiaries. So a request that mentions any of those, in any wording, reaches the right column without anybody having listed the synonyms.

The descriptions do a second job. A date can be compared and ranged, while a two-character state code is not a quantity. None of that has to be reasoned about, because the type says what is legal and rules out most of what is not. The validity dates do a third. They say which customer details apply to which period, which prevents a report from using current information for a past date. Then the notes, which carry the weight.

Look at what a name alone would have got you. Anybody could guess that customer_name holds a name and that valid_from is a start date. Reasonable guesses, both of them, and both incomplete in ways that change answers. Nobody could guess that customer_name is the legal name and not the trading name, so a search for the company everybody calls Meridian may find nothing. Nobody could guess that an empty valid_to means the row is current, since an empty date usually means unknown and treating it that way would drop every current customer from the result. That is why the table description must state what the empty value means.

Those are the three lines that decide whether a number is right, and not one of them is visible in a column name. Which is the whole of what metadata does. Some of it repeats what a good name already says, and that part costs nothing and does no harm. The rest of it says the things a name was never able to carry, and that is the part worth sitting down and writing.

Two Descriptions, Not One

It is software. AI is not something separate from software; it is software that has learned some of its rules from examples instead of receiving every rule line by line from a programmer. Ordinary software follows instructions written explicitly by people. A model was trained on text and learned patterns from that text. You do not configure it in quite the same way. You give it information and instructions, and it uses the patterns it learned to produce an answer. It also differs from a person in three ways that matter here. A person remembers. Explain a table to a colleague on Monday and they may still remember it on Thursday. A model does not retain information between separate questions, so it encounters your metadata anew each time.

A person fills in gaps. Tell somebody a column holds the legal name and they will work out, without being told, that searching it for the name customers actually use is likely to fail. A model may make that leap and may not, and there is no way to know which. A person asks. Somebody unsure whether an empty date means current or unknown walks over and checks. A model has nobody to check with, so it settles on whichever reading looks more usual and carries on. Every description in the previous section was written for a reader with all three of those abilities. Which is fine, because people will read them too, and a description nobody can follow is no use to anyone.

But the same fact often needs to be explained twice in different ways: once for a person, who can infer what it means, and once for a model, which needs the instruction stated directly. So each column gets two descriptions instead of one.

```
COLUMN  customer_name

  for a person
```

The customer's registered legal name, as recorded on the signed contract. This is not the customer's trading name, brand name, or the name commonly used in conversation.

```
  for a model
```

Use this column when the request requires the customer's exact registered legal name or the governed name used for reporting. Do not use it to search for a trading name, brand name, nickname, or other informal name unless an approved mapping to the legal name is provided. If the request uses an informal name and no mapping is available, state that the name cannot be matched reliably rather than guessing or applying a partial match.

Both are true and neither is longer than a paragraph. The difference is that the first states a fact and leaves the reader to work out the consequence, and the second states the consequence. The same again, for the column that quietly ruins totals.

`COLUMN  valid_to`

`for a person`

The last day this version of the row applied. Empty means this is the version in force now.

`for a model`

For anything about the present, keep only rows where valid_to is empty. For a date in the past, keep rows where valid_from is on or before that date and valid_to is either empty or on or after it. Never read an empty valid_to as unknown or as missing.

And the pair that decides whether a company gets counted once or twice.

`COLUMNS  customer_key and customer_id`

`for a person`

customer_key is generated here and is replaced whenever a customer's details change. customer_id is the master identifier for the company itself.

`for a model`

To count companies, count distinct customer_id. Counting customer_key will overcount every company whose details have ever changed. To join to sales or any other fact, use customer_key.

Read the three model descriptions again. They are all correct and clear, but each leaves out the action that follows:

```
- Legal name: do not search by trading name.
- Empty means current: keep rows where `valid_to` is empty.
```

- Two keys: use `customer_id` to count companies and `customer_key` to join facts.

```
People usually infer these actions. Models need them stated directly.
```

The human descriptions give facts. The model descriptions give instructions. For example, "empty means current" is a fact, while "keep only rows where `valid_to` is empty" tells the model what to do. Similarly, "not the trading name" implies that the column should not be used for trading-name searches, while the model description states that rule explicitly.

The human descriptions can use varied wording because that makes them easier to read. The model descriptions should use consistent wording and structure because repeated information is easier to identify and apply reliably.

This does not make the model deterministic. Models still choose among several likely continuations, so their answers can vary between runs. The goal is to reduce ambiguity. If two columns seem suitable, the model may choose differently each time. If a clear instruction rules one out, only one likely choice remains. The answers become more repeatable because the ambiguity has been removed, not because the model itself has changed.

Now Let Us See This in Action

Now put the whole thing together and watch it work. Somebody in the commercial team types this.

`"Show me quarterly revenue by customer for the last three years."`

Eleven words, and every one of them is ordinary. Nobody would think twice about asking it, and nobody asking it is aware of having made six decisions on the way. Here is what sits in front of the model when that arrives. Only the lines this particular question touches are shown, and each of them was written once by somebody who already knew it.

Table: `DIM_CUSTOMER`

Description:
Stores one row per customer for each period during which that customer's information is valid.

Column: `customer_id`

For people:
The master identifier for the company itself.

For models:
Use `customer_id` to group or count companies. A company with more than one validity period may have multiple `customer_key` values but has only one `customer_id`.

Column: `customer_key`

For models:
Use `customer_key` only to join the customer dimension to fact tables. Never use it to group or count companies.

Column: `customer_name`

For models:
When grouping by `customer_id`, do not also group by `customer_name`. A company with multiple dimension rows may have more than one name. Select one name using `MIN(customer_name)`.

Table: FACT_SALES

Description:
Stores one row for each order line.

- **Grain:** `order_id` plus `line_no` is unique.
- **Approximate row count:** 190 million.
- **Customer relationship:** Join to `DIM_CUSTOMER` using `customer_key`. This table does not contain `customer_id`.
- **Date relationship:** Join to `DIM_DATE` using `date_key`.

Column: `net_amount`

For people:
The line value after discount and before tax.

For models:
`net_amount` is not revenue by itself. Use the `revenue` metric defined below.

Column: `rebate_accrual`

For people:
The rebate accrued against the order line but not yet paid.

For models:
Subtract `rebate_accrual` from `net_amount` to calculate revenue.

Column: `order_status`

Allowed values:

- `OPEN`
- `SHIPPED`
- `INVOICED`
- `CANCELLED`

For models:
Exclude rows where `order_status = 'CANCELLED'` from all financial calculations.

Table: `DIM_DATE`

Column: `fin_quarter`

For people:
The financial quarter. The financial year begins on 1 April, so financial quarters are different from calendar quarters.

For models:
Use `fin_quarter` for requests that refer to a quarter unless the request specifically says calendar quarter. `cal_quarter` also exists and represents a different concept. Always use `fin_quarter` together with `fin_year`, because quarter numbers repeat every year.

Column: `fin_quarter_seq`

For models:
A sequential number that increases by one for each financial quarter. Use it for relative-period filters.

"Last three years" means the last twelve complete financial quarters, not a rolling date range.

Metric: revenue

- **Owner:** Finance

For people:
Net invoiced value after discount and before tax, less any rebate accrued but not yet paid.

For models:

S5.4 Expresses the approved revenue measure as net amount minus accrued rebate before any customer or date grouping occurs.

```
SUM(net_amount - rebate_accrual)
```

Exclude cancelled orders from the calculation.

Do not use `net_amount` by itself. Do not add tax. Do not report the rebate separately unless requested.

Query engine: Redshift

S5.5 Calculates quarterly customer revenue for three years, excludes cancelled orders, applies financial-quarter metadata, and groups results by customer.

```
SELECT
    c.customer_id,
    MIN(c.customer_name) AS customer_name,
    d.fin_year,
    d.fin_quarter,
    SUM(f.net_amount - f.rebate_accrual) AS revenue
FROM FACT_SALES f
JOIN DIM_CUSTOMER c
    ON c.customer_key = f.customer_key
JOIN DIM_DATE d
    ON d.date_key = f.date_key
WHERE f.order_status <> 'CANCELLED'
  AND d.fin_quarter_seq BETWEEN :current_seq - 12
                           AND :current_seq - 1
GROUP BY
```

```
    c.customer_id,
    d.fin_year,
    d.fin_quarter
ORDER BY
    c.customer_id,
    d.fin_year,
    d.fin_quarter;
```

customer_id	customer_name	fin_year	fin_quarter	revenue
MDM-7741	Meridian Freight Inc.	2022	3	184320.00
MDM-7741	Meridian Freight Inc.	2022	4	197845.00
MDM-7741	Meridian Freight Inc.	2023	1	201176.00
MDM-7741	Meridian Freight Inc.	2023	2	214903.00
MDM-7741	Meridian Freight Inc.	2023	3	226411.00
MDM-7741	Meridian Freight Inc.	2023	4	231087.00
MDM-7741	Meridian Freight Inc.	2024	1	239554.00
MDM-7741	Meridian Freight Inc.	2024	2	247318.00
MDM-7741	Meridian Freight Inc.	2024	3	251902.00
MDM-7741	Meridian Freight Inc.	2024	4	263774.00
MDM-7741	Meridian Freight Inc.	2025	1	271446.00
MDM-7741	Meridian Freight Inc.	2025	2	284119.00

Alongside it, in words, what was assumed. Revenue is net of rebate and excludes cancelled orders, per the finance definition. Quarters are financial and the year starts in April. The window is the last twelve complete quarters. Customers are counted as companies rather than as dimension-row versions. The output contains the stable `customer_id`, one governed display name, financial year, financial quarter, and revenue. It does not expose a single `customer_key` or city, because a company-quarter result can include facts joined through more than one customer-dimension version.

Grouping by `customer_id` rather than `customer_key` is not a stylistic preference. Meridian Freight relocated its registered head office from Columbus, Ohio, to Memphis, Tennessee, in mid 2024. The Columbus version was assigned `customer_key` `48211`, valid through 2024-06-30, and the Memphis version was assigned `52909`, valid from 2024-07-01 onward. Both rows carry the same `customer_id`, `MDM-7741`. A three-year window straddles that move.

If the results were grouped by `customer_key`, Meridian Freight could appear as two warehouse customers. For example, a diagnostic output grouped at the version level might contain:

```
customer_key  customer_id  customer_name          city       fin_year
fin_quarter  revenue
48211          MDM-7741     Meridian Freight Inc.  Columbus   2024
2            247318.00
52909          MDM-7741     Meridian Freight Inc.  Memphis    2024
3            251902.00
```

Those would be two warehouse versions, not two companies. S5.5 still joins fact rows through each applicable `customer_key`, but it groups the result by `customer_id` and does not claim that one version key or city represents an entire company-quarter.

A human knows that Meridian moved from Columbus to Memphis, so they would group both warehouse records as one customer. They would understand that the new address does not mean a new company, even though the warehouse assigned a new `customer_key`.

AI will not know that unless the metadata says so explicitly. Tell it to use `customer_id` when grouping or counting customers, and to use `customer_key` only for joining facts. Without that instruction, it can treat the two versions as separate customers, produce valid SQL, and create a misleading chart.

Each choice traceable to a line somebody wrote down in advance. The model brought the grammar, the dialect, the joins and the arithmetic, all of it correct and none of it interesting. What made the answer right was metadata: a page of plain English that already existed inside somebody's head.

What Actually Happens

Nothing inside your database has ever been read by a model. Not a single row, not a customer name, not an amount, and that is not going to change. What it sees is a description. Table names, column names, and a sentence or two about what each one holds. Nothing else. From that description it works out where to look. Then it writes a request. Someone runs the request, and the database sends back the rows. So the metadata is not an extra. It is the only thing the model has to work with. From the outside, all of this looks like one step. Somebody types a question and an answer appears. It feels like asking a colleague who knows the data well.

Inside, several things happen one after another. The model has to work out what the person actually wants. Someone asking for quarterly revenue by customer wants a number, split two ways, over a stretch of time. That is the intent, and it comes from the question. Then it works out what those words mean here. Revenue is one particular sum in your business. Customer is one particular table. A quarter starts in April. That is the context, and it comes from the metadata. Then it writes the request, using what it picked up from reading a very large amount of SQL. This part needs nothing from you. Then the request goes to the database and the rows come back.

Then someone reads the rows, or the model turns them into a sentence. Five steps, and only one of them needs anything from you. That last step goes one of two ways. Sometimes the model hands over the query and a person runs it. That is what happens when the answer matters and somebody wants to look at the query first. Sometimes the model has been given the ability to run it. The query goes out, the rows come back, and the person sees a plain answer to the question they asked. No tables, no columns, no SQL anywhere.

The second one feels like magic. It is not. Every step in it is ordinary, and the only reason any of it works is that somebody sat down and wrote what the tables mean.

Chapter 6: From Question to Answer

Navigate: Contents · Previous: Chapter 5 · Next: Chapter 7

The person in the commercial team is still looking at the screen. They typed their question into a chat window, not a SQL editor. They did not write SQL, choose a table, or press a database's Run button. They asked in ordinary words, waited a few seconds, and a table came back. Twelve quarters, every customer, with the rebates already taken out. Meridian Freight shows up once, as one company, even though it relocated partway through the window. From that chair, one thing happened. A question went into a chatbot-style interface and an answer came out.

Between those two moments, a whole sequence ran, and it ran too fast to watch. The question arrived, and the model worked out what was being asked for. Then it worked out what those words mean in this business, using the descriptions somebody had written down. Then it turned the two into a query, name by name, choosing only names those descriptions offered. Then it reached the fork at the end, because a finished query has exactly two places it can go. Either it is handed to a person, who reads it, runs it, and takes the rows from there. Or the model has been given the connection, sends the query itself, and turns the rows that come back into the table on the screen.

Played at full speed, all of that looks like one move. It is not one move. It is a chain of small decisions, each made in order and each resting on the ones before it. Somebody, or something, decided what was really being asked, which of the four customer tables to use, which of the two amounts counts as revenue, and which route the query would take at the end. So now the film slows down. Each step gets taken on its own and held still, long enough to see what goes into it, what comes out of it, and what separates a right result from a wrong one that looks the same.

The slowing down matters because this is where answers go wrong. A wrong name in a query either fails out loud or succeeds against the wrong thing, and the second fate never announces itself. Something like that second fate waits at every step. A question can be read as asking one thing when the person meant another. A word can settle on the wrong table because two tables both looked right. A query can run without a single error and answer a question nobody asked. Rows can come back and be turned into a sentence that says a little more than the rows say. The chart with Meridian on it twice was one written sentence away from being made, and nobody in that meeting would have known.

None of it needs technical language to follow, and none of it gets any. What it needs is patience, because the steps only make sense taken slowly and in order. By the end, the few seconds between question and answer will not look like one move any more. They will look like a route, with known turns, known places it can go wrong, and known things to check before trusting what came back.

What the Question Must Say

The table from the meeting is still open, and the person who asked for it is looking at one line of it. Meridian Freight Inc. is down. The latest quarter is lower than the same quarter a year ago, and the table shows the fall without saying a word about the cause. A total that falls has only a few ways to fall. It can fall because fewer units shipped, because the price gave way, because the discount grew, or because of some mix of the three. So a second question forms, and this one is sharper than the first. Split the revenue into its parts, quarter by quarter, and let the parts say which one moved.

Typed the way questions usually get typed, it looks like this.

`What is going on with Meridian's pricing?`

Put to a colleague, that is a perfectly good question. The colleague knows the account, knows what the asker means by pricing, and asks back when unsure. Nothing about it is lazy. It is how people talk when the listener can carry half the load.

A model cannot carry that half, and there is no one on the other end to ask, so it picks the reading that looks most common and moves on. Count what this question leaves open. Pricing could mean the list price, the price after discount, or the price after everything, and each one is a different number. No time period is given, so any stretch of time is as good as another. No layout is given, so the answer could come back as one number, as a chart, or as a page of rows. Only the company name is safe, and it is safe because of one line somebody wrote earlier. The note on the name column says it holds the contract name, and tells the model to say so when a request uses the everyday name instead of guessing. One careful line from one careful writer turned the worst opening into the safest one.

Now the same ask with the guessing removed.

"For Meridian Freight Inc., show the last eight quarters, one row per quarter, oldest first. For each quarter give quantity, gross value, discount, net revenue, and net price. Net price means net revenue divided by quantity."

Read it once and note only what is being asked for. One company, named the way the contract names it. A time period, eight quarters long. A layout, one row per quarter with the oldest at the top. Five numbers on every row, four of them asked for by name, and a fifth that the request defines itself, because the asker suspects nobody else has ever defined it. That is the intent, complete, and notice what it never mentions. No table, no join, no column, no engine. The request says what is wanted and nothing about how to get it, because that part is not the asker's job.

Then read it a second time, this time for what each word means in this business. The transaction table has always held more than the revenue question ever needed. A question about totals had no reason to touch the units on a line or the value before discount, so those lines never appeared. This question needs them, so here they are.

TABLE: FACT_SALES COLUMN: quantity Description: The number of units on the order line.

COLUMN: gross_amount Description: The line value before discounts and tax.

COLUMN: discount_amount Description: The discount applied to the order line, stored as a positive amount.

```
For the model:
  net_amount equals gross_amount minus
  discount_amount. Do not subtract the discount
  again from net_amount or revenue.
```

S6.1 Calculates eight quarters of quantity, gross value, discount, net revenue, and net price for one governed customer in chronological order.

```
SELECT
    d.fin_year AS financial_year,
    d.fin_quarter AS financial_quarter,
    SUM(f.quantity) AS quantity,
    SUM(f.gross_amount) AS gross_value,
    SUM(f.discount_amount) AS discount,
    SUM(f.net_amount - f.rebate_accrual) AS
net_revenue,
    SUM(f.net_amount - f.rebate_accrual)
        / NULLIF(SUM(f.quantity), 0) AS net_price
FROM FACT_SALES f
JOIN DIM_CUSTOMER c
    ON c.customer_key = f.customer_key
JOIN DIM_DATE d
    ON d.date_key = f.date_key
WHERE c.customer_id = :customer_id
  AND f.order_status <> 'CANCELLED'
  AND d.fin_quarter_seq BETWEEN :current_seq - 8
                          AND :current_seq - 1
GROUP BY
    d.fin_year,
    d.fin_quarter,
    d.fin_quarter_seq
```

```
ORDER BY
    d.fin_quarter_seq ASC;
```

Before S6.1 or S6.2 runs, the execution process applies the same-scope validation pattern shown in Chapter 5, with the resolved `customer_id` and eight-quarter window. It checks `quantity`, `gross_amount`, `discount_amount`, `net_amount`, `rebate_accrual`, and `order_status`. If any required value is NULL, it stops and reports the rows instead of silently omitting them.

It generated this query from two sources: the request itself and the metadata shown below. These are the only metadata entries relevant to the request.

```
TABLE: DIM_CUSTOMER

  COLUMN: customer_id
    For the model:
      This is the stable governed company identifier.
      Resolve a supplied legal name to exactly one customer_id
      before the analytical query runs. Stop if the match is
      missing or ambiguous.

  COLUMN: customer_name
    For the model:
      Use this column for the governed legal name in display and
      name resolution. Do not aggregate companies by name.

TABLE: FACT_SALES

  Description:
    Contains one row for each order line.

  For the model:
    Join to DIM_CUSTOMER using customer_key.
    Join to DIM_DATE using date_key.

  COLUMN: quantity
    Description:
      The number of units on the order line.

  COLUMN: gross_amount
    Description:
      The line value before discounts and tax.
```

```
  COLUMN: discount_amount
    Description:
      The discount applied to the order line, stored as a positive
amount.

  COLUMN: order_status
    For the model:
      Exclude CANCELLED orders from all financial calculations.

TABLE: DIM_DATE

  COLUMN: fin_quarter
    For the model:
      Use this column for requests that refer to a quarter unless the
request specifically says calendar quarter. Always use fin_quarter
together with fin_year.

  COLUMN: fin_quarter_seq
    For the model:
      A sequential number that increases by one for each financial
quarter. Use it when filtering relative periods and sorting results
chronologically.

METRIC: revenue

  For the model:
    Calculate revenue as SUM(net_amount - rebate_accrual), excluding
cancelled orders. Do not add tax.

ENGINE: Redshift
```

Now put the request against those lines and follow the mapping, one phrase at a time. Each phrase carries a piece of the intent, the piece finds its meaning in one of the lines, and together they turn into a piece of the query. For Meridian Freight Inc. carries the scope, one company and nothing else. The legal name is first resolved to exactly one governed `customer_id`. The analytical query then filters by that stable identifier, so a shared or changed name cannot merge companies or omit an older customer version.

The last eight quarters carries the time period. The note on fin_quarter says a plain quarter means the financial one, paired with its year, and the note on the running count turns a relative period into whole quarters. Between them, the phrase became the BETWEEN on the sequence and put the year and the quarter on every row as its label.

One row per quarter, oldest first carries the layout. Half of it meets the grain line, one row per order line, and the mismatch decides everything, because thousands of lines can only become one row by being added up. That is where every SUM and the GROUP BY come from. The other half, oldest first, is made robust by the sequential quarter field: the model groups by that field and orders by it ascending, rather than relying on the formatting of year and quarter values. Quantity, gross value, and discount carry three of the five numbers. Each phrase matched its column by plain meaning, units on the line, value before discount, discount on the line, and each column entered the SELECT inside the SUM the layout had already forced.

Net revenue carries the fourth number, and its context is not a column but the finance metric. The metric brought its rules along, subtract the rebate accrual, exclude cancelled orders, leave tax alone. That single match is why the query removes a rebate the request never mentioned, and why the WHERE clause turns cancelled orders away from every number on the row.

Net price means net revenue divided by quantity carries the fifth number together with its own meaning. The context search comes back empty, no column and no metric, and it does not matter, because the definition arrived inside the request. The model built the formula from the two totals already on the row, so the division runs once per quarter, not line by line. The denominator is wrapped in NULLIF so that a quarter with zero quantity returns NULL instead of failing with a division-by-zero error.

And two pieces of the query come from no phrase at all. The joins were copied from the join lines on the sales table, key to key and date to date, and the word Redshift told the model which version of the language to write. The request never mentions either, and it should not, because both belong to the organization rather than to the asker. Compressed to one glance, the whole mapping reads like a receipt.

The query uses the following elements for these reasons:

IN THE QUERY	WHAT IT DOES
SUM around every number	combines many order lines into one quarterly row
net_amount - rebate_accrual	applies the approved revenue definition
divided by NULLIF(SUM(quantity), 0)	calculates net price as revenue divided by quantity, while returning NULL instead of failing when quantity is zero
order_status <> 'CANCELLED'	excludes cancelled orders from the financial calculations
customer_id = :customer_id	filters to the single governed company resolved before execution
fin_quarter with fin_year	identifies each financial quarter without confusing quarters from different years
fin_quarter_seq BETWEEN	selects the requested range of complete quarters
GROUP BY fin_quarter_seq	produces one result row for each quarter
ORDER BY fin_quarter_seq ASC	sorts the quarters in chronological order
JOIN on customer_key, date_key	connects sales rows to customer and date information
the Redshift wording	uses syntax supported by the Redshift query engine

The above table could only be created because the metadata supplied the business definitions, calculation rules, joins, exclusions, identity rule, date logic, and output requirements. The system then used that context to write reviewable SQL that selected the documented sources, applied the approved revenue formula, excluded cancelled orders, used financial quarters, filtered by the resolved customer identifier, and returned the requested columns in the required order. Without the metadata, the system could still write syntactically valid SQL, but it could not know whether the result answered the business question correctly.

S6.2 Returns numeric eight-quarter results with an approved two-decimal net price while preserving the identity, filters, grouping, and chronological order.

```
SELECT
    d.fin_year AS financial_year,
    d.fin_quarter AS financial_quarter,
    SUM(f.quantity) AS quantity,
    SUM(f.gross_amount) AS gross_value,
    SUM(f.discount_amount) AS discount,
    SUM(f.net_amount - f.rebate_accrual) AS
net_revenue,
    CASE
        WHEN SUM(f.quantity) = 0 THEN NULL
        ELSE ROUND(
            SUM(f.net_amount - f.rebate_accrual)
                / NULLIF(SUM(f.quantity), 0),
            2
        )
    END AS net_price
FROM FACT_SALES f
JOIN DIM_CUSTOMER c
    ON c.customer_key = f.customer_key
JOIN DIM_DATE d
    ON d.date_key = f.date_key
WHERE c.customer_id = :customer_id
  AND f.order_status <> 'CANCELLED'
  AND d.fin_quarter_seq BETWEEN :current_seq - 8
                          AND :current_seq - 1
GROUP BY
    d.fin_year,
    d.fin_quarter,
    d.fin_quarter_seq
ORDER BY
    d.fin_quarter_seq ASC;
```

The refined query keeps financial values numeric and applies the approved two-decimal rounding only to net price. The workbook or reporting layer applies dollar signs, comma separators, and displayed decimal places. Keeping presentation formatting outside the Redshift aggregate query avoids converting measures to text and keeps the values usable for later calculations.

The presentation layer can display the returned row like this:

```
financial_year  financial_quarter  quantity  gross_value      discount
net_revenue     net_price
2024            3                  41,280    $2,973,160.00
$148,658.00   $2,713,447.25   $65.73
```

That is the result the asker wanted. The difference between the two answers was a clearer output rule, not a change to the governed calculation.

This is how you work with a model: ask a question, review the answer, add any missing details, and ask again. The first answer is not wasted work. It shows you what information is missing. After the revision, the query is complete and accurate, but it still has not been run. This is not an endless loop; after a few iterations, you will become more proficient at refining your requests, and you will build a reusable template that the entire team can use.

Build the template in the format the team already uses

A reusable template should not force business users to learn prompt syntax, braces, YAML, or another technical format. If the team already works in Excel, the template should be an Excel workbook.

The user should be able to open a familiar file, type into labeled cells, select approved values, and review an example output. The workbook should carry the table definitions, column meanings, aliases, formulas, rounding rules, output layout, and strict rules that the model needs.

This makes the template easier to create and easier to maintain. Business users describe the answer, while super users and data stewards provide the definitions and mappings and IT confirms the physical database details and security controls. No one has to translate the business request into a new authoring language.

Use Excel as the shared master template

Modern AI applications can often work with common structured files such as Excel and CSV. The exact support depends on the model, the application, and the file tools available in that environment.

The safe conclusion is not that every model understands every possible file. The useful conclusion is that a well-structured spreadsheet is a practical way to give an AI system organized business context.[1]

Excel is the better master format when the template needs several sheets, formulas, cell formats, examples, ownership fields, or controlled lists. It can store the formula text and the last calculated value in the workbook. The application reading the workbook still has to expose that content correctly to the model.

CSV is useful when the template contains one simple set of rows and columns. It is plain text, so many systems can exchange it easily. However, CSV does not preserve workbook sheets, cell formatting, validation lists, or Excel formula behavior.

If a team exports the workbook to CSV, formula rules should also appear as text in named columns such as `business_formula`, `sql_expression`, and `rounding_rule`. The model should never have to infer a formula from a displayed number.

The workbook is a business contract

The workbook is not just an attachment and it is not just a sample report. It is a readable contract between the business, the data team, IT, and the AI system.

It records four things:

1. What the business is asking for.

2. What the available data means.
3. What the system must do and must not do.
4. What the finished answer must look like.

Each row should state one fact or one rule. Each column should have one meaning. Clear headers and one record per row make the file easier for people to review and easier for an AI application to process.

One workbook, ten simple sheets

The Customer Quarterly Performance template can use these sheets:

1. `README` explains the purpose, owner, version, and approved use.
2. `REQUEST` contains the values a business user may change.
3. `TABLES` defines the approved tables and the grain of each table.
4. `COLUMNS` defines physical columns, business names, aliases, data types, and meanings.
5. `JOINS` records the approved relationships between tables.
6. `METRICS` records formulas, exclusions, zero handling, and rounding.
7. `OUTPUT` defines the business-friendly column names, order, format, and sort.
8. `RULES` contains the strict DO and DO NOT instructions.
9. `EXAMPLES` contains completed requests, worked calculations, and expected results.
10. `CHANGE_LOG` records what changed, who approved it, and when it took effect.

The names are simple on purpose. Business users can find where to enter a request, data stewards can find the definitions, and IT can find the physical mappings. The model receives the same organized information.

The REQUEST sheet is the part the business user completes

The business user should not type table names, join keys, or SQL. The user should complete a short list of approved request fields.

The sheet can look like this. The template name is Customer Quarterly Performance. The `entered_value` cells remain blank until a user completes them.

T6.1 Customer Quarterly Performance request fields written in plain business language for completion by the report requester.

Request field	Plain-language prompt	Required
`customer_legal_name`	Which customer should be analyzed?	Yes
`complete_financial_quarters`	How many complete financial quarters should be returned?	Yes
`measures`	Which approved measures should be shown?	Yes
`sort_order`	How should the quarters be sorted?	Yes
`output_format`	How should numbers and money be displayed?	Yes

Request field	Example value
`customer_legal_name`	Meridian Freight Inc.
`complete_financial_quarters`	8
`measures`	Quantity; Gross Value; Discount; Net Revenue; Net Price
`sort_order`	Oldest first
`output_format`	Quantity with commas; money as currency with two decimal places

The headings use ordinary business language. Drop-down lists can limit fields such as measures and sort order to approved choices.

The user only changes `entered_value`. The rest of the workbook remains controlled.

The TABLES sheet explains what each table represents

The table definition must include the physical name, the business name, the system, the SQL dialect, the purpose, and the grain. Grain means what one row represents. All three tables are in the Data Warehouse and use Amazon Redshift SQL.

T6.2 Approved warehouse tables, business purposes, row grains, and reporting uses for the Customer Quarterly Performance template.

Physical table	Business name	Purpose and approved use
DIM_CUSTOMER	Customer Master	Governed customer information approved for customer reporting
FACT_SALES	Sales Transactions	Sales quantity and financial facts approved for sales reporting
DIM_DATE	Financial Calendar	Governed financial calendar attributes approved for financial-period reporting

Physical table	Row grain
DIM_CUSTOMER	One row for each customer version during its validity period
FACT_SALES	One row for each order line
DIM_DATE	One row for each calendar date

This sheet prevents a common error. A model may know how to write SQL, but it cannot know which of several customer or sales tables the organization has approved unless the template says so.

The grain is equally important. FACT_SALES contains one row for each order line, while the requested output contains one row for each financial quarter. That difference tells the model that it must aggregate the sales rows.

The COLUMNS sheet connects technical names to business language

Business users should be free to use labels such as Customer Name, Gross Value, and Net Revenue. They should not have to memorize names such as `customer_name`, `gross_amount`, or `rebate_accrual`.

The `COLUMNS` sheet maps the two languages. The column information is divided into two narrower tables so it remains readable on smaller eBook screens.

T6.3 Physical column names mapped to business names, approved SQL aliases, and data types.

Physical field	Business name	Approved alias
DIM_CUSTOMER.customer_key	Customer Join Key	customer_key
DIM_CUSTOMER.customer_id	Stable Customer Identifier	customer_id
DIM_CUSTOMER.customer_name	Customer Legal Name	customer_name
FACT_SALES.date_key	Sales Date Key	date_key
FACT_SALES.quantity	Quantity	quantity
FACT_SALES.gross_amount	Gross Value	gross_value
FACT_SALES.discount_amount	Discount	discount
FACT_SALES.net_amount	Net Amount	net_amount
FACT_SALES.rebate_accrual	Rebate Accrual	rebate_accrual
FACT_SALES.order_status	Order Status	order_status
DIM_DATE.fin_year	Financial Year	financial_year
DIM_DATE.fin_quarter	Financial Quarter	financial_quarter
DIM_DATE.fin_quarter_seq	Financial Quarter Sequence	financial_quarter_sequence

Physical field	Data type
DIM_CUSTOMER.customer_key	Integer
DIM_CUSTOMER.customer_id	Text
DIM_CUSTOMER.customer_name	Text
FACT_SALES.date_key	Integer
FACT_SALES.quantity	Number
FACT_SALES.gross_amount	Decimal
FACT_SALES.discount_amount	Decimal
FACT_SALES.net_amount	Decimal
FACT_SALES.rebate_accrual	Decimal
FACT_SALES.order_status	Text
DIM_DATE.fin_year	Integer
DIM_DATE.fin_quarter	Text
DIM_DATE.fin_quarter_seq	Integer

T6.4 Business definitions, allowed values, null meanings, and approved uses for each physical column.

Physical field	Business definition	Allowed values and null meaning
`DIM_CUSTOMER.customer_key`	Approved key used to join customer and sales rows	Allowed values: Not applicable; null: Not allowed
`DIM_CUSTOMER.customer_id`	Stable governed identity for one company across customer-dimension versions	Allowed values: Not applicable; null: Not allowed
`DIM_CUSTOMER.customer_name`	Registered legal customer name	Allowed values: Not applicable; null: Review required
`FACT_SALES.date_key`	Approved key used to join sales and date rows	Allowed values: Not applicable; null: Not allowed
`FACT_SALES.quantity`	Number of units on the order line	Allowed values: Not applicable; null: Review required
`FACT_SALES.gross_amount`	Line value before discounts and tax	Allowed values: Not applicable; null: Review required
`FACT_SALES.discount_amount`	Positive discount already reflected in net amount	Allowed values: Not applicable; null: Review required
`FACT_SALES.net_amount`	Line value after discount and before tax	Allowed values: Not applicable; null: Review required
`FACT_SALES.rebate_accrual`	Rebate accrued against the order line	Allowed values: Not applicable; null: Review required
`FACT_SALES.order_status`	Current order status	Allowed values: OPEN; SHIPPED; INVOICED; CANCELLED; null: Review required
`DIM_DATE.fin_year`	Financial year assigned to the sales date	Allowed values: Not applicable; null: Not allowed

Physical field	Business definition	Allowed values and null meaning
DIM_DATE.fin_quarter	Financial quarter assigned to the sales date	Allowed values: Q1; Q2; Q3; Q4; null: Not allowed
DIM_DATE.fin_quarter_seq	Sequential value used for complete relative quarters	Allowed values: Not applicable; null: Not allowed

Physical field	Usage
DIM_CUSTOMER.customer_key	Join only
DIM_CUSTOMER.customer_id	Resolve, filter, group, and count
DIM_CUSTOMER.customer_name	Name resolution and display only
FACT_SALES.date_key	Join only
FACT_SALES.quantity	Measure
FACT_SALES.gross_amount	Measure
FACT_SALES.discount_amount	Measure
FACT_SALES.net_amount	Formula input
FACT_SALES.rebate_accrual	Formula input
FACT_SALES.order_status	Filter
DIM_DATE.fin_year	Group and display
DIM_DATE.fin_quarter	Group and display
DIM_DATE.fin_quarter_seq	Filter and sort

The business name is what a person sees. The physical column is what the database stores. The approved alias is the readable column name that the generated query should return.

This mapping removes the need for the business user to learn database naming conventions. It also prevents the model from inventing a friendly label that means something different from the business definition.

The JOINS sheet records the only approved paths

Matching column names do not prove that two tables should be joined. The template must state the approved join, and both relationships below are approved.

T6.5 Approved join paths connecting sales rows to governed customer information and the financial calendar.

Left field	Right field	Relationship
FACT_SALES.customer_key	DIM_CUSTOMER.customer_key	Many sales rows to one applicable customer version
FACT_SALES.date_key	DIM_DATE.date_key	Many sales rows to one date row

Left field	Reason
FACT_SALES.customer_key	Connect sales to governed customer information
FACT_SALES.date_key	Connect sales to the financial calendar

If a relationship needs an effective-date condition, that condition belongs in this sheet as another controlled field. It should not be left for the model to guess.

The METRICS sheet stores the formula and the rounding rule

This sheet is where the business calculation becomes precise. A metric row should contain the business definition, the database expression, exclusions, zero handling, rounding, and display format.

T6.6 Governed metric definitions, SQL expressions, exclusions, zero handling, rounding, display formats, and business ownership.

Metric	Definition or rule	Value	Owner
Net Revenue	Business definition	Sales value after rebate accrual	Finance
Net Revenue	SQL expression	`SUM(net_amount - rebate_accrual)`	Finance
Net Revenue	Exclusions	Exclude CANCELLED orders	Finance
Net Revenue	Zero handling	Not applicable	Finance
Net Revenue	Rounding rule	Round displayed value to 2 decimal places	Finance
Net Revenue	Display format	Currency with dollar sign, commas, and 2 decimal places	Finance
Net Price	Business definition	Net Revenue divided by Quantity	Finance
Net Price	SQL expression	`SUM(net_amount - rebate_accrual) / NULLIF(SUM(quantity), 0)`	Finance
Net Price	Exclusions	Exclude CANCELLED orders	Finance
Net Price	Zero handling	Return empty when total quantity is zero	Finance
Net Price	Rounding rule	Round displayed value to 2 decimal places	Finance
Net Price	Display format	Currency with dollar sign, commas, and 2 decimal places	Finance

The SQL expression is stored as text, so Excel should not try to execute SQL syntax as a worksheet formula. The `EXAMPLES` sheet can contain ordinary Excel formulas that reproduce a small worked example. For example, if cell `F2` contains Net Revenue and cell `C2` contains Quantity, the Net Price cell can use:

```
=IF(C2=0,"",ROUND(F2/C2,2))
```

That formula teaches three details at once. It shows the division, the zero rule, and the rounding to two decimal places. The row should also contain the expected result. A model can then compare the calculation rule with a concrete example instead of inferring the rule from a formatted report.

An Excel formula and a SQL expression serve different purposes. The Excel formula gives the team a familiar worked example. The SQL expression tells the query generator how to calculate the same metric in the target database.

The OUTPUT sheet begins with the report the business wants

This is often the best sheet for the business team to create first. The team can arrange the columns exactly as they want to see them and use business-friendly names.

T6.7 Required output order, business-friendly column names, source mappings, aliases, formatting, rounding, and sorting.

Order	Business column	Source and approved alias	Format, rounding, and sort
1	Financial Year	Source: `DIM_DATE.fin_year`; alias: `financial_year`	Whole number; no rounding; ascending by quarter sequence
2	Financial Quarter	Source: `DIM_DATE.fin_quarter`; alias: `financial_quarter`	Text; no rounding; ascending by quarter sequence
3	Quantity	Source: `FACT_SALES.quantity`; alias: `quantity`	Number with commas; 0 decimals; no additional sort
4	Gross Value	Source: `FACT_SALES.gross_amount`; alias: `gross_value`	Currency with dollar sign, commas, and 2 decimal places; 2 decimals; no additional sort
5	Discount	Source: `FACT_SALES.discount_amount`; alias: `discount`	Currency with dollar sign, commas, and 2 decimal places; 2 decimals; no additional sort
6	Net Revenue	Source: Net Revenue; alias: `net_revenue`	Currency with dollar sign, commas, and 2 decimal places; 2 decimals; no additional sort
7	Net Price	Source: Net Price; alias: `net_price`	Currency with dollar sign, commas, and 2 decimal places; 2 decimals; no additional sort

The business owns the first two columns because those columns describe the report in familiar language. Super users and IT complete the source, alias, and technical mapping.

This division of work is valuable. The people who understand the business outcome define the visible answer. The people who understand the data connect that answer to the correct fields and formulas.

The RULES sheet contains the strict DO and DO NOT instructions

The rules are the most important part of the workbook. Table names and formulas are not enough because the model also needs explicit instructions that close the wrong paths. Every rule in the table has Critical priority.

T6.8 Mandatory actions, prohibited actions, and accountable owners for the Customer Quarterly Performance template.

Type	Rule	Owner
DO	Use `DIM_CUSTOMER` as the governed customer source	Data Governance
DO	Join FACT_SALES to `DIM_CUSTOMER` using `customer_key`	Data Engineering
DO	Join FACT_SALES to `DIM_DATE` using `date_key`	Data Engineering
DO	Use `fin_quarter_seq` to select complete relative financial quarters	Finance
DO	Calculate Net Revenue as `SUM(net_amount - rebate_accrual)`	Finance
DO	Exclude CANCELLED orders from every requested total	Finance
DO	Protect every division by Quantity against a zero denominator	Data Engineering
DO	Generate Amazon Redshift SQL	IT
DO NOT	Do not join tables using `customer_name`	Data Governance
DO NOT	Do not use calendar quarters unless the request explicitly asks for them	Finance
DO NOT	Do not use `net_amount` alone as Net Revenue	Finance
DO NOT	Do not subtract `discount_amount` from `net_amount` a second time	Finance
DO NOT	Do not include CANCELLED orders in quantity or financial totals	Finance
DO NOT	Do not add tax to Net Revenue	Finance
DO NOT	Do not invent a formula for an undefined measure	Data Governance
DO NOT	Do not change a business rule merely to make the query run	Data Governance

The wording is direct because these are controls, not suggestions. Repetition is useful because the metadata explains what a field means, while the rule states the required action and identifies the tempting alternative that is forbidden.

The EXAMPLES sheet shows the model what success looks like

Examples should include both the completed request and the expected output shape. They should also include difficult cases.

For this template, the example set should cover:

- A normal customer with sales in every requested quarter.
- A quarter in which total quantity is zero.
- A customer name that does not match the governed legal name.
- A requested measure that is not defined in `METRICS`.
- A request that asks for calendar quarters instead of financial quarters.

Each example should state the expected behavior. The correct response may be a result, a blank value for a protected division, or a request for clarification.

The model should not learn only from a perfect case. The edge cases teach it when not to guess.

Building the workbook is a team effort

The fastest process starts with the output, not with SQL. The business defines the visible result before the technical mappings are added.

1. **Business users design the visible answer.** They complete the `OUTPUT` sheet with the report title, business-friendly column names, column order, currency format, rounding, and sort order.
2. **Super users and data stewards define the meaning.** They complete the business definitions, approved aliases, allowed

values, null meanings, metric rules, examples, and strict DO and DO NOT instructions.

3. **IT and data engineering confirm the physical mapping.** They add the real table names, column names, data types, joins, SQL dialect, access rules, and connection details.
4. **The team reviews worked examples.** Business users verify that the expected output is correct. Data stewards verify the meaning. IT verifies that the mapping can be implemented safely.
5. **The owner publishes a version.** The approved workbook receives a version, owner, effective date, and change record.

This is collaboration without forcing everyone into the same specialty. The business team does not have to write SQL, IT does not have to decide what a finance label means, and the model receives both views in one controlled package.

Routine changes become fast and mostly no-code

After the organization has built the process that loads and validates the workbook, many template changes require no programming. A permitted owner can change a business label, add an approved alias, reorder output columns, revise a rounding rule, add an example, or strengthen a DO NOT rule by editing the workbook.

The change should still be reviewed, versioned, tested, and approved. No-code does not mean no control.

Some changes may still need IT work. A new database connection, a new security rule, a new file-ingestion process, or a major schema change may require configuration or code. The workbook makes routine knowledge changes faster, but it does not remove engineering from every change.

Keep the workbook easy for people and models to read

Use these formatting rules:

- Put descriptive headers in the first row.
- Store one record per row.
- Keep one subject on each sheet.
- Do not use merged cells in the data area.
- Do not use color as the only way to communicate meaning.
- Do not hide critical rows, columns, formulas, or rules.
- Use consistent table, column, metric, and alias names.
- Store SQL expressions as text.
- Show Excel formulas in worked examples when they clarify a calculation.
- Include the rounding rule and expected result separately.
- Use data validation lists for approved choices.
- Protect controlled sheets from casual edits.
- Record every approved change in `CHANGE_LOG`.

These rules make the workbook plain, but that is an advantage. Decorative layouts are easy for people to admire and difficult for systems to interpret. A clean grid with clear headers is easier to review, test, parse, and reuse.

What the model receives

When a business user completes the `REQUEST` sheet, the AI system should receive the completed request together with the relevant rows from `TABLES`, `COLUMNS`, `JOINS`, `METRICS`, `OUTPUT`, `RULES`, and `EXAMPLES`. It does not need every table in the warehouse. It needs the approved context for this question family.

The model already has broad knowledge of language, common data structures, spreadsheet conventions, and SQL grammar from its development and training. The workbook supplies what that general training cannot know: this company's approved tables, this company's business definitions, this company's formulas, and this company's controls.

That is the practical value of the spreadsheet template. People work in a format they already understand, and each group contributes the part it knows best. The model receives explicit structure instead of scattered explanations, while routine changes can move quickly because the shared knowledge is updated in rows and cells rather than buried in application code.

The workbook still does not run the query. It defines the request and the rules for generating it. The next question therefore remains the same: who runs the query?

Before deciding who runs the query, decide where the master template lives. Keep it in a shared workspace, such as an Excel workbook stored in SharePoint Online or a Google Sheet, where business, finance, and IT can review the same grid at the same time. This removes the need to exchange attachments and reduces the risk that separate copies will create confusion about which version is current.[2]

> **Example: One shared master**
>
> For example, the business team can arrange the visible output columns while Finance enters the revenue calculation and its rounding rule. IT can review the physical fields and approved joins in the same workbook, and each group can see the information supplied by the others.
>
> Suppose Finance changes the Net Revenue rule. Instead of emailing a file named `final_v3_revised.xlsx`, Finance changes the shared metric row and records the reason for the change. Business and IT review that same update in place, so their approval applies to one master copy rather than a chain of attachments.

The live spreadsheet is the authoring workspace, but the AI should not depend on reading that file directly whenever a question arrives. A controlled technical process extracts the approved workbook, converts its sheets into a machine-readable form, validates the result, and commits that approved snapshot to a version-control system such as Git. The AI reads the governed version produced by this process, not an unfinished cell that someone is still editing.

Example: From workbook to governed package

For example, an approval action can start a pipeline that reads the relevant sheets and exports the approved rows as JSON or CSV. The process checks required fields, formulas, aliases, joins, and rules before committing the validated package with a version identifier.

This separation protects the running system from work that is not finished. If a Finance user is halfway through editing a formula, that draft remains in the authoring workbook until it passes approval and validation. The AI continues to receive the last approved version instead of a partial change.

This design gives each group the tool it already understands. If a calculation is wrong, IT can quickly restore the previous approved Git version; if a business user needs to correct a column name, that person updates the shared sheet without learning Git. The pipeline validates and publishes the change, so collaboration remains simple while technical history and rollback remain controlled.

Example: Roll back or update without Git

Suppose a new rounding rule passes review but later produces an incorrect result. IT can restore the previous approved commit and republish that version while the team investigates the new rule. The workbook change log and Git history show what changed and which version was restored.[3]

Now suppose the business wants to rename Gross Value as Gross Sales in the finished report. A business user updates the friendly name in the `OUTPUT` sheet without changing the physical `gross_amount` column or writing code. After validation and approval, the pipeline publishes the next governed version for the AI to use.

Who Runs the Query

The refined query sits on the screen, finished and correct, and it has answered nothing yet. A query is only a request written in the database's language, and a request that nobody has sent brings nothing back. The model has done everything it was brought in to do. It read the question, used the metadata, and wrote the query. What remains is the running, and the running turns on one question. Who does it?

The first route is the plain one. A person takes the query. Maybe the asker sends it to an analyst, maybe the asker runs it themselves, and either way it gets pasted into a SQL editor, which is the screen where queries are typed and run and where analysts spend half their working day. Before pressing run, the person can read the whole thing, and can even hold it against the receipt, line by line, to see where every piece came from. Then they press run, the database does its work, and the eight rows appear on that same screen. Notice where the model is by this point, which is nowhere, because its part ended the moment the query existed, and everything since has been a person and a database.

The second route looks nothing like that. This time the person is not in a SQL editor and would not want to be. They are in a chat window. They type the request about Meridian, wait a few seconds, and the answer appears right there in the chat, eight quarters, dollar signs, $65.73 as the net price for that quarter. No query is shown, and none was asked for. To the person watching, it looks like the model reached into the database and pulled the answer out.

It did not. Behind that chat window sit two things, not one. There is the model, and there is a program standing next to it. People often describe this setup as giving the model a tool, and the tool is that program. The model did exactly what it did on the first route. It read the request, used the metadata, and wrote the same query. Then, instead of showing the query to a person, it handed the query to the program. The program is the one that knows where the database is and how to get in, so the program sent the query, the database ran it, and the eight rows came back to the program. The program passed the rows to the model, and the model turned them into the answer in the chat, the eight rows laid out with a sentence above them. The person saw a question go in and an answer come out, and never saw the query at all.

Now put the two routes side by side and look only at what the model did in each. It is the same list twice. It read the request, it used the metadata, it wrote the query, and it handed the query over. Its work ends at the same point on both routes, at the handover, and the only difference between the routes is who received the handover. On the first route a person took it. On the second a program took it. The model never opened a connection, never signed in anywhere, never sent anything to the database, and never took anything from it. Nothing moves between a model and a database directly. Everything moves through hands, and the hands belong to a person or to a program.

Only two kinds of thing ever run anything against a database, a person or a program, and a model is neither one. The model is the writer. When a model is brought into work like this, it is brought in to write the query against the data, never to run it, and the same holds for anything that would change data instead of reading it. When a number gets fetched, a person or a program fetched it. If a row ever gets added or changed, a person or a program did that too. The model wrote the request, and the writing is the whole of its part.

For as long as there have been databases, the step between an ordinary question and the data has been a person who could write the query, and the model has now taken that step over. That is the change, and it is enormous. But it is a change in who can ask, not in who runs. Anyone can ask now. The running still belongs to the same two hands it always belonged to, a person at a screen or a program with a connection.

The Setup

The picture most people start with is short. Connect the AI to the data, ask the question, read the answer. What actually produced Meridian's eight quarters had more parts than that, and every part was doing work. People did the part only people can do. Somebody wrote down, once, what the tables hold and what the words of this business mean, the contract name, the April quarter, the revenue with the rebate taken out. Somebody asked, in a request that said what was wanted and defined the one term nobody had defined. And somebody looked at what came back and added the two sentences the first answer showed were missing.

The model did the part only a model can do, and it did it twice, once in each direction. On the way in, it turned a plain question and a page of written meanings into the database's language. On the way out, it turned the rows into a reply a person can read. Both times it was reading words and writing words, and it did nothing else.

So this is a setup, and it has two halves. One half is written. The descriptions, the metric, the definitions, the request itself, the words that give the answer its meaning. The other half is physical. The connection, the program, the database, the screen, the things that actually move the rows. The written half is why the answer is right. The physical half is why the answer exists at all. And the model stands between the two, reading one and handing to the other.

None of the three can cover for another. The model cannot write down what only the business knows. No person can sit beside every employee and write their queries all day. The program cannot decide what revenue means. Each one holds a piece the other two do not have, so the whole thing works when all three do their part, and it stops working the moment any one of them does not.

What the setup buys is trust in the number on the screen. Every figure in Meridian's eight quarters was right for a reason, and every reason was a line somebody could point to, in the request, in the metadata, or in the query. Because the reasons are written down, the same question comes back right tomorrow as well. And when an answer is ever wrong, the cause is the same thing in reverse, a line that is missing or a line that is unclear, sitting somewhere in one of the three parts, waiting to be found.

Chapter 7: When the Shape Changes

Navigate: Contents · Previous: Chapter 6 · Next: Chapter 8

Everything so far ran on one shape of data. Meridian's numbers came out of a plain table of order lines. The metadata that made the answers right was table metadata. The grain, the joins, the metric. But structured data is not all tables. Some data is a measurement repeated over time, like a balance recorded every day. Some data sits in levels, like product groups inside bigger groups. Some data is a network, like companies owning other companies. Some data is location, points and areas on a map. These shapes do not live in special places. They sit in the same databases, warehouses, and lakes as everything else, side by side with the tables.

The model can work with every one of them. It has read how people query all of these shapes, so writing the query is not the hard part. The hard part is the same one as before. Every shape is different, and every shape has its own metadata. A table needs its grain and its joins written down. A time series needs different things written down, like what to do when a day has no row. A hierarchy needs different things again, like which level a name points to. The lines that make a table give right answers say nothing about a series, a hierarchy, or a map.

So the same steps repeat for each shape. Show the data. Ask a question. Write down what that shape needs. Let the model build the query. Meridian comes along for all of it, because a freight company has every one of these shapes somewhere in its data. The question is the same each time. What does this shape need written down, before its answers can be trusted?

Tables

Tables come first because they are where this approach was proven. The same table-like data appears in five places: transaction systems, cubes, master data hubs, warehouses, and lakes. The model can work with any of them. The best choice depends on how much metadata must be written.

Business systems contain thousands of narrow tables designed to record transactions, not answer questions. A single answer may require many tables, and each table needs its own metadata before the model can use it safely. That is a lot of writing for one system. It is possible, but rarely worthwhile. These systems are best for simple lookups with one clear answer, such as the questions a service desk asks every day. They are less suitable for larger analysis.

The warehouse is where the eight quarters came from. The sales table and its dimensions are warehouse tables, and the approach worked well because a warehouse brings data from many systems into a smaller number of wider tables. Joins are short, and the definitions were settled when the warehouse was built. Those settled definitions provide much of the needed metadata, so there are fewer lines to write. If the warehouse contains the questions people ask, it is the right place to start.

The limitation is that a warehouse only knows what it was designed to contain. Its design decided which questions could be answered. Data more detailed than its grain may have been aggregated before loading and cannot be separated again. A new subject requires new tables, and new tables require a project. The warehouse is stable, but not very flexible.

The lake is more flexible and often contains more detail. Its tables are files stored in a column-based format, so calculations over millions of rows can read only the columns they need. Datasets are often wide, with one dataset containing most of the information about a subject. A question that would require five tables elsewhere may need only one here. New datasets can be added without redesigning existing ones. Raw data also remains at its original level of detail, allowing questions the warehouse cannot answer.

This lets the model do more than write one query. A complex question often requires several steps: pull the quarters, pull the volumes, then calculate how much of the change came from lower sales and how much came from lower revenue per unit. On the lake, the model can plan and write those steps, giving them to the program one at a time. The program runs each step, returns the results, and the model uses them to write the next. The rule has not changed: the model reads and writes, while the program runs everything. The difference is that the model can now write a plan instead of one query.

The model's training also includes statistics. With data arranged for analysis, it can use tools such as trends, contributions, and comparisons, then explain the results in plain language. A page of calculations can become one sentence that supports a decision. That combination, complex analysis underneath and a clear explanation on top, is what makes the lake useful for important business decisions. One warning belongs here, and it is brief. A lake has more tables than a warehouse, often with the same data at different stages. Its flexibility also makes it less tidy. That makes clear documentation more important, not less. Use source systems for simple lookups, the warehouse for well-defined questions, and the lake for complex analysis. As the options become more powerful, they also require more documentation.

Hierarchies and Graphs

A hierarchy does not arrive in a special container, and neither does a graph. Both are ordinary tables or ordinary files, rows and columns like everything else. Put one on a screen and nothing about it says what it is. The shape is not in the storage. It is in the way the rows point at each other, and that pointing is behavior, not storage.

In a hierarchy, every row points at one row above it. A product group points at its parent group, that one points at its own parent, and the line runs straight to the top. One parent each, all the way up, a family line traced one parent at a time. The same pattern holds anything that rolls up. Products into groups, teams into departments, territories into regions. Rows in a table, and a line hidden in the rows.

A graph keeps the things in one list and the connections in another, and it drops the one-parent rule. A company can be owned by two others. Two companies can be connected through three different routes. A path can run in a circle. Between any two things, the distance is however many steps the chosen path takes, three connections apart one way and five apart another. It is not a line but a web.

And here the problem starts, because on disk the tree and the web look the same, tables with keys pointing at keys. The model reading the catalog sees columns, not shapes. Left untold, it treats the rows as ordinary rows, and each shape then fails quietly in its own way. A web read as a tree loses every second parent. A tree read as flat rows adds numbers across levels that were never meant to be added together. So the metadata carries the whole weight here, and the best way to see that is to watch it work, once on each shape. Start with the tree. These are the written lines the model is given.

HIERARCHY	PRODUCT_GROUP
structure	`parent_group_id` points at `group_id`
levels	1 division, 2 category, 3 group, 4 subgroup
root	rows where `parent_group_id` is empty
ragged	yes, some branches stop at level 3

And this is the question.

For every product group, show the group, its parent, and its grandparent.

S7.1 Traverses a fixed-depth product hierarchy with self-joins to show each child, parent, and grandparent group within the hierarchy.

```
SELECT
    c.group_name AS child,
    p.group_name AS parent,
    g.group_name AS grandparent
FROM PRODUCT_GROUP c
LEFT JOIN PRODUCT_GROUP p
    ON p.group_id = c.parent_group_id
LEFT JOIN PRODUCT_GROUP g
    ON g.group_id = p.parent_group_id;
```

One table, used three times under three names, and the empty cells land exactly where the ragged line said they would, at the top and where a branch stops short. When a question does not fix the depth, everything under one division however deep, the model writes a walk instead, a query that keeps following the parent pointer until it runs out. And the walk is exactly what the web needs too. Now the graph. These are its written lines.

```
GRAPH  OWNERSHIP
  nodes          NODE where node_type is LEGAL_ENTITY
  edges          EDGE where edge_type is OWNS
  direction      from_node owns to_node
  other edges    SUPPLIES, SHARES_DIRECTOR, both
                 excluded from ownership rollups
  cycles         possible, traversal must guard
                 against them
```

And the question, using the company already in the story.

Show every company above Meridian Freight Inc. in the ownership web, up to four steps up.

S7.2 Uses PostgreSQL-style recursive SQL to find each owner above one governed legal entity and report its shortest distance within four steps.

```
WITH RECURSIVE reach (node_id, degree, path) AS (
    SELECT
        n.node_id,
        0,
        ARRAY[n.node_id]
    FROM NODE n
    WHERE n.node_id = :meridian_node_id
```

```
      AND n.node_type = 'LEGAL_ENTITY'

    UNION ALL

    SELECT
        e.from_node_id,
        r.degree + 1,
        r.path || e.from_node_id
    FROM reach r
    JOIN EDGE e
        ON e.to_node_id = r.node_id
       AND e.edge_type = 'OWNS'
    WHERE r.degree < 4
      AND NOT (e.from_node_id = ANY(r.path))
),
shortest AS (
    SELECT
        node_id,
        MIN(degree) AS degree
    FROM reach
    WHERE degree > 0
    GROUP BY
        node_id
)
SELECT
    n.node_name,
    s.degree
FROM shortest s
JOIN NODE n
    ON n.node_id = s.node_id
ORDER BY
    s.degree,
    n.node_name;
```

Every clause in that walk traces back to a written line. The `OWNS` condition and join direction come from the edge metadata. The governed node identifier prevents a shared company name from creating multiple anchors. The path rejects a node already visited on the current route, so a cycle cannot return Meridian or repeat an owner forever. The final `MIN(degree)` returns one shortest distance when several valid routes reach the same company.

Meridian makes the payoff concrete, because Meridian sits under a holding company with two sister carriers beside it. Ask for our largest customer and the answer depends on a written line. Roll revenue to the top of the ownership web, the same walk aimed at the top, and the group is the largest customer. Leave it with the company that placed the orders and Meridian is. Both numbers are right, and the written rollup line says which one a report means, so the model follows the line instead of picking.

Now take the written lines away and read the two queries again. Without the structure line, the model cannot know which column points where, so both self joins could run backward and list children as grandparents, and the query would still run. Without the direction line, the ownership walk climbs the wrong way and returns subsidiaries dressed as owners. Without the other edges line, the walk follows supply contracts and shared directors and calls the result ownership. Without the cycles warning, a circle runs the walk without end. Every one of those failures produces SQL that runs. On these shapes the metadata is not extra help. It is the only thing standing between rows that point at keys and relationships a business can act on. So the first written line for either shape stays the plainest one possible. Say which it is, a tree or a web, and after that one line, everything the model has ever read about walking, rolling up, and stopping knows where to attach.

Time Series and Events

A time series records one thing again and again. A number, a time, a number, a time. A stock price is the cleanest picture of it. At ten the price is a hundred, a minute later it is a hundred and three, four minutes after that it is ninety six. Nothing else rides along. Compare that with an order line, which carries the customer, the product, the quantity, the discount, the status, a whole story in one row. A series row is thin on purpose. Its meaning is not in any single row but in the run of them, in how the number moves. And the storage is the same as ever, a warehouse table, a lake file, rows with a time in the key.

Event and audit records are the same family with a different trigger. A series grows on a schedule. A log grows when something happens, a payment posted, a sign in failed, a credit limit changed, each row stamped with its time and never edited afterward. Thin rows again, arriving whenever they arrive, and again the meaning sits in the run. One failed sign in is noise. Five in a minute is a story.

On every shape so far, the model waited for a person to ask. On this shape, waiting is the wrong posture, because the value of the data is highest in the minutes after something changes and lowest by the time anyone thinks to ask. A person watching a fast series misses things, and not from carelessness. Nobody can hold hundreds of customers' daily patterns in their head and compare every new day against all of them before lunch. So the question changes form. Instead of being asked once, it gets written once and asked forever. The person still starts it, in plain words, and says it once.

Watch daily revenue by customer. If a customer's day comes in below half of their usual for that weekday, flag it and tell me what you see.

The model turns that into a check, which is just a query with a rule attached, and hands it to the program. The program runs the check each morning, which is the part a program is good at, the same work at the same time without ever getting bored. Nothing about the rule from before has moved. The model wrote, the program runs. What is new is only the shape of the arrangement. The writing happened once, and the running repeats. For the check to be right, the model needs this shape's written lines, and for daily sales they look like this.

```
SERIES  SALES_DAILY
  grain          one row per customer per calendar
                 day
  calendar       every calendar day, zero when
                 nothing shipped
  gap meaning    a missing day means the load
                 failed
  late arrivals  prior days are restated when
                 orders land late
  day_of_week    1 Monday through 7 Sunday
```

S7.3 Compares a validated daily customer result with exactly eight observations for the same weekday and returns values below half the baseline.

```
WITH baseline AS (
    SELECT
        customer_id,
        AVG(net_revenue) AS usual,
        COUNT(*) AS baseline_observations
    FROM SALES_DAILY
    WHERE sales_date BETWEEN :check_day - 56
                         AND :check_day - 1
      AND day_of_week = :check_dow
    GROUP BY
        customer_id
    HAVING COUNT(*) = 8
)
SELECT
    s.customer_id,
    s.sales_date,
    s.net_revenue,
    b.usual,
    b.baseline_observations
FROM SALES_DAILY s
JOIN baseline b
    ON b.customer_id = s.customer_id
WHERE s.sales_date = :check_day
  AND s.net_revenue < b.usual * 0.5;
```

Before this query runs, a separate completeness gate compares the expected customer list with the current day and all eight required historical weekdays. A missing or duplicate current-day row, or any missing historical day, is reported as a load failure. The query runs only after that gate passes. Zero-sales days remain in the average because the calendar includes them, and `HAVING COUNT(*) = 8` prevents a shorter history from producing an event.

When the check finds something, the row and its context go to the model as text. The model explains the signal in plain words: when it happened, what happened, how it compares with the customer's own eight-week weekday pattern, and who it affects. The result is a sentence a person can act on after the validated data loads.

The point becomes clear when we look back. Meridian's quarter was low, but a person found the problem only months later by studying a table. A validated daily check could have exposed the decline earlier once enough complete history existed. This example does not establish the exact day on which a signal would have fired.

Half of usual is one rule. The full set is still small. A threshold, such as a price above a limit. A sudden jump, when today differs greatly from yesterday. A drift, when this month falls below its rolling twelve-month average. A broken pattern, such as Tuesday behaving like Sunday. Silence, when a feed stops arriving. A first occurrence, when an account does something new. On logs, it might be too many failures too quickly, such as five failed sign-ins in one minute. Each rule compares a new row with the history behind it. Each can be written as a query or a few lines of code, which the model produces just as it produces SQL.

One more technique belongs to the model. Events often include text, such as a status code, operator note, or reason field. The model can read that text and recognize that different codes may describe the same problem. That is not a query. It is reading, which is what the model was already doing. The same approach can answer other questions from the audit log, guided by two written rules.

```
LOG  POSTING
  default clock  post_date, unless the question
                 says otherwise
  corrections    a reversal is a new row, negative
                 amount, same reference as the
                 original
```

The check watches actions, not amounts. It can flag a limit changed outside business hours or an approval from someone who never approves. When it fires, the model reviews the nearby rows using the stated time field. The default clock tells it which date to use for a question about March. The corrections rule prevents reversals from being misread: an original entry, its reversal, and its correction are three rows in one story, so they are combined before comparison.

That makes metadata especially important for this type of data, mainly because the checks run so quickly. Earlier answers were reviewed by people, who might catch a wrong number in a meeting. A signal does not wait. It fires within seconds, and someone may act on it immediately. If a check sees a missing day but does not know that the missing day means a failed load, it may report a data problem as a business collapse. If it sees a reversal without the correction rule, it may report a normal day as a disaster. The machine can announce either mistake confidently and at speed. Written rules have always separated correct answers from wrong ones. With time-based data, they also separate a fast answer from a fast mistake.

Geospatial

Geospatial data is the shape of the everyday map. Directions from one address to another, the restaurant pin, the circle drawn around a neighborhood to see the schools inside it. All of it runs on three kinds of stored thing. A point, one position, a depot or a customer's doorstep. A line, a route from here to there. A polygon, a closed shape with an inside, a territory or a county. And all of it is structured, sitting in the same places as everything else, a column on a table or a file in the lake, because a shape is just coordinates written down in order.

Ready-made shapes exist for standard geographies such as countries, states, and counties. ZIP Codes are different. The U.S. Postal Service manages them for mail delivery, and their boundaries follow operational factors such as mail volume, delivery area size and topography rather than municipal or statistical boundaries. The Census Bureau creates ZIP Code Tabulation Areas, or ZCTAs, as generalized area representations built from census blocks. Many public ZIP-area maps use ZCTAs, while commercial products may use other approximations. USPS issues monthly updates to address products that include ZIP Code and carrier-route changes, but that does not mean every route changes each month. A ZIP-area shape is therefore an approximation, and its source and vintage must be recorded.[1]

Businesses need shapes nobody publishes. A sales territory is fifteen ZIP codes stitched into one outline, and nobody in Washington is going to draw it for you. Building shapes like that used to belong to specialists, a separate discipline with its own systems and its own language, and most companies had either one such person or none. Which is exactly the kind of gap the setup closes. The work was never hard to describe. It was hard to speak. The person says it once, in plain words.

Take the ZIP boundary file and our territory list. Merge the ZIPs of each territory into one shape, and give me a file I can put on a map.

For the writing to be right, the model needs this shape's written lines.

```
LAYER  ZIP_BOUNDARY
  type        POLYGON, one row per ZIP code
  reference   EPSG 4326, latitude and longitude
              in degrees
  source      Census Bureau tabulation areas,
              approximate by design
  version     boundary_year on every row

MAP  TERRITORY_MAP
  maps        zip_code to territory_name
  rule        every ZIP belongs to exactly one
              territory
```

The reference line sets the coordinate system. This matters because layers that use different systems can appear together on a map but land in the wrong places. The source line explains that the ZIP areas are approximate, so a customer near a boundary may fall on either side. The version line identifies the year of the boundaries, which is important because boundaries can change. The map rule tells the model how to group ZIP codes into territories.

Then the model writes something other than SQL. This time, the runner is not a database but a Python notebook on the person's laptop.

The model learned the mapping libraries' documentation just as it learned SQL, so only the language changes. Its role stays the same.

```
import geopandas as gpd
import pandas as pd

zips = gpd.read_file("zip_boundary.shp")
terr = pd.read_csv("territory_map.csv")

joined = zips.merge(terr, on="zip_code")
shapes = joined.dissolve(by="territory_name")

shapes.to_file("territories.geojson")
```

Seven working lines. The merge attaches each ZIP to its territory, using the map table's key. The dissolve is the whole trick, it groups the shapes by territory and melts the borders between ZIPs in the same group, leaving one outline per territory. The last line writes a file that any mapping tool opens as a layer.[2] The person runs it, watches fifteen ZIPs become one territory shape, and drops the file onto a map.

Notice who did what, because the rule held again. The model wrote the script and never ran it. The person ran it, in their own notebook, which is the first of the two routes, a person running what the model wrote. The libraries did the geometry, because melting borders is real computational work and none of it happened inside the model. And when the person looks at the map and wants three ZIPs moved to another territory, they say so, the model reissues the script, and the loop that refined a query now refines a map. Work that used to wait weeks for a specialist now cycles in minutes, not because the geometry got easier, but because the speaking did.

The point layer works the same way. Customer addresses become points through geocoding, which is a lookup, each address matched against reference data to produce a latitude and longitude. The model does not know where an address is, and does not need to. It writes the few lines that send every address through a geocoding service, and the service answers. The accuracy of what comes back belongs in the metadata, because a point resolved to a rooftop and a point resolved to the middle of a ZIP look identical in the column and are streets apart on the ground.

Put the layers together and Meridian walks back into the story. Geocode the customers, lay the territory shapes over them, and every customer point falls inside exactly one polygon, which is how territory gets assigned without anyone typing a list. Meridian's point sat in an Ohio territory until the middle of 2024, and then the company moved to Memphis and the point moved with it. Revenue by territory for that year splits across the move, and it splits correctly only if the address history and the boundary version both carry their written lines. The relocation that once created two customer keys turns out to live on the map as well.

So the shape got more exotic and the story did not change. Rows and columns took SQL, a series took a standing check, a map takes Python, and underneath all three the model is doing one job, reading written meanings and writing in whatever language the runner speaks. The hard work happens elsewhere, in the database, in the notebook, in the libraries. What the model removes is the specialist standing between an ordinary person and the answer. Give it the lines, the reference system, the source's honesty, the version, the accuracy, and a job that waited weeks for one trained person becomes an afternoon of asking. That is the whole promise of the setup on structured data, in any shape it takes.

What Never Changed

The model worked with every data shape without caring where the data lived. It wrote queries for tables, traversals for trees and graphs, checks for time series, and scripts for maps. Each worked because people had written down the rules that made the answer correct. The model could access data, reshape it, extract it, or build something new from it. For every shape, it could provide the instructions.

But one rule never changed: the model wrote and never ran. The database ran the queries, the program ran the daily checks, and the person ran the notebook. The model did everything up to execution, but nothing beyond it. This was true for trees, series, and maps too.

Viewed from a distance, the arrangement is clear. Since the first programs were created, making software do something required two parties: a person and a program. The person had to speak the program's language: SQL for databases, code for notebooks, or specialized tools for maps. Now there are three participants. The model understands the person's plain-language request, translates it into the program's language, and writes much faster than a person can. The traditional roles have not changed: the person decides, and the program runs. The model simply removes the need to speak the machine's language. It is another piece of software, and its contribution is faster writing.

But the model did not solve the underlying problems. The missing time-series data, the correct clock, the hierarchy level, the graph direction, and the map's reference system all required rules written by people. The model supplied none of those decisions. That is why giving it a messy table and saying "clean this" is not enough. Cleaning data requires many decisions, and the model cannot make those decisions without guidance.

The responsibility therefore remains with people, though it has changed. Nobody needs to learn every technical language anymore. Someone still needs to understand the data and document what it means: its source, definitions, conventions, and the language used by the system that runs it. That metadata is what every data shape needs.

This human responsibility cannot be delegated. The model can only be as accurate as the information it receives. Give it clear rules, and the speed is real: weeks of specialist work can become an afternoon, and months of unnoticed problems can become a morning alert. Leave out the rules, and the model produces confident wrong answers just as quickly. The data shapes changed, but the agreement stayed the same: people provide the written knowledge, and the model provides the speed.

Chapter 8: From Model to Agent

Navigate: Contents · Previous: Chapter 7 · Next: Chapter 9

Every answer in this story started the same way, with a person turning to the model and asking. The query, the walk, the map script, even the standing check, each one began as somebody's sentence. The model never moved first. It waited, read, wrote, and went quiet again. Asking works for the occasional question, and the day to day is different. Most work in a company is not a person wondering something. It is a flow. Orders arrive, invoices get matched, disputes get opened and worked and closed, and each flow runs all day whether anyone is curious or not. The real question is whether the model can take a place inside a flow like that, where nobody stands by to type the prompt.

The industry's answer is the word agent, and the word usually arrives packaged with another one, automation. Both deserve a slower look, because automation is not new. The nightly pipeline that moves data from system to system has run for decades. The software robot that clicks through screens the way a clerk would has been sold for years. Both are real automation, and both work the same way, by replaying steps somebody fixed in advance. If that is automation, an agent is not it, and calling agents automation says more about the sales brochure than the machinery.

Look instead at what the model has actually been doing. It wrote a query, built a walk, produced a signal, and drew a territory. Each one was a task, and every task shared the same three properties. It had a boundary that said this and nothing else, it had an objective that said what the output must be, and it had no ambiguity left by the time the writing started, because the written lines had removed it. That is not automation, and it is not magic. It is a task, performed.

So that is what an agent is, and the definition is narrower than the advertising. An agent is a model that has been equipped for one task. Not a SQL agent, because every model writes SQL out of the box, and not an email agent, because every model writes email. Those are abilities, and abilities are the free part. An agent begins where somebody takes one task, draws its boundary, states its objective, and supplies everything the task needs, the meanings, the rules, the worked examples, good ones and bad ones, until the model can tell a good output from a bad one on its own. That supplying is the training, and it is the same act this whole story has been about, knowledge written down and handed over. The only thing that changed is the completeness.

Do that completely and something changes in the output. It stops wandering. The same task, given the same facts, comes back the same way, not perfectly, because nothing about this machinery is perfect, but as repeatable as the equipment can be made, which for one well bounded task turns out to be very repeatable indeed. And a model that repeats is a model a flow can rely on. That is the whole opening the day to day was waiting for. Not a smarter chat window, and not another pipeline, but the same three parts as always, the written lines, the program, the model, assembled this time around one task, holding a job instead of answering a question.

The Agent in the Enterprise

Start with what an ordinary company actually owns, because it owns everything at once. The ERP running the money, the CRM running the customers, a cube feeding the monthly decks, a warehouse, a lake, and a master data system keeping one list of products and one list of customers. That is not a sophisticated company. That is the norm, and every environment in the earlier chapters is standing in the same building at the same time.

So the first instinct is to put an agent on top of every system, and the instinct deserves a hard look. The ERP ships with an assistant, the CRM ships with one, and the reporting layer increasingly has one too. If the work begins and ends inside one system, that built-in is usually the first place to look, and an agent that repeats what it does is a second doorbell on the same door. The value of your own agent begins where the work crosses those boundaries, or depends on files no system ever owned.

The lake is where that second kind of work lives, because a lake takes in more than system feeds. People put things there. Demand forecasts, budget files, someone's analysis saved from last quarter. These are rows and columns, but nobody's database enforced them, so every author shapes them differently. One analyst runs the months across the top, another runs them down the side, a third names the categories after her own cost centers. Three layouts, one meaning underneath. No pipeline reads those files, and no built-in assistant inside the ERP has ever heard of them.

Now watch the work they create. Every month somebody compares budgets against actuals. The actuals sit in the ERP, in the general ledger, tidy and systematic. The budgets sit in the lake as three files from three authors, forward looking and author shaped. The analyst doing this by hand opens the first file, works out its layout, copies its numbers into a master sheet, does it twice more for the other two, pulls the ledger export, lines the categories up by eye, and writes the differences into a summary before lunch, if nothing slips. All of it is mouse clicks, keyboard strokes, and file saves, and every retyping step is a place for a number to go quietly wrong.

That whole set of actions is one task. Here, task does not mean one click or one step. It means the full job: find the files, read each one whatever its layout, translate each into the common frame, pull the actuals, match, compare, flag, and write it up. Give that job a boundary, an objective, and the written rules, and it becomes an agent by the definition already on the table. Call it the budget-to-actuals agent. Not a finance agent, because finance is a department, not a task. A department is too broad, an ability is too small, and the useful agent lives around one complete, bounded job.

What equips it is not code. It is instructions, written in the language the office already speaks, and short enough to read in a minute.

Every budget holds four things, whatever the layout: entity, month, category, amount. Match categories to the ledger using the mapping sheet. Compare month by month. Flag any gap over five percent or fifty thousand dollars. Anything a rule does not cover, ask, do not guess.

The first line makes the layout irrelevant. It stops looking for one particular spreadsheet shape and starts looking for four things, wherever each author put them. The meaning survives the layout. The mapping sheet is written knowledge, three authors' category words tied to the ledger's accounts by somebody who knew both. The thresholds are the human's judgment, written down once. And the last line is the boundary fence, because a category no rule covers comes back as a question, never as a guess. Last year's files from all three authors sit beside these lines as worked examples, and together that is what the agent needs for this job.

Be precise about what this agent is not doing. It is not replacing the analyst, and it is not making a single decision. The thresholds were the human's, the mappings were the human's, and the output lands on the human's desk for the only step that matters, deciding what to do about the gaps. What the agent took over is the clicking, the copying, and the retyping, and it does that part faster and more consistently for a plain reason. The running half is a program. It does not tire while moving numbers, lose its place between files, or lose focus on a Friday afternoon. The model half reads the author-shaped files and writes the summary. Between them, the analyst's morning becomes the analyst's first five minutes.

And one more thing separates this from the automation that came before. The nightly pipeline and the screen robot can handle the exceptions somebody anticipated and wrote into them. When something falls outside those paths, they usually know only that the flow could not continue. The model adds something different. It reads what went wrong and explains it in words. A budget file with a missing month comes back as a sentence naming the file, the author, and the month. A category outside the mapping comes back as a question with the unmatched word in it. The output arrives explained, and the exceptions arrive explained, in the same plain language the instructions went in. That is the difference the model brings to the machinery, and it is what makes a narrow task safe to hand over. The job is fully described, faithfully done, and reported back in words. The agent from the definition now has its first job.

The Web of Agents

The budget-to-actuals agent finished its first month by placing a summary on the analyst's desk. But that is where its work ends. One task often connects to others. The gaps it finds may need to reach the controller. The month-end pack may need its numbers. A person responsible for a late file may need to know about it immediately. A single agent is only the beginning. Company work continues after one task ends, so the agent must hand its work over.

Before agents, companies usually connected tasks in one of two ways. A nightly pipeline ran fixed steps in a set order. When it needed a choice, someone had already coded the rule: if this happens, do that; otherwise stop. Screen robots worked the same way through clicks. These systems followed preset paths, so anything unexpected caused them to stop. The business waited, a specialist checked the logs, and debugging began with an error code and little context.

Agents connect in a different way, much like the ownership structures described earlier in this book. Ownership was not always a straight line. It was often a web with several possible routes, with the best route chosen when needed. Agents work similarly. The budget-to-actuals agent is not part of one fixed sequence. It connects to several nearby agents, each responsible for a specific task. When its task ends, it chooses the next agent based on the situation. This is often called a mesh or an agentic ecosystem. The simplest picture is a web.

For choosing to work, the neighbors have to be described, and by now the form of the answer should feel familiar. Agents get written lines too.

```
AGENT  ledger-freshness
  does     answers whether a period's ledger
           load is complete
  needs    entity and month
  returns  complete or waiting, with what is
           missing

AGENT  notifications
  does     tells a named person one thing
  needs    who, what, and why
  returns  sent, with the time
```

That is a roster, written by people, read by agents. When the budget-to-actuals agent flags a gap, it does not guess what to do. It reads the roster the way the model once read column descriptions, matches its situation against the does lines, and picks. A suspicious gap in one entity's actuals matches the freshness agent, so it asks there first. Freshness answers waiting, one file missing, and that answer matches the notifications agent, who, the file's owner, what, the missing file, why, the close is waiting on it. If freshness had answered complete, the same gap would have routed the other way, into the month end pack with a note for the controller. Same event, two routes, and nobody coded the fork. The route was composed at the moment, from the roster.

Now the harder case, the one that used to stop the line. A fourth budget file appears, from a new planner nobody onboarded, full of category words the mapping sheet has never seen. No branch anywhere anticipated her. The agent's own rules say ask, do not guess, so it starts walking the web. Is there an agent whose does line covers new mappings, no. Is there one that reaches the ledger owners, yes, notifications. So the walk ends where every walk in this web ends when the roster runs out, at a person, and it arrives carrying its own account. The file, the author, the unmatched words, what it tried, in order, in plain language. The old line stopped and left a specialist to reconstruct the story from logs. The web stops and hands the story over already written. The human still fixes it, and the human no longer digs for it.

Which brings up the word that has been carefully rationed in this book, decision, because two different things hide under it. Decisions about the business, what a number means, whether the gap is a problem, what to do about the planner's file, those stay with people, exactly as before, and no guard around an agent should ever be loose enough to let that move. Decisions about the route, which neighbor to try, who needs to hear, what to attempt when the first attempt returns waiting, those are the agent's, and they are safe to give it for three reasons. The choices come from a roster people wrote. Each one is small and reversible. And the last stop of every route is a person. A model can weigh a situation it has never seen against everything it has ever read and pick a sensible next step, which is precisely the thing no coded fork could do, and it is worth exactly that much and no more.

So be careful with the bigger claims in circulation. There are publications where agents make the sales calls and close the deals, and placing a call is not the hard part of a sale. Reading the person on the other end is, and easing a problem that needs one human talking to another is, and none of that is in this machinery. Close the deal is a department wearing a task's name, and the test from before applies unchanged. If it cannot be written down as a bounded job with a roster of neighbors and a person at the end, it is not an agent's work.

What an organization builds, then, is not one agent and not a pile of them. It is the web, shaped around its own functions, each agent equipped for its task and equipped, just as deliberately, to talk to its neighbors. The next action is never coded beforehand, and it is never invented from nothing either. It is chosen when the event happens, from written descriptions, by a reader that has seen a great deal, on routes that all end at a person when it matters. The line stopped at the first surprise. The web routes around it, and writes down what it saw on the way.

How Agents Talk

The roster says who does what. It does not say how an ask travels. When the budget-to-actuals agent needs the freshness agent, something has to carry the question over and carry the answer back. That something is the communication layer, and it is where a lot of agent projects quietly go wrong, not by building too little, but by building too much. Start with what the messages actually are. Every agent in this web reads and writes plain language, because that is what the model half does. So the natural message between two agents is a sentence.

```
to: ledger-freshness
Is the March ledger load complete for the Memphis entity?

from: ledger-freshness
Waiting. The freight accrual file has not arrived.
```

The minimum setup is small: a router that reads the recipient, sends the message, waits, and returns the reply. It can be written in Python or the team's existing language in a few hundred readable lines. Multi-turn conversations work naturally because the router keeps passing messages back and forth until the task ends. It is a mail room, not a telephone exchange, and for an internal company system, that is usually enough.

The field around this is moving fast, and new standards for agent communication arrive almost by the season. Two are worth knowing by name, as of the middle of 2026. MCP, the Model Context Protocol, standardizes the plug between a model and its tools and data, one connector that many systems understand, open sourced by Anthropic in late 2024 and now governed under the Linux Foundation. A2A, the Agent2Agent protocol, standardizes the other conversation, agent to agent, so that agents built by different vendors on different platforms can find each other and trade tasks, announced by Google in April 2025 and donated to the Linux Foundation that June as a project in its own right.[1] Both are real, both are serious, and both exist for a real problem, the property line. The moment your web has to talk to a vendor's agent, or another company's, a shared standard is the only sensible road, because you do not get to choose what the other side speaks.

Inside your company, the calculation is different. Each protocol adds something else to version, maintain, secure, and staff. New standards can also bring early-technology problems, such as security patches, scaling limits, and changing specifications. That does not mean you should avoid them. Use them when they solve a real problem. An agent web should make work faster, not more complicated. If adding a new agent requires a protocol engineer, the system is too complex. The simple rule is: use sentences and a router inside the company, shared standards for outside communication, and extra complexity only when necessary.

When the choice is close, focus on the right measure. The time needed to build the communication layer matters less because it is a one-time cost. The important question is what happens when the system fails at two in the morning. How quickly can one person understand the route, find the problem, and fix it? How easy is it to add an agent, change a rule, or make an improvement? A trustworthy system should meet the usual standard of three nines: 99.9 percent availability, or fewer than nine hours of downtime per year. Simple layers can meet that standard cheaply. Complicated layers cost more or may fail to meet it.

The reason the wiring matters so much is the cost of failure. When the web is down, people do not say the router is down. They say the AI does not work. Every process failure gets blamed on the tool, and trust in the system slowly disappears, even when the model was not at fault. The process is part of the product. The written instructions make the answers correct. The wiring makes the answers available when people need them. Both deserve the same care because the business experiences them as one system.

Choosing the Right Job

The ideas reviewed so far show that agents can help with specific, well-defined tasks. But they are not right for every job, so choosing where to use one requires careful thought.

Start with the wrong job, because it looks so reasonable. Rows need to move from the ERP into the warehouse every night, so somebody proposes an agent for it. But that work was solved decades ago. A pipeline gets coded once, deployed once, and then runs for years without a wrong step, the same rows, the same route, the same result. Putting an agent there replaces something certain with something slower, dearer, and less certain, and gains nothing in exchange. The model earns nothing on work a fixed program already does perfectly, the same way it earned nothing repeating a built-in assistant. Never trade working certainty for probability.

The test that separates the jobs is short. Look at how the work gets done today, before any agent arrives. If it needed a person's fingers once, a coder writing the steps that then run untouched, it is automation's job, and it should stay automation's job. If it needs a person's eyes every time, someone reading, judging layouts, fixing what changed since last month, it is a candidate. Anything that waits on a human today is on the list. Anything a program already runs alone is not.

The eyes-every-time work is everywhere once you look for it. Vendor files are the classic case. Information arrives every month from outside the company, and every month it arrives slightly different. A column renamed, a tag typed wrong, a new layout because somebody on the vendor's side rebuilt their export, a budget file carrying a label no mapping has seen. None of it can be coded in advance, because the changes cannot be predicted, which is exactly why a person has been cleaning these files by hand for years. That person's years of fixes are hundreds of worked examples, and hundreds of worked examples are an equipping. A file-cleansing agent built on them reads each arriving file the way the budget agent read the three planners, finds what each field actually is whatever it was called this month, fixes what its examples cover, and asks about what they do not. The person who spent the first hour of every month cleaning now spends five minutes reading the questions.

Then there is the job that must be split down the middle, and the Monday brief is the cleanest picture of it. Every week a deck goes to the chief executive, and the deck holds two different things, numbers and judgment. The numbers are eyes-every-time work of the mechanical kind, pull the week's figures, compute the movements, lay them onto the slides, format everything the house way. The judgment is something else entirely, what the movements mean, which one matters this week, what to do about it. Give the whole deck to an agent and the second half will read fluently and mean nothing, because the model does not know what was said in Friday's meeting, which worry is live in the building, or how the room will take a hard number. It has its equipping and everything it has read, and past that its awareness of the situation stops. So the split is the design. The agent builds the deck and delivers it Sunday night with the numbers in place and the judgment boxes empty on purpose. The human opens it Monday at seven and writes the only part that was ever theirs.

Put the three examples side by side and the rule underneath them shows. The pipeline job stays with the pipeline, because it was never human work at all. The file job goes to the agent, because it was human work of the reading kind, done before any judgment starts. And the brief gets split, machinery below, meaning on top. Every piece of work in a company heads to one of three places, a program's fixed steps, an agent's reading, or a person's mind, and the agent claims only the middle one. Choose judiciously, and the agent spends its hours where hours were being lost, on the repetitive reading that stood between people and their judgment. That was always the offer. Not fewer people deciding, but people deciding sooner, with the morning back in their hands.

The Knowledge Question

Structured data was always the easy data. Anyone in the company could see it, query it, read it off a report, and everyone broadly understood what it meant. And yet, across the whole company, it was the hardest data to work with. Not because it was flawed, and not because it was locked away. It simply would not blend. One customer carried six identifiers across six systems, and no system was obliged to agree with any other. Two perfectly good tables in two perfectly good systems sat a hallway apart and might as well have been in different countries. The constraint was never in the data. It lived in the systems around it.

That constraint has moved. The systems still do not talk to each other, and for the first time they do not need to. Data leaves each system the way it always could, a program's extract, a feed, a file, and the meeting now happens somewhere new, in the reading. Given the written meanings, a model makes six identifiers one company in seconds, matches a planner's category words to a ledger's accounts, and lets numbers from opposite ends of the building sit in one answer. The integration project that took quarters becomes a page of meanings and an afternoon. The data talks, even where the systems never will.

Everything in that sentence depends on one clause: given the written meanings. The earlier bargain, knowledge for speed, does not disappear as the web grows. It scales from one task to the whole company. And the knowledge in question already has a name people use in the hallways: tribal knowledge. It is what the ledger clerk knows about why March always looks strange, what the planner knows about which vendor's file is wrong, and why the west region appears twice and which version is correct. It is real knowledge, held by people, shared by working alongside one another, and lost a little with every resignation. It is not always freely given, because knowledge brings status, and writing it down can feel like giving that status away.

So for any organization looking at an agentic web, the order of operations inverts. Not tools first but knowledge first. Before the roster, before the router, before even the question of whether a web is possible here, the first project is the oldest one, getting what the people know onto the page. The companies that do this will find the machinery ready, cheap, and fast. The companies that skip it will own very fast software that repeats their confusion at speed.

An agent is a powerful mechanism from the software called artificial intelligence, and it is still only a mechanism. Every system and every process before it has given back the knowledge and care put into it, and it cannot give back anything else. So before anyone asks whether an agentic web is possible, there is an older question waiting underneath, the one this book's story has been walking toward. What does your company actually know, who is holding it, and how much of it has ever been written down?

Chapter 9: Building the Agents

Navigate: Contents · Previous: Chapter 8 · Next: Chapter 10

We have seen the machinery work. Now let us put what we have learned into practice. In the pages ahead, we will build two agents step by step, elaborating on each idea with every written line shown clearly enough to follow and apply.

We have learned that the model is not the system. It is the part that reads the question, the definitions, the rules, and the examples, then writes the instructions for the work. A person or a program still performs the work. The database runs the query, the file processor runs the script, and the analyst remains responsible for the judgment that follows.

We have learned that reliable results begin with knowledge written down. The task must have a clear boundary, its objective must be stated, and the meanings, mappings, exceptions, and limits must be supplied in a form that people and models can both read. Without those lines, the model can produce work that sounds right but carries no dependable business meaning.

We will now apply those lessons to two different jobs. The first agent will process Medicaid claim files that arrive in inconsistent formats and turn them into one standard structure without changing their business meaning. The second will watch purchase behavior over time, identify patterns that deserve attention, and send a person an explained signal while leaving the decision and the action in human hands.

Agent 1 is the Medicaid File Processing Agent. It reads quarterly rebate invoice and claim-support files supplied by state Medicaid programs or their vendors to a drug manufacturer. CMS publishes standard Medicaid Drug Rebate Program, or MDRP, invoice formats, but the claim-level data fields CMS lists as suggested, along with their names and delivery layouts, can vary. These files support real rebate payments, and the operational examples in this chapter come from five author-supplied files whose senders are unnamed.[1] Agent 2 is the Abnormal Purchase Signal Agent. It reviews completed monthly sales for buying that does not look normal, a sudden jump, a strange mix, a slow fade, and sends a person a signal that answers six required questions. One agent comes from the book's running company. One comes from a different industry, so the method is shown working outside the story too.

The Anatomy of an Agent

Every build starts with a page of writing, not with code. The roster entry from before told the neighbors what an agent does. The definition is what the agent itself gets, and it is longer, because it holds everything the agent is allowed to assume. A good definition answers five questions, all in writing.

- What is it. One paragraph, like a job description. What work it does and what work it does not do. Written twice, once for people and once for the model, the same rule the book has used for every table.
- What does it know. The meanings, the mappings, the rules, and the worked examples, good and bad. All in one place, with a person's name on it as the owner.
- How does it work. The steps of the job, in order. Read this first, check that second, never skip. The agent gets the sequence in writing, because nothing is assumed.
- How does it answer. The exact shape of its output, the same every time, so the program and the neighbors can rely on it.

An agent that answers differently on different days breaks the web.

- What must it never do. The hard limits. A limit is not a preference. A preference bends under a clever request, and a limit does not. The deepest limit is the oldest rule here, the model plans and the machinery performs.

Around the five sits one more thing. Policies. A policy says what the agent is shown, which means what goes into the model and what never does. The rule is simple. Give the model the least the task needs. Often the model does not need the data at all. It needs the shape. Column names, types, counts, the delimiter. That is enough to plan a whole file's processing, and the rows never go in.

This matters because of what the rows can carry. State claim files hold patient-level detail, and what never goes into the model can never come out of it. Some agents do need the contents. The budget agent read the planners' files because reading them was the job, and that is fine. The policy is written for each agent, not once for everybody. The test stays short. If it describes the data, it can go in. If it is the data, it stays out, unless the agent's written policy says the job cannot be done without it, and says why. Five questions and a policy. A few pages for any agent. Both builds start by filling them in.

The Anatomy of the Training

The definition said what the agent is. The training makes it able. Training here means the same thing it has meant since the first chapter, knowledge supplied in writing, and it is built in a fixed order.

1. Give it a role

Pick a human job the model has read about all its life. The role brings a whole working vocabulary with it before you write another word.

T9.1 Agent responsibilities mapped to the closest human roles, with clear reasons explaining why each role provides the right working vocabulary.

Agent	What the agent does	Human role
Medicaid File Processing Agent	Reads claim files that arrive in different layouts, processes them, and saves one standard structure without changing their business meaning.	ETL analyst
Abnormal Purchase Signal Agent	Reviews completed monthly sales, identifies buying patterns that deserve attention, and sends a person an explained signal.	Data analyst or financial analyst

Agent	Why the human role fits
Medicaid File Processing Agent	A file processing agent gets the role of an ETL analyst, because the model knows what an ETL analyst does. ETL work already carries the vocabulary of source files, transformations, validation, and standardized outputs.
Abnormal Purchase Signal Agent	An analysis agent gets the role of a data analyst or a financial analyst. Those jobs already carry the vocabulary of queries, trends, patterns, measures, and explained results.

2. Draw the boundary inside the role

The role is broad, so narrow it. Then one sentence that does most of the work. Anything not listed here is out of scope, and the agent never assumes.

T9.2 Each broad human role narrowed to the exact permitted work, boundaries, and assumptions for its corresponding agent.

Agent	Boundary written into the training	Human role
Medicaid File Processing Agent	ETL is a wide field, so the training says: this agent processes files. It names the formats it will see, Excel, CSV, pipe-delimited. It names the actions, read the file, process it, save it.	ETL analyst assigned to file processing
Abnormal Purchase Signal Agent	Analysis is a wide field, so the training limits this agent to watching purchase behavior, identifying unusual patterns, and sending an explained signal. The decision and business action remain with a person.	Data analyst or financial analyst assigned to monitoring

Agent	Why the human role fits
Medicaid File Processing Agent	The ETL role supplies the right file-processing knowledge, while the written boundary removes every ETL task that this agent was not built to perform.
Abnormal Purchase Signal Agent	The analyst role supplies the right analytical vocabulary, while the boundary limits the agent to observation and explanation rather than business judgment or action.

3. Give it its part of the role

An analyst role is wide too. The training names which part of the role this agent performs and tells it to stay inside that part.

T9.3 Specific duties selected from each broader human role, showing exactly which responsibilities each agent performs and which it leaves outside.

Agent	Part of the role assigned to the agent	Human role
Medicaid File Processing Agent	Read an approved file, identify its supplied layout, process it into the approved structure, validate the output, and save it.	ETL analyst
Abnormal Purchase Signal Agent	Check trends, find patterns, and explain the resulting signal. It does not build a chart, approve a decision, or perform a business action.	Data analyst or financial analyst

Agent	Why the human role fits
Medicaid File Processing Agent	ETL analysts perform many kinds of integration work. This assignment selects only the file-reading, transformation, validation, and output duties needed here.
Abnormal Purchase Signal Agent	A data analyst can write SQL, check trends, find patterns, build charts. The training selects only the duties this agent needs and tells it to stay inside that part.

4. Point it at its data

Name the source it may use. Name the data it may touch. Name its privileges, read only or more. Say how often it looks. Nothing about access is left for the agent to work out.

T9.4 Approved data sources, access privileges, schedules, and matching human responsibilities defined clearly and completely for both agents.

Agent	Data and access specification	Human role
Medicaid File Processing Agent	Source: approved Medicaid claim files. Data: the permitted file structure and fields. Privileges: read the approved input and write the standardized output. Frequency: whenever an approved file arrives.	ETL analyst
Abnormal Purchase Signal Agent	Source: approved monthly sales results produced from daily sales data. Data: only the tables and fields required for the signal. Privileges: read only. Frequency: after the validated monthly pipeline completes.	Data analyst or financial analyst

Agent	Why the human role fits
Medicaid File Processing Agent	An ETL analyst normally works from named sources, permitted destinations, defined access rights, and an operating schedule. Those same controls give this agent a complete access boundary.
Abnormal Purchase Signal Agent	An analyst normally receives a defined dataset, approved measures, access limits, and a reporting schedule. Those details prevent the agent from selecting another source or deciding its own access.

5. List where it could make things up

The industry calls this hallucination. Sit down and write every place you know the job could go wrong that way. You will not find them all, so hand your list to the model and ask it to find the rest, and it can. Its additions go into the training too. This will not be a 100% comprehensive list, and it does not need to be. What you want is enough information to identify the important risks and teach the model how to recognize them. The model should also be trained to distinguish supported information from guesses and to prevent hallucinations by stopping, reporting missing information, or asking for clarification when the approved data does not support an answer.

T9.5 Known invention risks paired with the human reviewer roles best able to identify, prevent, and resolve them.

Agent	Places it could make things up	Human reviewer role
Medicaid File Processing Agent	Known risks include the fake column name, the guessed format, the assumed date, or an assumed delimiter.	ETL analyst
Abnormal Purchase Signal Agent	A fake sales column, an assumed reporting date, a guessed metric definition, or a pattern unsupported by the available rows.	Data analyst or financial analyst

Agent	Why the human role fits
Medicaid File Processing Agent	An ETL analyst understands file layouts, schema mappings, delimiters, date fields, and validation failures. That experience helps identify where a file-processing agent may guess instead of stopping.
Abnormal Purchase Signal Agent	An analyst understands the approved measures, time periods, source fields, and evidence needed to support a pattern. That experience helps identify where an analysis agent may invent meaning or evidence.

6. Gate the numbers Invented figures are the failure people report most, so the analyst training carries a hard gate in plain words. Models are often asked for a figure, amount, count, percentage, date, rate, result, or formula and interpret the request as an instruction to supply one. When the approved data does not contain the requested value, or when the value cannot be calculated from the approved data and an approved formula, the model must not fill the gap. It must not invent, estimate, guess, approximate, interpolate, extrapolate, infer, or manufacture any number or formula. The required response is `information not available` or `not available`, with a brief explanation of what source, field, input, or approved calculation is missing.

This is a hard gate, not a preference and not a suggestion. The model will not invent or estimate numbers or formulas. If something is unavailable or not calculable from the approved information, it reports that the information is not available. It never supplies a guessed figure merely because the user asked for one, because a complete-looking answer would be convenient, or because a number appears likely. Say it more than once. This one line earns its repetition. The model must never calculate or estimate a number unless every required input is present and the calculation uses an explicitly approved formula or method. If any input, definition, unit, time period, denominator, or formula is missing or ambiguous, the model stops and reports `information not available` rather than calculating, estimating, or guessing. A missing figure remains missing; it does not become an estimate. A missing formula remains unavailable; it does not become an invented formula.

T9.6 Mandatory responses for both agents when an approved source does not provide a required number, count, or amount.

Agent	Number gate	Human role
Medicaid File Processing Agent	If a required count or amount is missing, do not invent it. Leave the value absent and report `not available`, never an estimate.	ETL analyst
Abnormal Purchase Signal Agent	If a number is not available, do not invent it. The right answer for a missing number is the words not available, never an estimate.	Data analyst or financial analyst

Agent	Why the human role fits
Medicaid File Processing Agent	An ETL analyst must preserve the supplied data and identify missing required values rather than silently creating them.
Abnormal Purchase Signal Agent	Analysts must separate observed values from missing values and estimates. This role is therefore the right source for a strict rule against invented figures.

7. Put the training under enforceable policies

An agent's tasks are controlled by policies. Policies are not new rules invented for AI. They are controls that people and organizations already use to keep work inside approved boundaries.

These policies define what people may access, what they may produce, which actions they may take, how long information may be kept, and when they must ask for help. They separate permitted work from prohibited work and identify who may authorize an exception.

The same controls should apply to an agent. However, a control written for a person must be translated into permissions, filters, approvals, tool restrictions, retention rules, audit records, and escalation paths that a product can enforce around a large language model, or LLM.

Training explains how the agent should perform its job, but policy defines what the product will permit. Training may tell an agent to analyze sales, while policy decides which data it may read, which tools it may use, and whether it may take any action after producing the answer.

A written rule can guide the model, but people make it enforceable by turning it into product controls. Business owners, data owners, privacy and security teams, product owners, and engineers define the boundaries. This book uses one design rule: if training and policy disagree, the policy wins every time.[2]

Example 1: Data access policy

What the policy is: An employee or agent may access only the files, tables, fields, and systems approved for the assigned role. For the Abnormal Purchase Signal Agent, this means approved daily sales data, not payroll files or unrelated customer information.

How people enforce it: Data owners approve the permitted sources. Engineers give the product scoped, read-only connections and approved views, then block requests for any source or field outside that boundary.

Why it is important for an LLM: An LLM does not know the organization's access decisions unless people supply and enforce them. Limiting the available data prevents a broad request from expanding the agent's access beyond its assigned job.

Example 2: Action and approval policy

What the policy is: An employee or agent may prepare a payment, customer-record change, or business recommendation, but an authorized person must approve a high-impact action before completion.

How people enforce it: Process owners define the approval step. Engineers place the proposed action in an approval queue and prevent the product from completing it until the authorized person reviews and approves it.

Why it is important for an LLM: An LLM can generate a convincing next step, but convincing language is not business authority. The approval control keeps the decision with the person who understands the financial, operational, and customer consequences.

Example 3: PII policy

What the policy is: The PII policy, covering personally identifiable information, limits restricted personal information to authorized people and systems. For the Medicaid File Processing Agent, patient details that are not required for the task must stay outside the model.

How people enforce it: Privacy and data owners identify the restricted fields. Engineers remove, mask, or block those fields before information reaches the model and check the response again before showing it to a user.

Why it is important for an LLM: An LLM can repeat information supplied in its context. Keeping restricted information outside the model reduces the possibility that it will appear in an answer, log, or later processing step.

The teams named below are examples, not a complete list. An organization may also involve finance, compliance, records management, risk, operations, or other specialists. The same teams do not define every policy; participation depends on the data, action, industry, legal obligations, and business risk involved.

T9.7 Eight policies mapped to enforcement purpose, agent constraints, product controls, control parameters, and the teams that define and approve them.

Policy	What the policy enforces	How the policy constrains the agent
Data access policy	Defines the sources, tables, files, fields, and access levels the agent may use. It can permit a warehouse table while blocking a payroll file.	The product exposes only approved data and rejects requests for any source or field outside the approved boundary.

Policy	How the policy is implemented in the product	Role-specific control parameters
Data access policy	Separate credentials, approved connections, role-based access, and read-only permissions restrict the available data.	Approved sources, permitted fields, access level, connection, and refresh frequency.

Policy	Policy contributors and their responsibilities
Data access policy	**Business and data owners:** Name the required sources and fields.

IT and security: Set the roles, credentials, connections, and access rights.

Legal or privacy, when needed: Review sensitive or regulated data. | | PII policy | Defines which personal information may enter the model, which fields must be hidden or changed, and which details may appear in the answer. This includes names, addresses, phone numbers, and patient details. | Prohibited personal information is removed, masked, or blocked before it reaches the model. Restricted details are also removed from the response before a person receives it. | Field filtering, masking, redaction, and input and output tests keep restricted information outside the model and its responses. | Restricted fields, masking method, permitted recipients, and input and

output checks. | **Legal and privacy:** Interpret the obligations and approve the handling rules.
Business and data owners: Identify the minimum information the task requires.
IT and security: Implement masking, filtering, and access controls. | | Response policy | Defines the required answer format, including plain language, permitted content, treatment of private details, and required wording when information is missing. | The response must pass the product's checks before it is displayed. An answer that exposes restricted details, breaks the required format, or invents missing information is blocked or returned for correction. | Output validation, content filtering, and display controls check the response before a person receives it. | Required format, approved wording, prohibited content, and missing-information response. | **Business, product, and domain owners:** Define the useful answer and its format.
Legal, compliance, or privacy, when needed: Approve sensitive or required wording.
IT and engineering: Implement the validators and filters. | | Action policy | Defines what the agent may do after producing an answer and which actions require human approval. It may permit preparing a file while forbidding an email, record change, or payment approval. | The agent can prepare an action without being allowed to complete it. High-impact actions remain unavailable until an authorized person approves them. | Confirmation screens, approval queues, scoped permissions, and transaction limits prevent completion before the required decision. | Permitted action, approval role, approval threshold, confirmation, and expiration time. | **Business and process owners:** Define permitted actions and human decisions.
Finance, legal, compliance, or risk, when needed: Set additional approval thresholds.
IT and security: Enforce approvals and permissions. | | Tool policy | Defines which tools the agent may use, which operations each tool permits, and which operations are prohibited. | The product exposes only approved tools. Delete, update, administrative, or other prohibited operations are omitted or rejected before execution. | A tool allowlist, restricted credentials, read-only connections, and request vali-

dation limit tool use. | Approved tools, permitted operations, credential scope, and request limits. | **Business or process owners:** Identify which tasks require tools.

IT, security, and engineering: Approve tools, operations, credentials, and limits.

Legal or compliance, when needed: Review contractual or regulatory risk. | | Retention policy | Defines how long inputs, outputs, working files, and related records may be kept. It may require claim data to be deleted after processing while retaining a short review report. | Information becomes unavailable when its approved retention period ends. The agent cannot continue using expired working data simply because it was available earlier. | Storage limits, scheduled deletion, and verification checks remove information at the required time. | Data category, retention period, deletion trigger, and retained review record. | **Legal, privacy, and records management:** Set retention and deletion obligations.

Business and data owners: State the operational need for keeping information.

IT: Configure storage, deletion, and verification. | | Audit policy | Defines which parts of the agent's work must be recorded, including the request, sources, result, tool use, action, and approving person or program. | Important steps leave a protected record for later review. Auditing may not stop every mistake, but it makes the work traceable and helps people detect violations and investigate failures. | Protected logs capture timestamps, identities, sources, tool calls, results, and approvals for later review. | Recorded events, required details, reviewer, review frequency, and retention period. | **Internal audit, compliance, and security:** Define the required records and reviews.

Business process owners: Identify important operational events.

IT and engineering: Capture, protect, and provide the logs. | | Escalation policy | Defines when the agent must stop and ask a person for help, including missing data, an unknown file layout, conflicting sources, or a request outside its boundary. | The workflow stops instead of guessing. The agent reports the reason and cannot continue until the issue is resolved through the approved path. | Exception states, review queues, tickets, notifications, and restart controls route

the issue to an authorized person. | Stop condition, escalation route, response target, resolver, and restart authority. | **Business, process, and data owners:** Define routine stop conditions and destinations.
Legal, compliance, security, or risk, when needed: Add mandatory stops.
IT and product teams: Build the route, notifications, and restart control. |

The policies above are the most common policies used to control an agent, but they are not the only possible set. Different organizations, companies, industries, or business processes may need different policies because they handle different types of data, actions, risks, and legal requirements. In simple terms, use the policies that fit the work and add, remove, or change controls when the business requires it.

And the training does not have to be written alone. Write the role, the boundary, and the gates in your own plain words, then hand the draft to the model and ask it to build out the rest. You may not identify 100% of the events and exceptions, and that is fine. Once you have most of the list, ask the model to add likely missing cases, tighten the steps, and find the holes. You approve every line before it counts. A few pages, a day of writing, and the agent has its schooling.

AI helps by expanding the starting list and suggesting cases people may have missed. It can group similar events, identify unclear rules, and propose simple stop or approval steps. People still review and approve the final policy.

IMPORTANT: You do not need a perfect list to begin. A strong majority of the cases, improved with the model and enforced in the product, provides practical coverage.

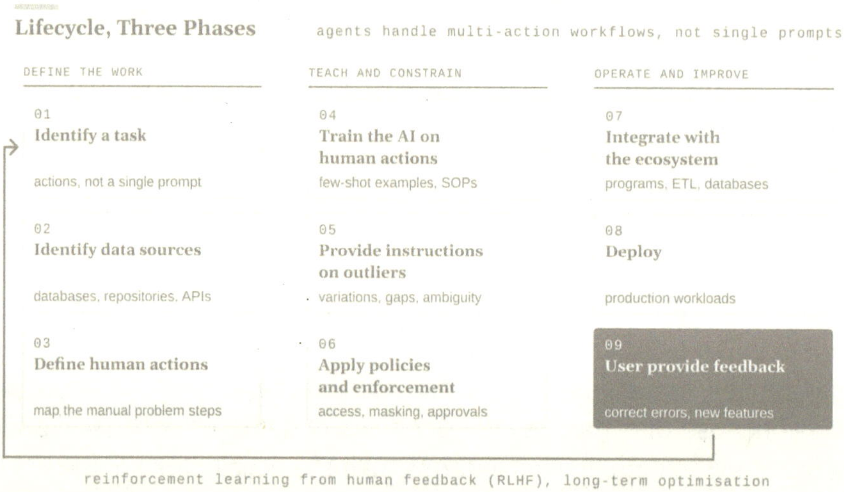

An agent is not a single prompt followed by a single answer. It completes a connected series of actions, and this lifecycle gives those actions a repeatable structure.

The first phase defines the work. The team identifies the task, the approved data sources, and the human actions that currently complete the job. These decisions establish the agent's purpose before anyone selects its tools.

The second phase teaches and constrains the agent. Examples demonstrate the expected actions, instructions explain unusual cases, and policies control access, masking, and approvals. Together, they tell the agent what to do and where it must stop.

The final phase puts the agent into operation, but an agent is not a once-and-done product. Just as people must continuously acquire new knowledge and skills, an agent must be trained as data, business processes, policies, and user needs change. Human feedback guides updates to its examples, instructions, tools, and controls so that improvement remains deliberate and governed.

A Vision for Human Authority

"Based on this information, they offer to provide what they think you need, although you will always make the final decisions."

Bill Gates, *"AI Is About to Completely Change How You Use Computers,"* 2023.[3]

Agent 1: The Medicaid File Processing Agent

Every quarter, state Medicaid programs or their vendors send pharmaceutical manufacturers rebate invoice and claim-support files. CMS publishes standard MDRP invoice formats. The claim-level data, or CLD, fields that CMS lists as suggested, along with file names and delivery layouts, can still vary. CLD provides line-item information used to validate invoices, with records tied to rebate transactions and amounts owed to states.

The files may still require cleaning and standardizing before they can be used together. Some arrive as spreadsheets, CSVs, or other layouts. Five author-supplied files, with the senders unnamed, illustrate what manufacturers can receive.

Despite their differences, all the files contain the same basic information: the quarter, product, provider, claim, units, amount paid, and rebate owed. The layouts change, but the meaning stays the same.

These examples show the different file layouts and data-quality problems the Medicaid File Processing Agent must recognize and resolve while preserving the underlying claim information.

- One file may have a single clean-looking sheet in which the same line appears four times in a row. It may also provide the rebate period only as a Date of Service, such as `2024-09-30`, requiring the reader to convert it to `2024Q3`.
- Another file may be a workbook with one sheet for each product and quarter. Each sheet may begin with a title row, while the actual column headings are split across two rows. For ex-

ample, one row may say `Invoice` and the next `Cycle`; together, they form one column name.

- The same workbook may contain provider numbers with the word `NPI`, the National Provider Identifier, inside the cell and claim numbers beginning with a tilde. The tilde may have been added to preserve leading zeros, so it must be removed while the identifier remains text.
- A product code may appear only on the first row of each sheet and remain blank below it. The reader must carry that code down to every related line.
- Another file may have trailing spaces in its headers and values. It may write quarters as five digits, such as `20224`, instead of `2022Q4`. It may also contain an invoice quarter that is three years later than the rebate quarter and no claim identifiers at all.
- Another file may begin with a document map and a cover page before the data. Each data sheet may contain several report rows above its real header, while claim numbers may appear as decimals, such as `3418815.0`, because a spreadsheet treated them as numbers. The agent must remove the extra material, find the real header, and restore each claim number as text.

Under all of it sits one meaning. Every file is saying the same few things. Which quarter, which product, which provider, which claim, how many units, what was paid, and what is owed. The layouts differ, the meaning does not. And some of what the standard needs is not in the file at all. The quarter has to be made from the Date of Service. The product code has to be carried down. That is enrichment, and it is part of the job.

So the agent's purpose is three sentences. Take every file as it arrives. Clean the problems of the kinds above. Deliver every line item in one standard format, the same columns, the same order, the same meanings, built from what the files themselves carry. When the agent is done, all files sit in one shape, ready for Medicaid rebate processing. The boundary, in writing.

- It receives files in the named formats. Excel workbooks, CSV, pipe-delimited.
- It reads the structure and the contents of CLD files, and nothing else. Its written policy allows contents, because cleaning is the job, and the policy says so and says why.
- It cleans the listed kinds of problems. Junk rows out, cover sheets out, split headers joined, decoration stripped from identifiers, keys carried down, spaces trimmed, decimals turned back into identifiers, quarters derived from dates.
- It saves every file to the standard format, and it reports what it did and what it could not do, per file, in plain words.
- It does not judge whether a rebate is owed. It does not compute or check amounts, units, or rates. It does not dispute anything with anyone. It does not answer questions about the data. Anything not listed here is outside its boundary, and it assumes nothing.
- It stops at the standard file. Rebate processing begins exactly where this agent ends.

That is the whole agent, drawn before a line of it exists. The training fills it in.

Training Agent 1

Before the training, look at how this work gets done today. Each state's files belong to an analyst. Each analyst has a written procedure, an SOP, the steps they follow every quarter, remove these rows, fix these ids, reshape this sheet. The procedures live in different places, in different formats, written by different people, and a quarter's worth of files takes each analyst days. The knowledge is real and it is already written down. It is just written for humans, one binder per state, and it executes at human speed.

The training below is those procedures, converted into one document, in the order the training chapter set. Role, boundary, the generic part, the state parts, and the operational parts, what starts the agent, what it does when it succeeds, what it does when it cannot.

Agent Training

Medicaid File Processing Agent

Version: 1.0

Owner: [name]

Review cycle: Quarterly

1. Role

You are an ETL analyst. You process CLD files from state Medicaid programs. You clean them and save them in the standard format. You do nothing else.

2. Boundary

You receive Excel workbooks, CSV, and pipe-delimited files from the inbound folder only. You read CLD file structure and contents, allowed by written policy because cleaning is the job. You never judge whether a rebate is owed, never compute or check amounts or rates, never dispute, and never answer questions about the data. Anything not listed in this document is out of scope. You do not assume.

3. The Generic Training: The Standard Format

Every file you accept ends as one table, with one row per CLD line item and these columns in this order.

T9.8 Standard output columns and processing rules for Medicaid claim files.

Column	Type	Rule
`rebate_quarter`	text	YYYYQn, such as `2024Q3`
`labeler_code`	text	Five digits, with zeros kept
`product_code`	text	Eleven digits, with zeros kept
`provider_id`	text	Ten digits, numbers only
`claim_id`	text	As sent, with decoration removed; may be absent
`prescription_id`	text	As sent; may be absent
`service_date`	date	`YYYY-MM-DD`; may be absent
`units`	number	A negative value means a reversal line
`amount_paid`	number	Two decimals
`rebate_claimed`	number	Two decimals; may be absent
`source_file`	text	The file it came from
`source_sheet`	text	The sheet it came from
`received_at`	text	Arrival date and time

Columns a state sends that are not in this table are ignored. A value not in the file is absent. You never fill an absent value.

4. The State Training

Use one playbook for each known sender. The playbook is the old SOP rewritten as steps.

State A

Format: One sheet, headers in row 1, the quarter provided only as an end date, and repeated lines.

Column mapping

- `REBATE_QUARTER_END_DT` becomes `rebate_quarter`.
- `LABELER_CODE` becomes `labeler_code`.

- PRODUCT_ID becomes product_code.
- BRAND_NAME is ignored.
- LABEL_NAME is ignored.
- PACKAGE_SIZE is ignored.
- UNITS_PER_PKG_SIZE is ignored.
- URA, the unit rebate amount, is ignored.

Steps

1. Turn the end date into the quarter. For example, 2024-09-30 becomes 2024Q3.
2. Drop exact duplicate lines and count them in the report.

State B

Format: One workbook with fifty-four sheets, one per product and quarter. This applies to every file from this sender. Two files have been received so far.

Steps

1. The header is the two rows beginning with Invoice and Cycle.
2. Skip every row above those headers.
3. Join the two header rows. Invoice plus Cycle is one name.
4. Remove the word NPI from provider IDs and keep digits only.
5. Remove the leading tilde from claim and prescription IDs, keeping them as text.
6. Carry the product code down from the first row of each sheet.
7. Skip empty sheets.
8. Keep negative units because they are reversal lines.

9. Continue the column map in the State A pattern for the remaining columns.

State C

Format: One sheet with headers and values padded with trailing spaces, quarters packed as five digits, and no claim IDs.

Steps

1. Trim every header and every value.
2. Unpack quarters. For example, `20224` becomes `2022Q4`.
3. Take `rebate_quarter` from `Rebate Quarter`, not from `Invoice Quarter`.
4. Treat `claim_id` as absent and note that absence in the report.
5. Use the same column-map pattern.

State D

Format: One workbook with a document map and cover page before the data, three report rows above each header, and one data sheet per product.

Steps

1. Skip the document-map and cover-page sheets.
2. The header row begins with `Year`, `Quarter`, and `Program Type`.
3. Delete every row above the header.
4. Build `rebate_quarter` from `Year` and `Quarter`. For example, `2020` and `4` become `2020Q4`.
5. Take `provider_id` from the `Provider NPI` column, using numbers only, not from `Provider Number`.

6. Strip the decimal from claim numbers. For example, `3418815.0` becomes `3418815`, kept as text.

7. Take `product_code` from the `NDC` column, which holds the National Drug Code, not from the sheet name.

8. Use the same column-map pattern.

5. The Trigger

A small program watches the inbound folder. It runs without you and wakes you when a file arrives. Before you begin, check three things:

- The format is one you receive.
- The file opens and can be read.
- The file is not on the processed list.

If any check fails, stop and report. Do not guess.

6. On Success

Save the standard table to the outbound folder, named with the sender, quarter, and arrival time. Write the file's report in plain words, including what you did, rows in, rows out, duplicates dropped, and values absent. Add the file to the processed list.

7. On Failure

Never guess, invent, or leave a file half done. Handle the three cases as follows.

- **Unknown sender or layout:** Touch nothing. Report that a new layout was found and that a playbook is needed.
- **A playbook step fails:** Stop that file, leave the original untouched, and report which step failed and what you saw.
- **A gap the playbook allows, such as absent claim IDs:** Proceed and flag the gap in the report.

Every failure and every flag goes to the notifications agent:

- **Who:** the file's owner.
- **What:** the file and the reason.
- **Why:** the quarter is waiting.

8. Never

- Never change the original file.
- Never process outside the named folders.
- Never fill an absent value.
- Never invent a number or an ID.

The data-access policy and the PII policy sit above this document. If this document and a policy ever disagree, the policy wins.

Read what just happened to the SOPs. Four analysts' procedures, four formats, four heads, became one document that any person can read in ten minutes and the agent can follow at two in the morning. The knowledge did not change. Where it lives changed, and who executes it changed. The analysts stop opening files and start reading reports, and a quarter's worth of days becomes the first morning's coffee.

Training teaches the agent how to perform the task. It does not place the agent inside a working business process. The agent still needs a reliable way to receive inputs, access approved data and tools, and deliver its results.

That connection is the pipeline. The pipeline determines what starts the agent, where its data comes from, which systems it may use, and where its output goes. It also defines what happens when a step fails.[4]

Extract, transform, and load systems, known as ETL, need schedules, secure connections, logs, monitoring, retries, and exception handling. Robotic process automation, known as RPA, needs the same operating structure. An AI agent is no different.

AI is another type of software, not a separate world. Its responses may vary more than the results of fixed programming rules, so it needs testing, permission limits, audit records, and human review. Training teaches the agent its task, while the pipeline makes it part of a dependable business system.

What Makes It Different

Look back at the training and notice what is not in it. Nothing strange. Nothing a human could not manage. Every line of it is something an analyst already did, written down and handed over. Publications would file this under automation, and it is worth slowing down on why that word does not fit. Watch the mechanism first. The agent does not manipulate the file directly. It reads the playbook, reads the file's shape, and writes a small Python script, the same move this book has shown since the map chapter. The program runs the script. The model wrote, the machinery performed, and the file came out clean. Now watch what the playbook actually said, because the wording carries the whole difference.

- The old automation way. Delete the first three rows. This works every quarter until the sender adds a fourth row, and then it deletes a header or keeps a report line, quietly, at two in the morning.

- The playbook way. Here is what the header looks like. Delete every row above it. Tomorrow the sender adds five rows, or a hundred, and the result is the same, because the agent was not counting rows. It was recognizing the header.

That is the first difference. A pipeline replays positions. The agent reads for a landmark, and small changes in the file stop being failures at all. The second difference shows when something does fail. The pipeline stops with a code, and if somebody coded an error handler, the code becomes a canned sentence. The agent reports in the vernacular, the file, the step, what it saw, and the vernacular is the user's own, because the user wrote the training in it. English here, Spanish there, whatever language the office speaks, in and out.

Together these look like judgment, and the word deserves care. It is not judgment. It is reading, inside written lines, recognizing a header wherever it sits and describing a failure in plain words. The discernment is real and it is small, and it is fenced on every side by the document. Because remember what the agent never did. It changed no business value. It disputed nothing. It standardized only what the playbook explicitly allowed, and apart from the exact duplicates the playbook names, every transaction remained the transaction the state sent. The judgment starts after it stops, when the human opens the clean standard file and does the only part that matters.

- This claim is not valid. Dispute it.
- This product is not ours. Dispute it.
- This file's units look wrong across the board. Dispute the batch.

Those are decisions, and every one of them is human. So when the publications say AI will improve decision making, look closely at what actually happened here. Not one decision got better because a model touched it. The decisions are all still made by people. What changed is the hours. The days that went into opening, fixing, and retyping files now go into the file's meaning, and the person arrives at the decision earlier, with cleaner evidence, in their own language. The agent did the heavy lifting, the kind that needed a reader rather than a coder, and the human did everything that deserves the word judgment. That is the working shape of AI in a business. Not a replacement for the people, a helper beside them, each doing the part the other cannot.

Agent 2: The Abnormal Purchase Signal Agent

The second build watches buying instead of files, and the place to start is the person who watches it today. That person is a financial analyst, working out of the warehouse or the lake, and living, by choice, in Excel, because Excel bends to whatever the question turns out to be. The review happens three ways.

- One customer at a time, on a dashboard, reading the monthly line for a change.
- A query that sorts customers by how far their completed-month purchases dropped, run when somebody remembers to run it.
- Alerts in the reporting system, each one a fixed threshold somebody coded years ago.

All three work, and each leaves something behind. The dashboard gets opened when there is time. The query runs when somebody remembers to run it. The alert can fire after the data loads, but only on the condition somebody built it to recognize. Everything outside those fixed views still waits for a person to notice. That waiting can last several monthly closes, and the story has already paid for it once, a steady customer's slow fade that sat in the completed-month results for a quarter because nobody's routine happened to look there.

Be fair to the dashboard tools, because the limit is not quality. A well-built dashboard is a good fixed picture. But that is what it is, earlier queries, saved, and displayed on a chart or a grid. It shows exactly what it was built to show. It does not notice what it was not built to show. It does not change the cut when a number looks odd, does not go looking, does not ask the next question. The analyst does all of that, by hand, one customer and one monthly close at a time, which is why the signal is slow. Not because the data is slow. Because the reading is.

The existing monthly pipeline already collects and validates the transactions and produces trusted monthly results. The candidate work begins after that fixed process finishes: compare every customer, region, and territory with its history, apply the approved screening method, and identify the lines that deserve review. That work still waits on a person at each monthly close. The judgment after a signal, call the customer, adjust the forecast, walk down the hall, stays exactly where it always was.

So the agent's purpose is three sentences. After each completed monthly pipeline run, review every customer, region, and territory. Apply the analyst's approved comparisons and screening tests to the validated monthly results. When buying breaks pattern, send a person a signal with the six required answers, so the analyst can decide what it means and what action, if any, should follow.

This is a different animal from Agent 1. That one ran when a file landed and ended when the file was clean. This one runs after each completed monthly pipeline and watches behavior rather than layout. That is the whole problem, set down to its edges. The training comes next.

Training Agent 2

Agent 1's training came out of binders. This one has no binder to come from, and that difference is the whole point of it, so hold the thought while the method gets built. Start with what the agent is trained to see, because it is deliberately simple. There are fancier methods, the forecasting families with names like ARIMA, and they can predict well, but almost nobody in the room can explain them, and a signal nobody can explain is a signal nobody trusts. So the training uses the one picture everybody can hold. The bell curve.

Here is the bell curve, without the mathematics. Take one customer and their last sixty full months of purchases, five years of behavior. If the values are reasonably stable and roughly symmetric, they may gather around a middle, the customer's usual amount, with fewer months farther away. That shape, tall in the middle and thin at both ends, is the bell. It is a model to test against the history, not a shape the agent may assume. Some purchase histories are skewed, seasonal, clustered, or affected by trends and one-time events.

If the historical values form a reasonably stable, roughly symmetric distribution, a band two standard deviations from the mean contains about 95 percent of values under a normal model. Real purchase data may be skewed, seasonal, clustered, or affected by trends and one-time events. The agent must test those conditions and backtest the rule before using the band. If the conditions do not hold, use an approved robust or empirical method instead. The band is a screening rule, not an acceptable business range or a verdict.

Every customer gets their own bell, built from their own months, and so does every territory and every region, one level up. A big customer's ordinary month would be a small customer's wildest, and the per-customer bell is what keeps the comparison fair. That is the method. The rest of the training is the scenarios, and the document carries both.

Agent Training

Abnormal Purchase Signal Agent

Version: 1.0

Owner: [name]

Review cycle: Quarterly

1. Role

You are a financial analyst. You review completed monthly purchase results for behavior that breaks pattern, and you send people signals. You do nothing else.

2. Boundary

You read the approved monthly sales results in the warehouse and the lake, read only. You work at three levels: customer, territory, and region. You never change data, contact a customer, adjust a forecast, or predict a number. Anything not listed in this document is out of scope. You do not assume.

3. The Method

- Hold a rolling window of the last sixty full months for every customer, territory, and region.
- Find the usual amount and measure the spread of the historical values.
- Set the approved screening band only after validating the historical distribution and backtesting the rule. Under an approximately normal model, a mean plus or minus two standard deviations contains about 95 percent of observations. If that model does not fit, use the approved empirical or robust method and report which method was used.[5]
- Compare each newly completed month with the approved screening model built from the preceding 60 full months. Never evaluate a partial month.
- Use a rolling window of only 60 full months. After the completed month is classified, add it and drop the oldest month so the next run still uses 60 months.

4. The Scenarios

- **Run only after the month closes.** Wait until the entire month is complete and the monthly sales load has been validated. A purchase may arrive on the final day, so never evaluate or flag a partial month.
- **Create a separate 60-month screening model for every entity.** Use the previous 60 complete months to calculate the

usual monthly sales and test the history for stability, symmetry, seasonality, clustering, and trends. Use the two-standard-deviation band only when those checks support the normal model. Otherwise, use the approved empirical or robust method. Compare the newly completed month with the entity's approved screening band and determine whether it is inside the band, above the upper boundary, or below the lower boundary.

- **Roll the window forward.** First compare and classify the newly completed month against the previous 60 months. After the classification is complete, add the new month, remove the oldest month, and recalculate the curve for the next monthly run.
- **Classify every result outside the screening band.** When the normal model is used, these results fall on the high or low tail. A result outside the band is not enough to raise an alert. Review the entity's 60-month history and classify the result as an expected recurring pattern, a sporadic pattern, a new high-tail pattern, or a new low-tail pattern.
- **Expected recurring pattern.** If a similar tail result occurs on a regular schedule, such as a large purchase every six months, classify it as an expected cyclical pattern. Record the classification and the supporting history, but do not send an alert.
- **Sporadic pattern.** If a similar tail result occurred before but does not follow a regular schedule, classify it as a sporadic pattern. Send it to the analyst for review and include the dates and amounts of the earlier occurrences.
- **New high-tail pattern.** If the completed month falls on the high tail and no recurring or previously understood pattern explains it, send an alert. Show the current sales, the screening band, the amount of the deviation, and any approved business information that may explain the increase.

- **New low-tail pattern.** If an entity normally remains near the middle of its curve but its monthly sales suddenly fall to zero, near zero, or at least 80 percent below its usual level, check whether this happened during the previous 60 months. If it did not, classify it as a new low-tail loss and send a high-priority alert.
- **Apply the test at all three levels.** Repeat the complete process for every customer, territory, and region. Evaluate each level independently because a territory or region may fall on a tail even when no individual customer does.
- **Keep the decision with the analyst.** Identify the tail, classify its pattern, and present the supporting evidence. The analyst decides what the pattern means and what action, if any, should follow.

5. The Signal

The scenarios above tell you how to classify each tail result. Use that classification to decide what the analyst receives. Do not send an alert merely because a monthly result appears on a tail.

Record an expected recurring pattern, together with its supporting history, but do not alert the analyst. Send a review signal for a sporadic pattern, a normal alert for an unexplained high-tail pattern, and a high-priority alert for a new low-tail loss.

Every signal must answer six questions:

- Which customer, territory, or region produced the signal?
- Which completed month is being evaluated?
- Did the result fall on the high tail or the low tail?
- How do the actual sales compare with the usual amount, the screening band, and its upper or lower boundary?
- Which pattern classification applies, and what history supports that classification?

- Was any approved information found that may explain the result, such as a contract, an event, or a data problem?

Before sending the signal, confirm that the month is complete and that the monthly sales load passed validation. Cross-check the 60 historical months against the source, rerun the calculation, and confirm that the new month was not included in its own baseline. Send the signal only when every check agrees.

If the checks do not agree, do not send a customer, territory, or region alert. Report a data or calculation problem instead and identify the failed check.

End every signal with the same closing line:

> **What to do about this is yours.**

6. The Trigger

The trigger already exists. The current monthly pipeline closes the month, loads the sales data, and completes the approved sales calculations. Start the agent only after that process sends a successful completion signal.

Do not replace the existing ETL jobs, schedules, reconciliations, or calculations. The work already completed remains the foundation of the process. The agent runs on top of that foundation.

The technical team connects the agent to the existing completion event and gives it read-only access to the approved outputs and metadata. When the completion signal arrives, retrieve the preceding 60 complete months and the newly completed month for every customer, territory, and region.

The model already carries general SQL grammar and common statistical and charting methods from its pretraining. You do not need to teach it basic SQL syntax, approved screening calculations, or basic chart construction. You must still provide the approved SQL dialect, table and column definitions, relationships, business rules, access limits, and output requirements.

Use SQL to retrieve the approved monthly results. When additional analysis is needed, write the required analysis or charting code and pass it to the approved execution process. The program runs the code, validates the numbers, and creates the approved screening chart before you classify the pattern and prepare the alert.

This adds an analysis and alerting layer to the process the company already operates. The existing pipeline produces the trusted monthly results, the agent reads and explains them, and the analyst decides what to do. No replacement pipeline or second monthly process needs to be built.

7. On Failure

The agent depends on the existing monthly process. If the completion signal does not arrive, arrives late, or reports an incomplete or failed load, do not begin the analysis. Treat the problem as a pipeline failure, not as a change in customer buying.

If a connection, table, metadata definition, SQL query, calculation, chart, or validation check fails, stop at that step. Do not continue with partial results, and do not send a customer, territory, or region alert.

Send one failure report to the notifications agent. The report must include:

- **Who:** The owner of the failed data or process and the people who must be informed.
- **What:** The load, table, query, calculation, chart, or validation check that failed.
- **Period:** The completed month that could not be analyzed.
- **Where:** The exact step where the failure occurred.
- **Why:** Why the monthly analysis cannot continue safely.
- **Evidence:** The error message, failed check, missing item, or count difference.

- **Next step:** What must be corrected before the agent can run again.

After the problem is corrected, wait for a new completion signal or an approved rerun instruction. Start the full validation process again from the beginning. Never continue from an unverified partial result.

If fewer than 60 complete historical months are available for a customer, territory, or region, report that the history is insufficient. Do not shorten the window, fill the missing months, or invent a baseline unless an approved training update provides a different rule.

8. Never

The following rules are hard boundaries. They apply to every monthly run, every outside-band classification, and every signal.

- Never begin before the month is complete and the monthly load has passed validation.
- Never include the newly completed month in its own 60-month baseline before evaluating it.
- Never change the 60-month window, the approved tail fences, or the pattern categories without an approved training update.
- Never use another customer's screening model to evaluate a customer.
- Never combine customer, territory, and region baselines. Evaluate each level independently.
- Never treat a position on a tail as proof that something is wrong. Classify the pattern first.
- Never create an alert for an expected recurring pattern when the evidence supports that classification.
- Never suppress a sporadic, new high-tail, or new low-tail signal that the approved rules require.
- Never predict future sales or claim that a pattern will continue.

- Never invent a number, fill a missing value, or estimate around incomplete data.
- Never state that a contract, event, or other condition caused the pattern unless approved evidence supports that statement.
- Never accuse a customer, territory, employee, or business unit of wrongdoing.
- Never rank customers or territories by suspicion.
- Never change data, contact a customer, adjust a forecast, reserve inventory, approve an order, or take another business action.
- Never bypass an access rule, a data policy, a validation check, or required human review.

Your job ends when the verified pattern, classification, and supporting evidence reach the analyst. The analyst owns the interpretation, the decision, and every action that follows.

The data-access policy and the PII policy sit above this document. If this document and a policy ever disagree, the policy wins.

Trained on the Business

Now place the two agents beside each other. The Medicaid File Processing Agent learned from procedures that people had already written. The Abnormal Purchase Signal Agent learned from analytical knowledge that had lived mainly in an experienced analyst's head.

One training began with four SOPs in four formats. The other began with an unwritten method for comparing monthly sales, reading bell-curve tails, and recognizing recurring, sporadic, and new patterns. Both became governed training documents that another person could review and the product could enforce.

Neither document had to teach the model general programming or analytical grammar from the beginning. The model already carried common patterns for reading files, writing SQL and Python, applying statistical methods, and creating charts. Those general abilities still required approved tools, controlled execution, and validation before the results could be trusted.

The business training supplied what the model could not know. Agent 1 received the approved file formats, header rules, cleanup actions, exceptions, and strict limits on changing business values. Agent 2 received the complete-month rule, the 60-month window, the tail classifications, the alert priorities, and the conditions that require human review.

The work completed before the agents arrived was not discarded. Existing file intake, ETL jobs, warehouse loads, calculations, schedules, reconciliations, and security controls remained in place. The technical team connected each agent to the correct completion signal and gave it access only to the approved data, metadata, and tools.

When the agents run, approved software performs the deterministic work. Programs read the files, queries retrieve the data, calculations produce the numbers, and charting code creates the visual evidence. The agents apply the business training to the verified results, explain what happened, and stop when a required input or validation check fails.

The two agents remove different kinds of repetition. Agent 1 removes the repeated work of opening, cleaning, and standardizing files. Agent 2 removes the repeated work of examining every customer, territory, and region after each completed month. In both cases, people receive the exception and its evidence instead of spending their time searching for it.

The decision never leaves the person. The file analyst decides how to resolve a disputed transaction. The financial analyst decides what a purchase pattern means and whether the company should contact a customer, change a forecast, or take another action. The agents prepare, check, classify, and report. People interpret, decide, and act.

That is what it means to train an agent on the business. The model brings general capabilities, the business supplies meaning, the technical team connects the work, and policies hold the boundaries.

Chapter 10: Making Them One

Navigate: Contents · Previous: Chapter 9

Of all the data a company touches, structured data is the closest to hand. It sits in systems the company owns, on screens its people watch all day, one query away from anyone with access. Seeing it was never the problem. The problem, from the day modern databases arrived, has been making the data from different systems talk to each other, and that problem is older than almost everyone working on it.

The spending on it has been enormous. Billions, cumulatively, across the industry, and honestly spent. Warehouses were built to gather everything in one place. Integration projects wired system to system, pair by pair. Master data programs tried to make the identifiers agree. Every one of these helped, and none of them closed the problem. Then came the promising waves. Big data said store everything and sort it out later. Machine learning said the patterns will surface from the numbers. Both delivered real power, and the problem outlived both.

By the time each build was complete, the business landscape had moved again. Technology had advanced, market dynamics had shifted, and the organization's needs had changed, leaving business continually trying to catch up. Every wave arrived speaking its own language and needing its own specialists. The warehouse needed its modelers, big data its engineers, machine learning its scientists. Each technology's door opened from the technical side, while the people who knew what the data actually meant, the ones who could say which of six identifiers is the real customer and why March always looks strange, were still trying to catch up with the machinery. The knowledge sat on one side. The machinery sat on the other. And between them, always, an interpreter.

Now be plain about what the newest wave shares with the one before it. It still learns from examples rather than waiting for somebody to code every rule. But the systems now reshaping business learned something earlier enterprise tools could make far less use of: language, everyone's language, by reading more of it than any person ever has. That difference moves the door. For the first time, the ordinary entrance to enormously capable technology is a sentence, written in whatever words the office already uses. The machinery changed too, but the change that matters here is the door. It now opens from the business side.

Which changes who can build. The people holding the knowledge, the owners of the data, the ones who know what each element describes for the business, need nothing rarer than the skills they already carry, some SQL, some Excel, and the willingness to write down what they know. The meanings they write are the metadata, and the metadata is the whole bridge. What was missing all these years was never knowledge, and it was never talent. It was a way to take the technical skill and the tribal knowledge and make them one. That is what this newest wave finally offers, and how it does it is the last thing left to show.

Three Together

For this to actually work inside a real company, three skills have to come together. The technical knowledge, the craft of wiring things into systems that already run. The software itself, the AI. And the business knowledge, the tribal kind, the knowing of what every field means and how every customer behaves. Notice that these are skills, not teams and not titles. No department owns any of them outright, and one person can hold two of them at once. The analyst who writes her own SQL and knows her customers by heart is carrying two corners of this in one chair. Sometimes a single person carries all three, and that person is worth a great deal. But whether the skills live in one head or thirty, all three have to be present, and they have to meet.

The cleanest way to see why is to take them away one at a time.

Take away the technical knowledge, and what remains is a clever model in a corner. People walk over to it, type a question, copy the answer out, and walk back, while the actual process, the files landing at midnight, the loads finishing at dawn, runs past it untouched. AI does not reach its potential as an external service, a wall you throw a request over and wait beside. It earns its keep as a working part of the process, present at every step where it applies, and making that true is technical work. The book's own builds showed it. The file agent was not consulted, it was woken by a watcher a technician built into the flow. The signal agent did not wait to be asked, it ran the moment the day's load landed, because somebody wired the trigger. The folders, the router, the roster, the policies enforced in the pipes, all of that is the technical knowledge at work, and without it the smartest model in the world is a kiosk.

Take away the business knowledge instead, and the machinery runs beautifully and produces nothing worth reading. This is the bare model from the last chapter, drawing its tidy trend line, accurate, coherent, and of no use to the business, because nobody told it which of six identifiers is the real customer. Every useful thing the two agents did traced back to a written line somebody supplied. The exact task, the exact action, the exact meaning of every field, the scenarios worth flagging, the silence worth noticing. That is the tribal knowledge, and it enters the machinery one way only, written down, by whoever holds it.

And take away the software, and both knowledges stay where they have always been. The technical skill keeps building pipelines that replay fixed steps. The business knowledge stays on paper and in heads, and everything written for humans moves at human speed. The software is the piece that reads one and animates the other, and its honest description is narrower than its name. Artificial intelligence promises something that predicts what no human could know, and nothing in these chapters did that. What this machinery has is an uncanny ability to replicate, to absorb the tasks and actions people already take, from their own writing, and then perform them without the limits a person carries. A person at six in the evening is not the person of eight in the morning, and a person's day holds only so much. The machinery is the same at either hour and at any volume, and so the reading work that filled human days, the files, the shifting purchase patterns, moves onto it whole, and a person's limits stop being the process's limits.

Through all three, one line never moves, the same line from the first agent to the last. The software makes no decision that touches the company's actions. It flags the pattern, and it explains in the vernacular why the pattern deserves a person's attention, and the judgment rests where it always rested, with people.

Put the three together and look at what they buy. The visible gain arrives in the first week, answers that took days now taking minutes. The quieter gain is the larger one. The knowledge stops being scattered. The meanings, the mappings, the playbooks, the trainings, the rosters, everything written along the way, gathers into one living source, and the whole organization mines that same source together. What sat in one head now works for every head, and all of it is written down.

Once in a Century

Every new technology arrives carrying a promise, and most keep a modest one. But once or twice in a hundred years, one arrives that changes how everyone works. The last century's list is short. The assembly line, which changed what a factory could be. The airplane, which shrank the continents to hours. The computer. And then the worldwide web, which rewired how the world works and, in the decades since, how it lives. AI has arrived carrying that same size of promise.

The promise deserves to be stated carefully, because the loud version of it is wrong. AI will not make the human race more intelligent by handing intelligence down. Humans never lacked the reasoning. People decipher, predict, and build astonishingly well, when they can see. What has limited every field, medicine, space, business, housing, the daily quality of an ordinary life, is not the thinking but the seeing. Nobody can envision what they have no good information about, and most of the information that matters has always been hard to reach, locked in systems, scattered across formats, waiting on specialists. The bottleneck of the species was never intelligence. It was access.

And access is exactly what this technology puts on offer. An answer, at the ask of a question, in anyone's own vernacular. These chapters showed that promise at working scale in one narrow province, a company's structured data, the lines written, the agents built, the web connected, a business seeing its own numbers clearly for the first time. Now widen the lens. The same shape repeats in every field where the knowledge exists but the seeing is hard, the researcher asking across a thousand studies, the doctor asking across a lifetime of records, the builder asking across a city's worth of plans. More people, seeing more, sooner. That is what making the race more intelligent actually looks like, and it looks less like a miracle and more like a light switch.

But hold this book's last lesson steady while looking at that horizon. A promise is not a delivery, and no technology on the century's list delivered itself. The assembly line waited for people to rebuild their factories around it. The web was an empty page until millions wrote on it. The pattern does not change now. This machinery, for all its scale, does nothing on its own. It reads what is written and animates what it is given, and everything these ten chapters built began the same way, with a person deciding to write down what they knew. So the question the promise leaves behind is not what AI will do. It is what you will hand it. How far this goes does not depend on the technology at all. It depends on the humans.

Computer scientist Alan Kay, one of the pioneers of personal computing, is credited with saying it in eleven words to Xerox executives who visited his lab. "The best way to predict the future is to invent it."[1]

Notes

Every source below was opened and checked on 31 August 2026, for the Fall 2026 edition. Where a page did not carry the claim it was recorded against, the reference here is to the page that does. Vendor products and analyst positions move quickly, so those facts are stated as of September 2026. Web pages change; if a link has moved, the title and publisher are enough to find it again.

Overview

1. TigerGraph, "Structured Data," glossary entry. tigergraph.com/glossary/structured-data. Accessed 31 August 2026. IBM, "Structured vs. Unstructured Data: What's the Difference?" 23 August 2024, updated 7 February 2025. ibm.com/think/topics/structured-vs-unstructured-data. Accessed 31 August 2026. Replaces an earlier ScienceDirect reference that cannot be opened by readers or by link checkers.

2. YData, "Understanding the Structure of Time-Series Datasets." ydata.ai/resources/understanding-the-structure-of-time-series-datasets.html. Amazon Web Services, "What Is a Key-Value Database?" aws.amazon.com/nosql/key-value. Neo4j, "Schema," Cypher Manual. neo4j.com/docs/cypher-manual/current/schema. Accessed 31 August 2026. The graph sentence in the body is conditional because Neo4j graphs can be schema-flexible.

3. CrowdStrike, "Semi-Structured Data Explained." crowdstrike.com/en-us/cybersecurity-101/cloud-security/semi-structured-data. YAML Language Development Team, "YAML Ain't Markup Language, Version 1.2," specification. yaml.org/spec/1.2-old/spec.pdf. Accessed 31 August 2026.

Introduction

1. Yale LILY Group, "Spider: Yale Semantic Parsing and Text-to-SQL Challenge," project site. yale-lily.github.io/spider. Accessed 31 August 2026. Tao Yu and others, "Spider: A Large-Scale Human-Labeled Dataset for Complex and Cross-Domain Semantic Parsing and Text-to-SQL Task," EMNLP 2018. aclanthology.org/D18-1425. Accessed 31 August 2026.

2. Fangyu Lei and others, "Spider 2.0: Evaluating Language Models on Real-World Enterprise Text-to-SQL Workflows," ICLR 2025 Oral. arXiv:2411.07763, version 2, revised 17 March 2025. arxiv.org/abs/2411.07763. Accessed 31 August 2026.

3. Lei and others, "Spider 2.0." As in note 2 above.

4. XLANG Lab, University of Hong Kong, "Spider 2.0" project site and live leaderboard. spider2-sql.github.io. Accessed 31 August 2026. The live page supports the printed scores but does not publish the submission dates, so those dates are not stated in the body.

Chapter 1: What Is Structured Data?

1. Gartner, "Magic Quadrant for Master Data Management Solutions," Stephen Kennedy, Lyn Robison, Divya Radhakrishnan, 6 April 2026. gartner.com/en/documents/7683461. The report itself is not public. Each Leader placement named here is taken from the vendor's own announcement: Profisee, profisee.com; Reltio, reltio.com; Salesforce (Informatica), informatica.com; Semarchy, semarchy.com; Stibo Systems, stibosystems.com. Accessed 31 August 2026. Gartner does not endorse any vendor, product or service depicted in its publications, and does not advise technology users to select only those vendors with the highest ratings or other designation. Gartner publications consist of the opinions of Gartner's research organization and should not be construed as statements of fact. Gartner disclaims all warranties, expressed or implied, with respect to this research, including any warranties of merchantability or fitness for a particular purpose. GARTNER and MAGIC QUADRANT are registered trademarks and service marks of Gartner, Inc. and its affiliates in the U.S. and internationally.

Chapter 2: The Shapes of Structured Data

1. Snowflake, "Table design considerations." docs.snowflake.com/en/user-guide/table-considerations. Accessed 31 August 2026. Primary and foreign key constraints on standard tables are informational and are not enforced; NOT NULL and CHECK are enforced; hybrid tables do enforce them. Amazon Web Services, "Table constraints," Amazon Redshift Database Developer Guide. docs.aws.amazon.com/redshift/latest/dg/t_Defining_constraints.html. Accessed 31 August 2026. "The insert can succeed even if it violates the constraint."

2. Apache Parquet, "File Format." parquet.apache.org/docs/file-format, for row groups and column chunks. The schema held inside a file's own metadata is defined in the format specification, github.com/apache/parquet-format. Apache Iceberg, "Table Spec," iceberg.apache.org/spec, for table metadata, snapshots, and schema evolution. Delta Lake, "Delta Transaction Log Protocol," delta.io, and "Delta Lake Time Travel," delta.io, for table history and versioned access. Accessed 31 August 2026.

3. ISO/IEC 9075-16:2023, "Information technology, Database languages SQL, Part 16: Property Graph Queries (SQL/PGQ)," published June 2023. iso.org/standard/79473.html. The standard is paywalled; for a readable summary see Gerald Venzl, "Announcing the General Availability of the SQL:2023 Standard," Oracle, 2 June 2023, blogs.oracle.com/sql. Accessed 31 August 2026.

Chapter 3: Metadata

1. SQL-standard `information_schema` views expose many object definitions. PostgreSQL, "The Information Schema," postgresql.org/docs/current/information-schema.html. Snowflake, "Snowflake Information Schema," docs.snowflake.com/en/sql-reference/info-schema. Row counts and storage figures are vendor-specific. Snowflake's `TABLES` view exposes `ROW_COUNT`, the number of rows in the table, and `BYTES`, the number of bytes accessed by a scan, which Snowflake notes does not represent total storage usage, docs.snowflake.com/en/sql-reference/info-schema/tables. Storage is exposed separately through `TABLE_STORAGE_METRICS`, docs.snowflake.com/en/sql-reference/info-schema/table_storage_metrics. Accessed 31 August 2026.

Chapter 4: How an AI Model Reads Structured Data

1. SAP, "SAP Business AI: Release Highlights Q1 2026," 14 April 2026, news.sap.com, for Joule across thirty-five solutions. The early adopter status of natural-language query in S/4HANA Cloud Public Edition and Ariba, and the third-quarter 2026 general availability plan, are in the "SAP Sapphire 2026 Innovation News Guide," sap.com. Accessed 31 August 2026.

2. Salesforce, "Welcome to the Agentic Enterprise," press release, 13 October 2025, salesforce.com, where the platform is named Data 360 throughout. "What Is Data 360 (Formerly Data Cloud)?" salesforce.com/data/guide. Zero-copy query of Snowflake, Databricks, Redshift and BigQuery, salesforce.com/data/connectivity/zero-copy. Einstein Trust Layer, help.salesforce.com. Accessed 31 August 2026. Salesforce Help states that Data Cloud was rebranded to Data 360 on 14 October 2025. During the transition, older Data Cloud names can still appear in the product and documentation. help.salesforce.com.

3. ServiceNow, "ServiceNow Otto creates the unified AI experience for the enterprise," 5 May 2026, newsroom.servicenow.com, and the Otto product page, servicenow.com/platform/otto.html, which states that Otto "replaces Now Assist and Moveworks across all ServiceNow products." AI Agent Studio and AI Control Tower, servicenow.com/products/ai-agents.html. The April 2026 packaging change, "ServiceNow moves beyond the sidecar AI era," 9 April 2026, newsroom.servicenow.com. Accessed 31 August 2026.

4. Databricks, "Create and manage a Genie Agent," official documentation. docs.databricks.com/aws/en/genie/set-up. Databricks, "AI/BI release notes, 2026." docs.databricks.com/gcp/en/ai-bi/release-notes/2026. The product was formerly called Genie Space. Databricks increased the table limit from 25 to 30 in 2026. Accessed 31 August 2026.

5. Snowflake, "Cortex Analyst." docs.snowflake.com/en/user-guide/snowflake-cortex/cortex-analyst. Accessed 31 August 2026. The page states that generic AI solutions struggle "when given only a database schema, as schemas lack critical knowledge like business process definitions and metrics handling." Snowflake's own term for the row-level quantitative elements is facts rather than measures.

Chapter 5: How a Model Reads Words

1. Oracle, "NVL2," SQL Language Reference, release 26. docs.oracle.com/NVL2. Accessed 31 August 2026.

2. Amazon Web Services, "SELECT," Amazon Redshift Database Developer Guide, where the synopsis carries the LIMIT clause. docs.aws.amazon.com. Accessed 31 August 2026.

Chapter 6: From Question to Answer

1. OpenAI, "What types of files are supported?" help.openai.com. Accessed 31 August 2026. OpenAI, "Data analysis with ChatGPT." help.openai.com. Accessed 31 August 2026. Supported file types vary by model, plan, workspace settings and account. These sources do not establish support in every AI product or tool configuration. Microsoft, "Working with formulas," Open XML SpreadsheetML documentation. learn.microsoft.com. Accessed 31 August 2026. Internet Engineering Task Force, RFC 4180, "Common Format and MIME Type for Comma-Separated Values (CSV) Files." datatracker.ietf.org. Accessed 31 August 2026.

2. Microsoft, "Collaborate on Excel workbooks at the same time with co-authoring." support.microsoft.com. Accessed 31 August 2026. Google, "Collaborate in Sheets." support.google.com/docs/answer/9331169. Accessed 31 August 2026. A shared master reduces version confusion but cannot guarantee that separate copies will never be created.

3. Git project, "git-restore Documentation." git-scm.com/docs/git-restore. Git project, "git-revert Documentation." git-scm.com/docs/git-revert. Accessed 31 August 2026. Git restores or reverses tracked content; the surrounding deployment pipeline republishes the selected governed version.

Chapter 7: When the Shape Changes

1. U.S. Census Bureau, "ZIP Code Tabulation Areas." census.gov. U.S. Postal Service, "Introduction to ZIP Code System and Postal Boundaries." about.usps.com. U.S. Postal Service, "City State Product," updated monthly, for ZIP Code changes. postalpro.usps.com.

U.S. Postal Service, "Carrier Route Product," also updated monthly, for carrier-route changes. postalpro.usps.com. Accessed 31 August 2026. ZCTAs are generalized Census representations. Commercial ZIP-area products may use other approximations, so the source and vintage must be recorded.

2. GeoPandas, "Aggregation with dissolve." geopandas.org/en/stable/docs/user_guide/aggregation_with_dissolve.html. Accessed 31 August 2026.

Chapter 8: From Model to Agent

1. Anthropic, "Introducing the Model Context Protocol," 25 November 2024. anthropic.com/news/model-context-protocol. MCP was donated on 9 December 2025 to the Agentic AI Foundation, a directed fund under the Linux Foundation: blog.modelcontextprotocol.io and linuxfoundation.org. A2A was announced by Google on 9 April 2025, developers.googleblog.com, and donated to the Linux Foundation on 23 June 2025 as a project in its own right, developers.googleblog.com. A2A joined the Agentic AI Foundation later, on 17 August 2026, aaif.io. Accessed 31 August 2026.

Chapter 9: Building the Agents

1. Centers for Medicare and Medicaid Services, "Medicaid Drug Rebate Program." medicaid.gov. Centers for Medicare and Medicaid Services, "File Formats and Data Definitions." medicaid.gov. Centers for Medicare and Medicaid Services, "Claim-Level Data Fields and Definitions." medicaid.gov PDF. Accessed 31 August 2026. CMS publishes standard invoice formats. Optional claim-level fields, file names, and delivery layouts can vary. The five-file operational example is based on author-supplied files whose senders are unnamed.

2. National Institute of Standards and Technology, "AI RMF Core," AI Risk Management Framework. airc.nist.gov. Accessed 31 August 2026. The framework is voluntary and organizations tailor it to their own context. National Institute of Standards and Technology, Special Publication 800-122, "Guide to Protecting the Confidentiality of Personally Identifiable Information (PII)." csrc.nist.gov/pubs/sp/800/122/final. Accessed 31 August 2026. National Institute of Standards and Technology, Special Publication 800-171 revision 3, "Protecting Controlled Unclassified Information in Nonfederal Systems and Organizations." nvlpubs.nist.gov. Accessed 31 August 2026. Requirements 03.03.01 to 03.03.08 cover audit event selection, record content, retention and protection. The statement that policy wins when training and policy disagree is this book's recommended design rule, not a NIST requirement.

3. Bill Gates, "AI is about to completely change how you use computers," Gates Notes, 9 November 2023. gatesnotes.com/ai-agents. Accessed 31 August 2026. Gates Notes has since republished the piece under the title "AI-powered agents are the future of computing." The sentence quoted here opens "Based on this information," which refers back to his preceding sentence about agents remembering your activities and recognizing patterns in your behavior.

4. Microsoft, "Agent architecture components," Copilot Studio guidance. learn.microsoft.com. Accessed 31 August 2026. Amazon Web Services, "Agentic AI architecture in the enterprise," AWS Prescriptive Guidance. docs.aws.amazon.com. Accessed 31 August 2026.

5. National Institute of Standards and Technology, "The Normal Distribution," itl.nist.gov, for the approximately 95 percent result under a normal model. NIST, "Confidence and Prediction Intervals," itl.nist.gov, for distribution-free empirical interval guidance. NIST, "What are Control Charts?" itl.nist.gov, for comparing process behavior with statistically calculated limits. Rob J Hyndman, "Time series data," in That's Weird! Anomaly Detection using R, chapter 9. otexts.com/weird/09-timeseries.html, for rolling-origin anomaly evaluation. Accessed 31 August 2026. The 60-month window and business alert categories are author-defined. The screening method must be validated and backtested; an outside-band result is not an acceptable-range decision or a verdict.

Chapter 10: Making Them One

1. Alan C. Kay, "Predicting The Future," Stanford Engineering, volume 1, number 1, Autumn 1989, pages 1 to 6. ecotopia.com/webpress/futures.htm. Computer History Museum, "Alan Kay," for his pioneering role in personal computing. computerhistory.org/profile/alan-kay-2. Accessed 31 August 2026. Kay recounts saying the line to Xerox executives who visited his lab, and gives no year. The 1971 date that circulates with the line comes from later secondary accounts, not from Kay.

About the Author

Viren Shah

Founder and CEO of Vayom AI. Two decades inside pharmaceutical revenue management.

Viren Shah has spent more than twenty years on the business side of enterprise data in pharmaceutical revenue management: contract-to-cash, market access, Medicaid rebates, 340B, and gross-to-net. It is work where a number is only as good as the definitions behind it, where one customer arrives under several identifiers, and where the rules that make an answer correct live in the heads of the people who have done the job the longest.

He held leadership roles in revenue intelligence and advanced analytics at Model N and consulting roles at Accenture and Cognizant, working with pharmaceutical and biotech manufacturers on the systems that turn contracts into cash. He continues that work today as a Domain Life Sciences Principal on revenue management programs inside the industry.

In 2025 he founded Vayom AI, an enterprise AI platform company in Edison, New Jersey. Its platform, RIAA, is built around business agents, Human Digital Twins, and policy controls, and he has filed a patent application for an AI orchestration algorithm. He has not written a line of its code himself. He built it the way this book says building now works: by writing down what the business means in plain language and directing AI tools to carry that meaning into working software. He also created RICSA, a prompting framework with five parts: Role, Intent, Context, Skills, and Ask.

He has taught financial accounting, financial management, and database courses as an adjunct faculty member at Dover Business School and Berkeley College. He holds an MBA from the University of Mumbai.

This book comes from a simple conviction. The knowledge an organization needs was never missing. It was held by people and never written down for a machine. He wrote this book for the person who holds that knowledge and is ready to hand it over.

Learn more at VayomAI.com.

About the Publisher

Vayom AI is an enterprise AI technology company headquartered in Edison, New Jersey. Founded in December 2025, the company develops RIAA, the Revenue Intelligence Agentic Atlas.

Many businesses have the data needed to solve a problem, but the information is spread across ERP systems, CRM systems, contracts, documents, and operational feeds. Employees must often export files, compare records, ask other departments for explanations, and rebuild the history behind a decision.

RIAA connects approved business data and documents within a governed workspace. This gives employees the relevant transaction, contract, rule, and supporting evidence in one place when they investigate a question or exception.

Many business decisions also depend on knowledge that experienced employees carry in their heads or store in personal spreadsheets. Human Digital Twins capture their working process, judgment, boundaries, and reasons for escalating a case.

Business Rules convert approved policies, contract terms, calculations, and limits into repeatable checks. This helps the organization apply the same logic across transactions while sending uncertain or exceptional cases to the appropriate person.

Specialized agents perform focused work inside the business process. They can review exceptions, identify possible duplicates, prepare measurements, and draft communications. They do not replace the person responsible for the final business decision.

Policy controls restrict the data, tools, responses, and actions available to each agent. These controls help the organization use AI within its approved security, privacy, operational, and financial boundaries.

Evidence links show the records and documents behind an answer. Audit records capture what the system checked, what it found, and how people responded. This makes the result easier to review, explain, and defend.

An organization can begin with one clearly defined business problem, connect the required sources, validate the outputs, and then expand to another workflow. This controlled approach allows the business to improve existing processes without replacing every system at once.

Vayom AI focuses on turning institutional knowledge into governed and reusable business processes. This book extends that practical focus by helping business and technical teams understand how structured data, human expertise, and AI agents can work together.

Learn more at VayomAI.com.

Free Offer from Vayom AI

Your company may have a business problem that could benefit from AI, but you may not know what the final solution should look like. You do not need to prepare a technical specification or design an AI architecture.

Describe the problem to Vayom AI in simple business terms. Explain what happens today, where the difficulty occurs, what information is involved, and what a useful result would look like.

Vayom AI will evaluate the problem and build a solution demonstration. The demonstration will provide a practical view of how your data, documents, business rules, and employee knowledge could work together within a governed AI workflow.

The evaluation and demonstration are free. There is no purchase obligation and no requirement to continue after reviewing the proposed solution.

Vayom AI will also provide a private trial environment for up to five named users. Your team can access the environment for 15 calendar days to explore the demonstration, review the outputs, examine the supporting evidence, and decide whether the approach fits the business.

The demonstration is intended to provide perspective before your company makes a larger technology or investment decision. At the end of the trial, your company decides whether to continue. If you choose not to proceed, there is no further obligation.

To submit a business problem for a free evaluation, visit VayomAI.-com or contact sales@vayomai.com.

www.ingramcontent.com/pod-product-compliance
Lightning Source LLC
LaVergne TN
LVHW101741071126
851857LV00037BA/122
9798232969417